Vorwort

Mit dem „Eckermann/Piert" haben viele Menschen in Kursen an Volkshochschulen, Spracheninstituten, Abendgymnasien und -realschulen, an berufsbildenden Schulen und im Selbstunterricht Englisch gelernt. Daneben hat sich das Werk auch bei fortgeschrittenen Kursteilnehmern als Wiederholungskurs bewährt.
Im Laufe der Jahre haben viele der mit „Eckermann/Piert" arbeitenden Kursleiter und -teilnehmer zu dem Werk kritisch Stellung genommen. Die Urteile und Anregungen wurden sorgfältig registriert und für die Neubearbeitung ausgewertet. Allen, die auf diese Weise zur Verbesserung des Buches beigetragen haben, sei an dieser Stelle herzlich gedankt.
Maßgebend für die Neubearbeitung des „Eckermann/Piert" war zweierlei: Zum einen sollte das in den letzten Jahren gewachsene Bedürfnis nach sozial- und politisch-orientierten Texten befriedigt werden, zum anderen sollte den lexikalischen und grammatikalischen Anforderungen des Zertifikats Englisch des Deutschen Volkshochschul-Verbandes voll Rechnung getragen werden — unter Beibehaltung der bewährten Vorzüge der bisherigen Ausgabe, wie z. B. des Doppelseitenprinzips.
Eckermann/Piert *Englisch* enthält aktuelle und praxisorientierte Texte zu sozialen und politischen Themen, amüsante und anregende Lesestücke und Texte, die einen Einblick in das kulturelle Leben Großbritanniens vermitteln. Das Werk berücksichtigt in vollem Umfang die Strukturenlisten des Deutschen Volkshochschul-Verbandes und den „Englischen Mindestwortschatz", d. h. den Grundwortschatz, dessen Kenntnis bei der Prüfung zum Volkshochschul-Zertifikat für Englisch vorausgesetzt wird. Es bietet methodisch vielfältige und abwechslungsreiche Übungen zu Aussprache, Wortschatz und Strukturen, die vor allem sprachpraktische Fertigkeiten wie die des verstehenden Hörens und des monologischen und dialogischen Sprechens fördern.
Zusammen mit dem *Lehrerheft* (Klettb. 50463), den *Übungen und Tests* (Klettb. 50465), dem *Schlüssel zu den Übungen und Tests* (Klettb. 50464), den *Tonträgermaterialien* (Schallpl. Klett-Nr. 50461, Compact-Cass. Klett-Nr. 50467, Tonb. Klett-Nr, 50468), den *Easy English Stories* (Klettb. 52462) und *English Stories Plus* (Klettb. 52465) eignet es sich auch für den Selbstunterricht.
Das *Lehrerheft* enthält methodische Erläuterungen, zahlreiche zusätzliche Übungen und den Schlüssel für die Übungen im Lehrbuch. Das Arbeitsbuch *Übungen und Tests* dient vor allem der individuellen häuslichen Vor- und Nachbereitung der Kursstunden, der Lernerfolgskontrolle durch Testaufgaben und der gezielten Förderung mit Hilfe von 'Revision Exercises'.
Schallplatten, *Compact-Cassette* und *Tonband* enthalten die Texte der ersten Lektionen zur Ausspracheschulung und zum Hörverstehen, sowie eine Auswahl dialogischer Lektionstexte.
Mit Eckermann/Piert *Englisch* liegt ein Englischkurs vor, der praktisch verwertbare Fertigkeiten und Kenntnisse vermittelt, wie sie für zahlreiche Tätigkeitsbereiche in Wirtschaft und Industrie als Qualifikationsnachweis erforderlich sind. Nach Durcharbeitung des Werkes ist der Lernende in der Lage, alle bei einem Auslandsaufenthalt sich ergebenden wichtigen Situationen sprachlich zu meistern, und er hat die Möglichkeit, weiterführende Kurse zu besuchen.

Trafalgar Square
with *Nelson's Column* on the left
and the *National Gallery*
on the right

The *Houses of Parliament*
with the famous clock tower, *Big Ben*

Buckingham Palace,
the London home of the Royal Family

Westminster Abbey

St. Paul's Cathedral

Tower Bridge
and the *Tower of London*

Oxford University,
the oldest of Britain's universities

Windsor Castle on the Thames,
a residence of Queen Elizabeth II

top left:
Hong Kong, one of the main trading centres in the Far East

top right:
Sydney, the first British settlement in Australia

left:
Canterbury Plain in New Zealand, with the *Southern Alps*

top left:
The *Capitol*, the meeting place of the American parliament

top right:
New York, Manhattan Island

left:
The *White House*, home of the American president

Colorado Plateau

Niagara Falls

Inhaltsverzeichnis

◙ Text auf Schallplatten, Cassette und Tonband

2-5046

1

A Visit
ə 'vizit

Mr Dent: "Is Mrs Sim in?"
mistə 'dent | iz misiz‿'sim‿'in? ‖

Ann: "Yes, Mr Dent, Mrs Sim is in. A minute,
'æn | 'jes | mistə 'dent | misiz‿'sim‿iz‿'in ‖ ə 'minit |

please. (To Mrs Sim) It is Mr Dent, Mrs Sim."
'pli:z ‖ tə misiz‿'sim | it‿iz mistə 'dent | misiz‿'sim ‖

Mrs Sim: "Fetch Mr Dent in, Ann."
misiz‿'sim | 'fetʃ mistə dent‿'in | 'æn ‖

Mr Sim is in bed. He is ill.
mistə 'sim‿iz‿in 'bed ‖ hi:z‿'il ‖

Mr Dent is an actor. Mr Dent and Mrs Sim have tea. Mrs Sim says: "Hand me cheese and biscuits, please."
mistə 'dent‿iz‿ən‿'æktə ‖ mistə 'dent‿ənd misiz‿'sim hæv 'ti: ‖ misiz‿'sim 'sez | 'hænd mi: 'tʃi:z‿ənd 'biskits | 'pli:z ‖

Mrs Sim has cheese, Mr Dent has an egg. Mrs Sim says: "Ken is ill in bed." — "Is he better?" — "Yes, he is better.
misiz‿'sim hæz 'tʃi:z | mistə 'dent hæz‿ən‿'eg ‖ misiz‿'sim 'sez | 'ken‿iz‿'il‿in 'bed ‖ — iz hi: 'betə? ‖ — 'jes | hi:z 'betə ‖

Give Mr Sim his tea, Ann."
'giv mistə 'sim hiz 'ti: | 'æn ‖

"And an egg?"
'ænd‿ən‿'eg? ‖

"Yes, and an egg." —
'jes | 'ænd‿ən 'eg ‖

Tea is finished.
'ti:‿iz 'finiʃt ‖

Mr Dent gets his hat.
mistə 'dent 'gets hiz 'hæt ‖

He gives Mrs Sim a kiss.
hi: 'givz misiz‿'sim‿ə 'kis ‖

Mrs Sim is Mr Dent's sister.
misiz‿'sim‿iz mistə 'dents‿'sistə ‖

Grammatik

I. Die Grundform (Infinitiv) und die Befehlsform (Imperativ)

Grundform		Befehlsform	
to hand	reichen	**Hand** me an egg, please.	Reich (od.: reichen Sie, reicht) mir ...!
to give	geben	**Give** Mr Sim his tea.	Geben Sie (od.: gib, gebt) ...!

Die Befehlsform hat dieselbe Form wie die Grundform (ohne *to*). Sie lautet in Einzahl und Mehrzahl gleich.

II. Das unbestimmte Geschlechtswort (unbest. Artikel) — Formen

a hat **a** minute **a** bed	ein Hut eine Minute ein Bett	Das unbestimmte Geschlechtswort ist für alle drei Geschlechter gleich: Es lautet:	***a*** vor Mitlauten (Konsonanten)
an actor **an** egg	ein Schauspieler ein Ei		***an*** vor Selbstlauten (Vokalen)

III. Bemerkungen zur Aussprache

Zeichen	Lautbeschreibung	Musterwörter
:	bedeutet, daß der Selbstlaut lang gesprochen wird	
[iː]	langes *i* wie in dt. *tief, fiel*	he tea
[e]	geschlossener als das *e* in dt. *nett*	egg fetch
[ə]	kurzes, unbetontes *e* wie in dt. *bitte*	a sister
[æ]	breiter und offener als in dt. *Männer, Hände*	hat hand
[t]	„breiter" als dt. *t*	hat better
[s]	stimmloses *ß* wie in dt. *muß;* auch am Wortanfang stimmlos	kiss sister
[z]	stimmhaftes *s* wie in dt. *Rose* (bes. zu üben von Südd.!)	is his
[v]	in jeder Stellung stimmhaft, also auch am Ende des Wortes	have give
[ʃ]	stimmlos wie *sch* in dt. *Tisch*	finished
[tʃ]	stimmlos wie *tsch* in *deutsch*	cheese
[d]	stimmhaft, vor allem auch am Ende des Wortes; unterscheide genau dt. *Hand* [t] und engl. *hand* [d]	bed hand
[g]	stimmhaft; unterscheide dt. *Weg* [k] und engl. *egg* [g]	give egg

Übungen

I. Wo sie sind und was sie tun 1. Mr Sim is ... 2. Mr Dent and Mrs Sim ... 3. Ann gives ... 4. Mr Dent gets ... 5. Mr Dent gives ...

II. Wer? 1. ... is in bed. 2. ... is an actor. 3. ... has an egg. 4. ... has cheese and biscuits. 5. ... gives Mr Sim his tea. 6. ... has a sister.

III. *A* oder *an*? 1. Mr Dent has ... hat. 2. Is Mr Dent ... actor? 3. Mr Dent has ... sister. 4. Hand me ... biscuit, please. 5. Mr Sim has ... egg.

IV. Was sie tun sollen 1. ... me a kiss, Ken. 2. ... me cheese and biscuits, please. 3. ... Mr Dent in, Ann. 4. ... a biscuit, Mr Dent. 5. ... Mr Dent his tea, Ann. 6. ... Mr Dent's hat, Ann.

V. Übersetze ins Deutsche: 1. Mr Dent has a sister. 2. Mr Dent and Mrs Sim have tea. 3. Mrs Sim has cheese and biscuits. 4. Mr Sim has tea. 5. Mr Dent has an egg.

VI. Ausspracheübung

[e] yes, says, egg, get, fetch
[ə] a, an, mister, sister, better, actor
[æ] hand, Ann, actor, hat
[t] tea, biscuit, minute, visit, Dent
[s] kiss, Sim, sister, gets, yes, biscuits
[z] please, is, cheese, says, his, gives, visit
[v] have, gives, visit
[ʃ] finished
[tʃ] fetch, cheese
[d] and, hand, bed
[g] give, get, egg

VII. Ergänze ein Reimwort

please	is	mister	he
cheese	...	...	...

2 A Stationer's Shop
ə 'steiʃnəz ʃɔp

Tom is an assistant in a shop. The shop is in the City. It is a
'tɔm‿iz‿ən‿ə'sistənt‿in‿ə 'ʃɔp ‖ ðə 'ʃɔp‿iz‿in ðə 'siti ‖ it‿iz‿ə

stationer's shop.
'steiʃnəz ʃɔp ‖

Who is the boss? Mr Smith is the boss.
'hu:‿iz ðə 'bɔs? ‖ mistə 'smiθ‿iz ðə 'bɔs ‖

What is in the shop? The shop sells newspapers, pens, pencils,
'wɔt‿iz‿in ðə 'ʃɔp? ‖ ðə 'ʃɔp 'selz 'nju:speipəz | 'penz | 'penslz |

picture postcards, tobacco and sweets.
'piktʃə 'pəustkɑ:dz | tə'bækəu | ənd 'swi:ts ‖

Betty White enters the shop. She is a typist in an office. The office
'beti 'wait‿ 'entəz ðə 'ʃɔp ‖ ʃi:z‿ə 'taipist‿in‿ən‿'ɔfis ‖ ði‿'ɔfis‿

is opposite the shop. Miss White is a nice little thing and has a nice face. She has white shoes on.
iz‿'ɔpəzit ðə 'ʃɔp ‖ mis 'wait‿iz ə 'nais litl 'θiŋ | ənd hæz‿ə 'nais 'feis ‖ ʃi: hæz 'wait 'ʃu:z‿ɔn ‖

Miss White wants a newspaper. The assistant shows two papers, *The Times* and
mis 'wait 'wɔnts‿ə 'nju:speipə ‖ ði‿ə'sistənt 'ʃəuz 'tu: 'peipəz | ðə 'taimz‿ənd

The Guardian. Mr Smith says: "Go away, Tom. Not these papers, Miss White.
ðə 'gɑ:djən ‖ mistə 'smiθ 'sez | 'gəu‿ə'wei | 'tɔm ‖ nɔt 'ði:z 'peipəz | mis 'wait ‖

Buy *The Daily Mail*. This paper has nice pictures and entertaining articles."
'bai ðə 'deili 'meil ‖ 'ðis 'peipə hæz 'nais 'piktʃəz | ənd ‿ entə'teiniŋ ‿ 'ɑ:tiklz ‖

He opens the paper. "This is a wedding, Miss White, and these are two actors."
hi:‿'əupənz ðə 'peipə ‖ 'ðis‿iz‿ə 'wediŋ | mis 'wait | ənd 'ði:z‿ə 'tu:‿'æktəz ‖

Miss White takes *The Daily Mail*. It is not expensive. "Many thanks, Miss White,
mis 'wait 'teiks ðə 'deili 'meil ‖ it‿iz 'nɔt‿iks'pensiv ‖ 'meni 'θæŋks | mis 'wait |

good-bye, Miss White." She leaves the shop. Mr Smith says: "I know Miss White
'gud'bai | mis 'wait ‖ ʃi: 'li:vz ðə 'ʃɔp ‖ mistə 'smiθ 'sez | 'ai nəu mis 'wait

better. Miss White and *The Times*, Tom! What nonsense!"
'betə ‖ mis 'wait‿ənd ðə 'taimz | 'tɔm ‖ 'wɔt 'nɔnsəns ‖

I. Die Mehrzahl des Hauptworts (Plural des Substantivs)

a shoe — two shoes [ʃu:z] a postcard — two postcards [-dz] a pencil — two pencils [-lz]	Die Mehrzahl wird gebildet durch Anhängen eines *-s* an die Einzahl.	Aussprache des *-s:* [z] = stimmhaft nach Selbstlauten und stimmhaften Mitlauten
a shop — two shops [-ps] a minute — two minutes [-ts]		[s] = stimmlos nach stimmlosen Mitlauten

II. Das bestimmte Geschlechtswort (best. Artikel)

Einzahl	Mehrzahl		Aussprache:
the boss der Chef **the typist** die Stenot. **the picture** das Bild	**the pictures** die Bilder	Das best. Geschlechtswort hat für alle drei Geschlechter in Einzahl und Mehrzahl nur eine Form: ***the***	[ðə] vor Mitlauten
the assistant der Verk. **the office** das Büro	**the expensive pictures**		[ði] vor Selbstlauten

III. Bemerkungen zur Aussprache

Zeichen	Lautbeschreibung	Musterwörter
[ɔ]	offenes *o*, noch offener als *o* in dt. *Torte*	Tom shop
[ai]	etwa wie in dt. *Ei*, *fein*, *Kaiser*	nice typist
[ei]	Doppellaut aus englischem [e] mit *i*-Nachschlag	paper face
[əu]	Doppellaut aus [ə] mit *u*-Nachschlag	go open
[ɑ:]	langes *a*, etwa wie in *Bar*	are card
[u:]	langes *u*, offener als in dt. *du* (Lippen kaum vorstülpen!)	two shoe
[ð]	stimmhafter Lispellaut; Zungenspitze leicht gegen die oberen Vorderzähne legen, die Luft hindurchstreichen lassen und im Kehlkopf summen	the this these
[θ]	stimmloser Lispellaut; gebildet wie [ð], aber Zungenspitze fest anlegen und Luft energisch hindurchpressen	Smith thanks
[ŋ]	wie *ng* in dt. *lang* (kein *k* am Ende hörbar werden lassen!)	thing
[w]	vom engl. [u] ausgehen und zum folgenden Laut hinübergleiten; nicht mit [v] verwechseln!	what sweets
[l]	1. helles *l* wie im Dt., am Wort- und Silbenanfang und zwischen Selbstlauten	leave politics
	2. dunkles *l*, bei dem die Hinterzunge gegen den weichen Gaumen gehoben wird; am Wortende und vor Mitlauten	sell little

I. Lies: the boss, the assistant, the office, the nice article, the expensive paper, the visit, the entertaining visit, the eggs, the two eggs, the expensive eggs, the biscuits, the actors

II. *This is — these are*

Bsp.: This is a pencil. — *These are* pencils.

postcard, nice picture, hat, newspaper, white shoe, sweet biscuit, shop, entertaining article, expensive pen, nice little thing

III. *Yes — no*

Bsp.: Is Mr Smith the boss? — *Yes, he is.*
Is Tom the boss? — *No, he is not* the boss, (he is an assistant).

1. Is Miss White a typist? 2. Is Tom an actor? 3. Is Betty his sister? 4. Is Mr Smith in bed? 5. Is Tom ill? 6. Is Mr Smith an assistant?

IV. *Who?* 1. Who is an assistant? 2. Who is a typist? 3. Who has a shop in the City? 4. Who is in the shop? 5. Who has a nice face? 6. Who shows *The Times* and *The Guardian*? 7. Who says "Go away, Tom"? 8. Who is ill? 9. Who is Mr Dent's sister? 10. Who gives Mr Sim tea? 11. Who gives Mrs Sim a kiss?

V. Ausspracheübung

[ai] — [ei] a nice face
Buy *The Daily Mail.*
Take *The Times.*

[ð] — [θ] this thing, these things
The Times, please, Mr Smith.
Many thanks, Mr Smith.

[v] — [w] a visit — a wedding
Give me a sweet.
Give it away.
An expensive wedding.

3 An Evening Out
ən‿'i:vniŋ‿'aut

Bill has free tickets for the Empire. That is a big cinema.
'bil hæz 'fri: 'tikits fə ði‿'empaiə ‖ 'ðæt‿iz‿ə 'big 'sinəmə ‖

"What about the pictures, Sally?" — "What's on, Bill?"
'wɔt‿əbaut ðə 'piktʃəz | 'sæli? ‖ — 'wɔts‿'ɔn | 'bil? ‖

"The Green Monster, darling." — "That's fine, Bill. Let's take a
ðə 'gri:n 'mɔnstə | 'dɑ:liŋ ‖ — 'ðæts 'fain | 'bil ‖ 'lets teik‿ə

taxi." — "Why not a bus? We have plenty of time."
'tæksi ‖ — 'wai nɔt‿ə 'bʌs? ‖ wi: hæv 'plenti‿əv 'taim ‖

"No, we haven't. The film begins in ten minutes."
'nəu | wi: 'hævnt ‖ ðə 'film bi'ginz‿in 'ten 'minits ‖

The streets are full of cars. It is the rush hour. Traffic lights at
ðə 'stri:ts‿ə 'ful‿əv 'kɑ:z ‖ it‿iz ðə 'rʌʃ‿auə ‖ 'træfik laits‿ət‿

every crossing. Piccadilly at last! Lights, theatres, cinemas! This is London's West End.
'evri 'krɔsiŋ ‖ pikə'dili‿ət 'lɑ:st ‖ 'laits | 'θiətəz | 'sinəməz ‖ 'ðis‿iz 'lʌndənz 'west 'end ‖

"Here we are," says Bill. The man at the cinema entrance looks at the
'hiə wi:‿'ɑ: | 'sez 'bil ‖ ðə 'mæn‿ət ðə 'sinəmə 'entrəns 'luks‿ət ðə

tickets, but he says: "What's this?" Bill says: "These are the tickets."
'tikits | bət hi: 'sez | 'wɔts 'ðis? ‖ 'bil 'sez | 'ði:z‿ə ðə 'tikits ‖

The man: "Sorry, these are bus tickets. They are no good. Box-office
ðə 'mæn | 'sɔri | 'ði:z‿ə 'bʌs tikits ‖ ðei‿ə 'nəu 'gud ‖ 'bɔksɔfis‿

on the left."
ɔn ðə 'left ‖

Bill looks in his pockets. He says: "I'm sorry, Sally, but the tickets
'bil 'luks‿in hiz 'pɔkits ‖ hi: 'sez | aim 'sɔri | 'sæli | 'bʌt ðə 'tikits

aren't in my pocket." — "Never mind, darling. Better luck next time."
'ɑ:nt‿in mai 'pɔkit ‖ — 'nevə 'maind | 'dɑ:liŋ ‖ 'betə 'lʌk 'nekst‿'taim ‖

"Are you sad, Sally?" — "No, I'm not. Let's have a drink instead."
ɑ: ju: 'sæd | 'sæli? ‖ — 'nəu | aim 'nɔt ‖ 'lets hæv‿ə 'driŋk‿in'sted ‖

Zeitwort in Grundform „to ….."
Personalform „……"

I. *to have* haben

		Frageform
I **have**	ich habe	have I?
you **have**	du hast, Sie haben	have you?
he **has**	er hat	has he?
she **has**	sie hat	has she?
it **has**	es hat	has it?
we **have**	wir haben	have we?
you **have**	ihr habt, Sie h.	have you?
they **have**	sie haben	have they?
Verneinte Form		**Kurzform**
I have not	ich habe nicht	haven't ['hævnt]
you have not		
he has not, etc.		hasn't ['hæznt]
Fragend-verneinte Form		**Kurzform**
have I not?	habe ich nicht?	haven't I?
have you not?		haven't you?

II. *to be* sein

		Frageform
I **am** (I'm)	ich bin	am I?
you **are**	du bist, Sie s.	are you?
he **is** (he's)	er ist	is he?
she **is** (she's)	sie ist	is she?
it **is** (it's)	es ist	is it?
we **are**	wir sind	are we?
you **are**	ihr seid, Sie s.	are you?
they **are**	sie sind	are they?
Verneinte Form		**Kurzform**
I am not	ich bin nicht	aren't [ɑ:nt]
you are not		isn't ['iznt]
he is not, etc.		
Fragend-verneinte Form		**Kurzform**
am I not?	bin ich nicht?	
are you not?		aren't you?

Die Kurzformen werden hauptsächlich in der Umgangssprache verwendet.

Merke: Have you a car? — Yes, *I have.* Ja. — No, *I haven't.* Nein.
Is she sad? — Yes, *she is.* Ja. — No, *she isn't.* Nein.

III. Das Geschlecht der Hauptwörter

Mr Smith has a shop.	**He** is the boss.	*he* steht für männliche Personen
Miss Green is a typist.	**She** is in the shop.	*she* steht für weibliche Personen
The paper has nice pictures.	**It** is entertaining.	*it* steht für Sachen

IV. Bemerkungen zur Aussprache

Zeichen	Lautbeschreibung	Musterwörter
[ʌ]	kurzer *a*-Laut, etwa wie in dt. *Mann, Matte*	bus luck
[iə]	Doppellaut aus [i] mit nachklingendem [ə]	here
[au]	Doppellaut aus hellem [a] mit nachklingendem [u]	out hour
[r]	Gaumen-*r* (kein Zäpfchen-*r* oder gerolltes Zungen-*r*); die Zungenspitze wird gegen den Gaumen angehoben und leicht zurückgebogen, der austretende Luftstrom erzeugt [r]. Im Auslaut wird *r* nur bei Bindung gesprochen: *here‿are* [hiər‿ɑ:], aber *here* [hiə].	rush every traffic drink the car‿is

I. Satzbautafel

Bsp.: We have plenty of time.

I Miss White We He Mr and Mrs Sim	(to have)	plenty of time a big car two free tickets ten postcards a nice picture

II. a) Verneine die Fragen

Bsp.: Is the Daily Mail expensive? No, it isn't.

1. Is the Empire a theatre? No, … 2. Is the Green Monster an entertaining film? 3. Are the streets full of cars? 4. Is Sally a typist? 5. Are Tom and Mr Smith actors?

b) Bejahe die Fragen

III. a) Verneine die Fragen

Bsp.: Have you a car? No, I haven't.

1. Has Bill free tickets for the theatre? No, he … 2. Has Bill Sally's picture in his pocket? 3. Have Bill and Sally plenty of time? 4. Have the streets traffic lights at every crossing? 5. Has Sally a newspaper?

b) Bejahe die Fragen

IV. Beantworte: 1. Has Bill a car? 2. Is the Empire in the West End? 3. Are taxis expensive? 4. Are the streets full of cars? 5. Is Sally a nice little thing? (Look at the picture.) 6. Has she a hat on? 7. Has Bill the cinema tickets in his pocket? 8. Is the man at the entrance an actor?

V. *On — at.* 1. Traffic lights … every crossing! 2. "Here we are … last." 3. The cinema is … the left. 4. The man … the entrance says, "Sorry." 5. Has Sally nice shoes …?

4 The Red Paint
ðə ˈred ˈpeint

Mr and Mrs Brown have a small house in Wimbledon. "Home, sweet home,"
mistər‿ənd misiz ˈbraun hæv‿ə ˈsmɔ:l ˈhaus‿in ˈwimbldən ‖ ˈhəum | ˈswi:t ˈhəum |
is Mr Brown's motto. He is downstairs in the sitting-room. Where is Mrs
iz mistə ˈbraunz ˈmɔtəu ‖ hi:z ˈdaunˈstɛəz‿in ðə ˈsitiŋrum ‖ ˈwɛər‿iz ˈmisiz
Brown? She is in the garden. There are beautiful flowers in the garden.
ˈbraun? ‖ ʃi:z‿in ðə ˈgɑ:dn ‖ ðər‿ə ˈbju:təfl ˈflauəz‿in ðə ˈgɑ:dn ‖
Mr Brown looks at the evening paper. There is nothing interesting in the
mistə ˈbraun ˈluks‿ət ði‿ˈi:vniŋ ˈpeipə ‖ ðəz ˈnʌθiŋ ˈintristiŋ‿in ðə
paper. He opens a book. It is boring, too. What about TV? Is there a good
ˈpeipə ‖ hi:‿ˈəupənz‿ə ˈbuk ‖ it‿iz ˈbɔ:riŋ | ˈtu: ‖ ˈwɔt‿əbaut ˈti:ˈvi:? ‖ iz ðər‿ə ˈgud
programme on today? No, there isn't.
ˈprəugræm‿ˈɔn təˈdei? ‖ ˈnəu | ðər‿ˈiznt ‖

Then he gets an idea. He thinks: "I have a brush and red paint. There are plenty of white bathrooms, but how many
ˈðen hi: ˈgets‿ən‿aiˈdiə ‖ hi: ˈθiŋks | ai hæv‿ə ˈbrʌʃ‿ənd ˈred ˈpeint ‖ ðər‿ə ˈplenti‿əv ˈwait ˈbɑ:θrumz | bət ˈhau meni
houses have a red bathroom?" He goes upstairs and begins to paint. After one hour the bath, the chairs, the floor, the
ˈhauziz hæv‿ə ˈred ˈbɑ:θrum? ‖ hi: ˈgəuz‿ʌpˈstɛəz‿ənd biˈginz tə ˈpeint ‖ ɑ:ftə ˈwʌn‿ˈauə ðə ˈbɑ:θ | ðə ˈtʃɛəz | ðə ˈflɔ: | ðə

walls and the window frames are all red. Mrs Brown knocks at the door. There
ˈwɔ:lz | ənd ðə ˈwindəu freimz‿ər‿ˈɔ:l ˈred ‖ misiz ˈbraun ˈnɔks‿ət ðə ˈdɔ: ‖ ðər‿
is no answer. She enters and cries: "What's this? What an awful colour!"
iz ˈnəu ˈɑ:nsə ‖ ʃi:‿ˈentəz‿ənd ˈkraiz | ˈwɔts ˈðis? ‖ wɔt‿ən‿ˈɔ:fl ˈkʌlə ‖
Mr Brown: "I'm sorry, Mary, but I like the colour." Mrs Brown: "What
mistə ˈbraun | aim ˈsɔri | ˈmɛəri | bət‿ˈai ˈlaik ðə ˈkʌlə ‖ misiz ˈbraun | ˈwɔt
nonsense! Why not paint the door green, this wall blue, that wall brown, these
ˈnɔnsəns ‖ wai nɔt ˈpeint ðə ˈdɔ: ˈgri:n | ˈðis wɔ:l ˈblu: | ˈðæt wɔ:l ˈbraun | ˈði:z
chairs yellow and those window frames pink? My hair goes grey when I look
ˈtʃɛəz ˈjeləu | ənd ˈðəuz ˈwindəu freimz ˈpiŋk? ‖ mai ˈhɛə gəuz ˈgrei | wen‿ai ˈluk‿
at it." Mr Brown: "This is a black day for my red bath."
ət‿it ‖ mistə ˈbraun | ˈðis‿iz‿ə ˈblæk ˈdei fə mai ˈred ˈbɑ:θ ‖

I. *there is, there are*

There is a bathroom upstairs. **There is** no theatre in Wimbledon.	Oben ist ... In W. gibt es ...	*There is* es ist, es gibt u. *there are* es sind, es gibt müssen oft auch dann stehen, wenn im Dt. „es" nicht notwendig ist.
There are plenty of white bathrooms. **There are** no pictures on the wall.	Es gibt ... An der W. sind ...	

Merke: Is there a stationer's shop in this street? — Yes, *there is.* Ja.
Are there two bathrooms in Mr. Brown's house? — No, *there aren't.* Nein.

II. *this — that, these — those*

This is a big house. (This house is big.	Dies (hier) ist ... Dieses Haus hier ...)	**That is** a small house. (That house is small.	Das (dort) ist ... Das Haus dort ...)
These are awful colours. (These colours are awful.	Dies (hier) sind ... Diese F. hier ...)	**Those are** awful colours. (Those colours are awful.	Das (dort) sind ... Die F. dort ...)

This, these bezeichnen das räumlich oder zeitlich Nahe.

That, those bezeichnen das Entferntere.

III. Einige Fragewörter

1. **What** is red? 2. **Who** is in the garden?	**what?** was? **who?** wer?	3. **Where** is Mr Brown? 4. **How many** cars have you?	**where?** wo? **how many?** wie viele?

Merke: **What colour is** the bath? — Was für eine, welche Farbe hat das Bad?
What colour are the chairs? — Was für eine, welche Farbe haben die Stühle?

IV. Zahlen 1—12

1 one	[wʌn]	**4** four	[fɔ:]	**7** seven	['sevn]	**10** ten	[ten]
2 two	[tu:]	**5** five	[faiv]	**8** eight	[eit]	**11** eleven	[i'levn]
3 three	[θri:]	**6** six	[siks]	**9** nine	[nain]	**12** twelve	[twelv]

V. Bemerkungen zur Aussprache

Zeichen	Lautbeschreibung	Musterwörter
[ɔ:]	langes, offenes *o*, wie in gedehnt gesprochenem dt. *Tor-te*	small floor
[ɛə]	Doppellaut aus *ä* wie in *Hälse* und nachklingendem [ə]	hair there
[b-p] [d-t] [g-k]	Der Unterschied zwischen den stimmhaften (weichen) Lauten [b-d-g] und den entsprechenden stimmlosen (harten) [p-t-k] ist in allen Stellungen, auch am Wortende, sehr stark. Vgl. dagegen das Dt.: *Leib* [p], *Hand* [t], *Tag* [k].	Bob shop red get egg black

I. Say where

Bsp.: There is a sitting-room *downstairs.*

1. There is a bathroom ... 2. There are flowers ... 3. There is nothing interesting ... 4. There are entertaining articles ... 5. There are many theatres and cinemas ... 6. There are traffic lights ...

II. *There is* and *there are*

Bsp.: (one flower in my sitting-room)
(many flowers in my garden)
There is one flower in my sitting-room, but *there are* many flowers in my garden.

1. (one sitting-room in Mr Smith's house) (two bathrooms) 2. (is nothing interesting on TV) (many entertaining articles in the Daily Mail) 3. (not many taxis free in the rush hour) (plenty of time) 4. (no tickets for the theatre) (a good programme on TV) 5. (a boring film on at the Empire) (plenty of books in the sitting-room) 6. (many good shops in the City) (not many cinemas)

III. Gegensätze (Opposites)

a) Setze sinngemäß ein: *awful, black, boring, small, upstairs*

Bsp.: This is an awful colour, that is a *nice* colour.

1. This is an entertaining book, that is a ... 2. This is a nice drink, that is an ... 3. This car is white, that car ... 4. This house is big, ... 5. This man has a room downstairs, ...

b) Bilde die Mehrzahl

Bsp.: These are awful colours, those are nice colours.

1. These are entertaining books, ... 2. These ...

IV. Fill in *who* or *where* and give answers

Bsp.: Who is in the garden?
Mrs Brown is in the garden.

1. ... is ill in bed? 2. ... is the box-office? 3. ... is Mr Brown's bathroom? 4. ... leaves the stationer's shop? 5. ... looks at the TV programme?

5 Spoilt Holidays
ˈspɔilt ˈhɔlədiz

It is two days before Mr Turner's holidays. He comes home from the office.
it‿iz ˈtu: ˈdeiz bifɔ: mistə ˈtə:nəz ˈhɔlədiz ‖ hi: ˈkʌmz ˈhəum frəm ði‿ˈɔfis ‖

He is very tired and he has a headache. Mrs Turner says: "Take a hot bath.
hi:z ˈveri ˈtaiəd | ənd hi: hæz‿ə ˈhedeik ‖ ˈmisiz ˈtə:nə ˈsez | ˈteik‿ə ˈhɔt ˈbɑ:θ ‖

It's good for your health. A hot bath does you good."
its ˈgud fə jɔ: ˈhelθ ‖ ə ˈhɔt ˈbɑ:θ ˈdʌz ju: ˈgud ‖

Mr Turner goes upstairs to the bathroom. He turns on the water. The water
mistə ˈtə:nə ˈgəuz‿ʌpˈstɛəz tə ðə ˈbɑ:θrum ‖ hi: ˈtə:nz‿ˈɔn ðə ˈwɔ:tə ‖ ðə ˈwɔ:tə

fills the bath. He takes off his jacket, his pullover, his tie, his shirt, his
ˈfilz ðə ˈbɑ:θ ‖ hi: ˈteiks‿ˈɔf hiz ˈdʒækit | hiz ˈpuləuvə | hiz ˈtai | hiz ˈʃə:t | hiz

trousers, his shoes, his socks, his pants. He gets in. The water is very hot. A few minutes, and it is just right.
ˈtrauzəz | hiz ˈʃu:z | hiz‿ˈsɔks | hiz ˈpænts ‖ hi: ˈgets‿ˈin ‖ ðə ˈwɔ:tər‿iz ˈveri ˈhɔt ‖ ə ˈfju: ˈminits | ənd‿it‿iz ˈdʒʌst ˈrait ‖

Mr Turner shuts his eyes. He enjoys the warmth. What a pleasure! — Now Mr Turner opens his eyes. He gets a
mistə ˈtə:nə ˈʃʌts hiz‿ˈaiz ‖ hi:‿inˈdʒɔiz ðə ˈwɔ:mθ ‖ ˈwɔt‿ə ˈpleʒə ‖ — ˈnau mistə ˈtə:nə ˈəupənz hiz‿ˈaiz ‖ hi: ˈgets‿ə

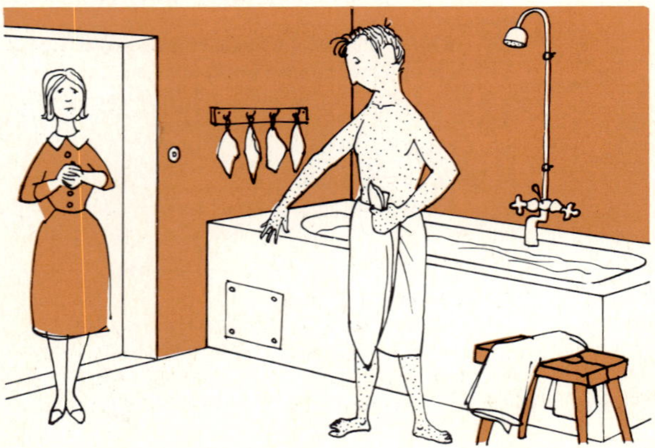

shock. His body is covered with red spots. There are spots on his
ˈʃɔk ‖ hiz ˈbɔdi‿iz ˈkʌvəd wið ˈred ˈspɔts ‖ ðər‿ə ˈspɔts‿ɔn hiz

hands, on his fingers, on his arms, on his legs, on his feet, on his
ˈhændz | ɔn hiz ˈfiŋgəz | ɔn hiz‿ˈɑ:mz | ɔn hiz ˈlegz | ɔn hiz ˈfi:t | ɔn hiz

chest. He jumps out of the bath. He takes a towel and rubs hard.
ˈtʃest ‖ hi: ˈdʒʌmps‿ˈaut‿əv ðə ˈbɑ:θ ‖ hi: ˈteiks‿ə ˈtauəl | ənd ˈrʌbz ˈhɑ:d ‖

The spots are still there. He calls his wife. Mrs Turner comes in.
ðə ˈspɔts‿ə ˈstil ˈðɛə ‖ hi: ˈkɔ:lz hiz ˈwaif ‖ misiz ˈtə:nə ˈkʌmz‿ˈin ‖

She sees her husband. He has red spots on his skin. She says: "Oh,
ʃi: ˈsi:z hə: ˈhʌzbənd ‖ hi: hæz ˈred ˈspɔts ɔn hiz ˈskin ‖ ʃi: ˈsez | ˈəu

John, you big baby! You have German measles. Our holidays are
ˈdʒɔn | ju: ˈbig ˈbeibi ‖ ju: hæv ˈdʒə:mən ˈmi:zlz ‖ auə ˈhɔlədiz‿ə

spoilt. What a pity."
ˈspɔilt ‖ ˈwɔt ə ˈpiti ‖

I. Die Gegenwart des Zeitworts (Präsens des Verbs)

Beispiel: **to open** öffnen	Aussprache der Endung *-s* der 3. Person Einzahl:	
I open — ich öffne you open — du öffnest, Sie öffnen he / she / it } opens — er / sie / es } öffnet	1. he sees [si:z] he calls [-lz] he rubs [-bz]	[z], d. h. stimmhaft, nach Selbstlauten und stimmhaften Mitlauten
	2. he jumps [-ps] he takes [-ks] he shuts [-ts]	[s], d. h. stimmlos, nach stimmlosen Mitlauten
we open — wir öffnen you open — ihr öffnet, Sie ö. they open — sie öffnen	to go — he goes [gəuz] to do — he does [dʌz] to say — he says [sez]	Merke die nebenstehenden Besonderheiten

Beachte: he (she, it) *can* — er (sie, es) kann; he (she, it) *must* [mʌst] — er (sie, es) muß } Diese Hilfszeitwörter haben kein *-s* in der 3. Person Einzahl (im Dt. kein *-t*).

II. Das besitzanzeigende Fürwort I (Possessivpronomen)

I	open	**my**	book(s)	mein Buch (meine Bücher)	Das besitzanzeigende Fürwort bleibt in seiner Form unverändert, gleichgültig ob es vor einem Hauptwort in der Einzahl oder Mehrzahl steht.
you	open	**your**	book(s)	dein, Ihr Buch (deine, Ihre B.)	
he	opens	**his**	book(s)	sein Buch (seine Bücher)	
she	opens	**her**	book(s)	ihr Buch (ihre Bücher)	
(the house)		**its**	window(s)	sein Fenster (seine Fenster)	
we	open	**our**	book(s)	unser Buch (unsere Bücher)	
you	open	**your**	book(s)	euer, Ihr Buch (eure, Ihre B.)	
they	open	**their**	book(s)	ihr Buch (ihre Bücher)	

Merke: He shuts **his eyes.** — schließt **die** Augen
Mr Turner takes off **his shoes.** — zieht **die** Schuhe aus
Bei Körperteilen und Kleidungsstücken steht immer das besitzanz. Fürwort.

III. Bemerkungen zur Aussprache

Zeichen	Lautbeschreibung	Musterwörter
[əː]	ein dem dt. *ö*, wie z. B. in *Mörder*, verwandter Laut, aber ohne Lippenrundung gesprochen	turn shirt
[ɔi]	Doppellaut aus [ɔ] und nachklingendem *i*	boy spoilt
[ʒ]	stimmhafter *sch*-Laut wie in gut gesprochenem *Garage*, *Journal*	pleasure
[dʒ]	[ʒ] + *d*-Vorschlag	John German

I. Satzbautafel

Bsp.: Bill and Sally want two tickets.

Bill and Sally	(to want)	two tickets
The typist	(to leave)	the shop
We	(to like)	this picture
Mrs Turner	(to knock)	at the door
Her husband	(to come)	home tired

II. Setze die Zeitwörter in die Gegenwart

Bsp.: Bill (to come) home. — Bill comes home.

a) 1. Bill (to come) home from the office. 2.Sally, his wife, (to be) not in the sitting-room. 3. Bill (to go) upstairs. 4. He (to enter) the bathroom. 5. (to be) she in the garden? 6. He (to call), "Sally, where (to be) you?" 7. There (to be) no answer. 8. Sally (not to be) in the house.

b) 1. Darling Ann, Bill and I (to be) now husband and wife. 2. We (to have) a small house in Wimbledon. 3. Bill (to have) a hobby, he (to paint). 4. He (to come) home from the office in the evening and (to go) upstairs to the bathroom. 5. I (to say), "What about tea?", but Bill (to have) no time for tea. 6. He (to take) a brush and (to begin) to paint. 7. He (to do) that every evening.

III. ***My, your, his,*** **etc.:** 1. Mr and Mrs Turner like ... home. 2. The house is small, but ... rooms are very nice. 3. Mrs Turner and ... husband are in the garden. 4. They have beautiful flowers in ... garden. 5. Mr Turner is not in ... office today. 6. Mrs Turner says: "Is ... headache better?" 7. Mr Turner says: "Yes, ... headache is better."

IV. Wandle um

Bsp.: I have a big garden. My garden is big.

1. I have a green car. 2. You have a yellow pullover. 3. He has a red face. 4. She has pink shoes. 5. It has big windows. 6. We have beautiful flowers.

6 Red Riding Hood and the Wolf
ˈred ˈraidiŋ hud‿ənd ðə ˈwulf

Betsy is standing in front of the mirror. What is she doing? She is putting on her red dress,
ˈbetsi‿iz ˈstændiŋ‿in ˈfrʌnt‿əv ðə ˈmirə ‖ ˈwɔt‿iz ʃi: ˈduiŋ? ‖ ʃi:z ˈputiŋ‿ˈɔn hə: ˈred‿ˈdres |
her red cap, her best stockings and red shoes. Her mother says: "Go and see Grandma, Betsy.
hə: ˈred ˈkæp | hə: ˈbest ˈstɔkiŋz | ənd ˈred ˈʃu:z ‖ hə: ˈmʌðə ˈsez | ˈgəu‿ənd ˈsi: ˈgrænmɑ: | ˈbetsi ‖
She is ill in bed. Take the number eleven bus. Here is a basket with cake and fruit in it."
ʃi:z‿ˈil‿in ˈbed ‖ ˈteik ðə nʌmber‿iˈlevn bʌs ‖ ˈhiər‿iz‿ə ˈbɑ:skit | wið ˈkeik‿ənd ˈfru:t‿in‿it ‖
Betsy, a young lady of eighteen, is a nice girl.
ˈbetsi | ə ˈjʌŋ ˈleidi‿əv‿eiˈti:n | iz‿ə ˈnais ˈgə:l ‖
A lot of people are waiting at the bus stop. A young man comes to Betsy and asks, smiling:
ə lɔt‿əv ˈpi:pl‿ə ˈweitiŋ‿ət ðə ˈbʌs‿stɔp ‖ ə ˈjʌŋ ˈmæn ˈkʌmz tə ˈbetsi | ənd‿ˈɑ:sks | ˈsmailiŋ |
"Are you waiting for a bus? It's not nice to wait. Let's take my car." Betsy says:
ɑ:‿ju: ˈweitiŋ fər‿ə ˈbʌs? ‖ its ˈnɔt ˈnais tə ˈweit ‖ lets ˈteik mai ˈkɑ: ‖ ˈbetsi ˈsez |
"Thank you. You are very kind." They go round the corner and get in.
ˈθæŋk‿ju ‖ ˈju:‿ə ˈveri ˈkaind ‖ ðei ˈgəu raund ðə ˈkɔ:nə | ənd ˈget‿ˈin ‖

The car starts. Betsy says: "My grandma lives near Hyde Park. This is not the way
ðə ˈkɑ: ˈstɑ:ts ‖ ˈbetsi ˈsez | mai ˈgrænmɑ: ˈlivz niə ˈhaid ˈpɑ:k ‖ ðis‿iz ˈnɔt ðə ˈwei
to Hyde Park. Where are you going?" The young man: "We are driving to a nice little
tə ˈhaid ˈpɑ:k ‖ ˈwɛər‿ə‿ju: ˈgəuiŋ? ‖ ðə ˈjʌŋ ˈmæn | wi:‿ə ˈdraiviŋ tu‿ə ˈnais litl
snack-bar." Betsy: "Please stop the car." The young man, laughing: "I'm the big bad
ˈsnækbɑ: ‖ ˈbetsi | ˈpli:z‿ˈstɔp ðə ˈkɑ: ‖ ðə ˈjʌŋ ˈmæn | ˈlɑ:fiŋ | ˈaim ðə ˈbig ˈbæd
wolf and you are Red Riding Hood." Betsy cries. The car is driving on. There is
ˈwulf | ənd ˈju:‿ə ˈred ˈraidiŋ hud ‖ ˈbetsi kraiz ‖ ðə ˈkɑ:r‿iz ˈdraiviŋ‿ˈɔn ‖ ðəz‿
a red traffic light. The car stops. Betsy jumps out and runs away. — But where is
ə ˈred ˈtræfik lait ‖ ðə ˈkɑ: ˈstɔps ‖ ˈbetsi ˈdʒʌmps‿ˈaut | ənd ˈrʌnz‿əˈwei ‖ bət ˈwɛər‿iz
the basket for Grandma? Betsy runs back. The traffic light is green. The car is gone.
ðə ˈbɑ:skit fə ˈgrænmɑ:? ‖ ˈbetsi ˈrʌnz ˈbæk ‖ ðə ˈtræfik lait‿iz ˈgri:n ‖ ðə ˈkɑ:r‿iz ˈgɔn ‖
Poor Betsy! Poor Grandma!
ˈpuə ˈbetsi ‖ ˈpuə ˈgrænmɑ: ‖

I. Die ing-Form des Zeitworts (Partizip Präsens)

Grundform		ing-Form		
to wait to look	warten schauen	waiting looking	wartend schauend	Die ing-Form des Zeitworts wird gebildet durch Anhängen der Endung *-ing* an die Grundform (Infinitiv)
a) to drive to smile b) to begin to shut to rub	fahren lächeln beginnen schließen reiben	driving smiling beginning shutting rubbing	fahrend lächelnd beginnend schließend reibend	Besonderheiten in der Schreibung: a) stummes End-*e* fällt weg b) nach einfachem, kurzem, betontem Selbstlaut wird der Endmitlaut verdoppelt

II. Die Verlaufsform I

1. I am waiting / we are waiting you are waiting / you are waiting he (she, it) is waiting / they are waiting	**1. Formen:** Die Verlaufsform wird gebildet aus *to be* + ing-Form
2. Betsy **is standing** in front of the mirror. Betsy steht (gerade) ... Lots of people **are waiting** at the bus stop. Viele Leute warten (gerade) ... Where **are** you **going**? Wohin gehen (fahren) Sie (gerade)? We **are driving** to a tea-room. Wir fahren (sind gerade auf dem Weg) zu ...	**2. Gebrauch:** Die Verlaufsform bezeichnet eine Handlung, die **gerade vor sich geht.** Sie hat begonnen und ist noch nicht abgeschlossen. (Vgl. dt. „ich bin beim Schreiben, beim Packen“)

Merke: Are you waiting for a bus? — *Yes, I am.* Ja. — *No, I'm not.* Nein.

III. *in front of — behind; before — after*

1. The car stops **in front of** the house. There is a garden **behind** the house.	1. örtlich: *in front of* vor *behind* hinter
2. It is two days **before** Mr Turner's holidays. Let's go to the cinema **after** tea.	2. zeitlich: *before* vor *after* nach

Übungen

I. *before — after, in front of — behind*
1. Mr Turner takes a hot bath two days ... his holidays. 2. ... ten minutes he jumps out of the bath. 3. Lots of people are standing ... the cinema. 4. You cannot see Mr Brown from here; he is standing ... the door. 5. Is there a bus stop ... the theatre? 6. ... tea Mr Dent gets his hat.

II. Satzbautafel (Vgl. L 5, Übung I)
Bsp.: Grandma *is waiting* for Betsy.

Grandma	(to wait) for Betsy
I	(to drive) home from the City
You	(to have) a bath
The young man	(to stand) at the entrance
The girls	(to have) tea
Mother and I	(to shut) the windows

III. Bilde die ing-Form: to put — putting, to call, to leave, to know, to rub, to live, to come, to sit, to knock, to run, to look

IV. It is the rush hour
Bsp.: A lot of people *are standing* at the bus stop.
1. A man (to run to the bus stop) 2. A lot of people (to wait at the crossing) 3. A bus (to come round the corner) 4. A lady (to wait for a taxi) 5. A young man and a girl (to stand in front of the cinema) 6. Many people (to look at the shop windows) 7. Two ladies (to come out of a shop)

V. Give answers
1. Where is Betsy standing? 2. What is she doing? 3. Who is Betsy? 4. What are the people doing at the bus stop? 5. Where is the young man's car standing? 6. Why isn't the young man driving to Hyde Park?

VI. Übersetze; *verwende für alle mit * bezeichneten Zeitwörter die Verlaufsform:* 1. Betsy und ihre Großmutter sitzen* im Garten. 2. Der Garten ist hinter dem Haus. 3. Sie trinken* Tee. 4. Auf dem Tisch (*table* [ˈteibl]) sind (!) Kekse, Eier, Käse, Kuchen und Obst. 5. Ein roter Wagen steht* vor dem Haus. 6. Der junge Mann in dem Wagen wartet* auf Betsy. 7. Betsy sagt: „Auf Wiedersehen, Oma.“ 8. Sie geht zum Wagen und steigt ein. 9. Der Wagen fährt an. 10. Betsy sagt zu dem jungen Mann: „Sie sind sehr freundlich.“

7 A Letter

ə 'letə

29 Greenleaf Road
'twenti'nain | 'gri:nli:f 'rəud ‖
London, E. 17
'lʌndən | 'i: sevn'ti:n ‖
Sunday, June 5th
'sʌndi | 'dʒu:n ðə 'fifθ ‖

Stamp

Mr Dudley Walker
34 Christchurch Road
Bromley
Kent
BRI 3PH

Dear Dudley,
'diə 'dʌdli ‖

At last we are in our new home. It is a nice house with
ət 'lɑ:st wi:‿ər‿in‿auə 'nju: 'həum ‖ it‿iz‿ə 'nais 'haus wið
five rooms. It is in the same road as my parents' house.
'faiv 'rumz ‖ it‿iz‿in ðə 'seim 'rəud | əz mai 'pɛərənts haus ‖
Downstairs we have a sitting-room, a dining-room and a
'daunstɛəz wi: hæv‿ə 'sitiŋrum | ə 'dainiŋrum | ənd‿ə
kitchen, upstairs three bedrooms and a bathroom with a
'kitʃin | 'ʌpstɛəz 'θri: 'bedrumz | ənd‿ə 'bɑ:θrum wið‿ə
lavatory. There is a little front garden, but we have a back
'lævətəri ‖ ðəz‿ə 'litl 'frʌnt 'gɑ:dn | bət wi: hæv‿ə 'bæk
garden, too. It runs down to the railway. Every minute
gɑ:dn | 'tu: ‖ it 'rʌnz 'daun tə ðə 'reilwei ‖ 'evri 'minit
we hear the trains, but we take no notice, as the rent is
wi: 'hiə ðə 'treinz | bət wi: 'teik 'nəu 'nəutis | əz ðə 'rent‿iz
cheap. The landlord is my wife's brother.
'tʃi:p ‖ ðə 'lænlɔ:d‿iz mai 'waifs 'brʌðər ‖

In the evening we are often at home. Sometimes Shirley's
in ði‿'i:vniŋ wi:‿ər‿'ɔfn‿ət 'həum ‖ 'sʌmtaimz 'ʃə:liz‿
sister calls on us. She always talks about new clothes.
'sistə 'kɔ:lz‿ɔn‿əs ‖ ʃi:‿'ɔ:lwəz 'tɔ:ks‿əbaut 'nju: 'kləuðz ‖
Visitors are welcome, but even without friends' visits
'vizitəz‿ə 'welkəm | bət‿i:vn wi'ðaut 'frendz 'vizits
we are never bored. There are the flowers to water, a
wi:‿ə 'nevə 'bɔ:d ‖ ðər‿ə ðə 'flauəz tu 'wɔ:tə | ə
curtain to hang up or a carpet to nail down. Shirley
'kə:tn tə hæŋ‿'ʌp | ɔ:r‿ə 'kɑ:pit‿tə neil 'daun ‖ 'ʃə:li
writes a letter or reads a book, and sometimes she plays
'raits‿ə 'letə | ɔ: 'ri:dz‿ə 'buk | ənd 'sʌmtaimz ʃi: 'pleiz
the piano. Fortunately the walls are thick. The neighbours
ðə 'piænəu ‖ 'fɔ:tʃnitli ðə 'wɔ:lz‿ə 'θik ‖ ðə 'neibəz
say nothing. (Only their dog howls sometimes!) So we say
sei 'nʌθiŋ ‖ əunli ðɛə 'dɔg 'haulz‿sʌmtaimz ‖ səu 'wi: sei
nothing about their children's noise.
nʌθiŋ‿əbaut 'ðɛə 'tʃildrənz nɔiz ‖

Come and spend an evening with us. Write or phone
'kʌm‿ənd 'spend‿ən‿'i:vniŋ wið‿əs ‖ 'rait‿ɔ: 'fəun |
before you come.
bifɔ: ju: 'kʌm ‖

Give my love to Aunt Sarah and Uncle Henry. All the best,
'giv mai 'lʌv tu‿ɑ:nt 'sɛərə‿ənd‿ʌŋkl 'henri ‖ 'ɔ:l ðə 'best

Yours,
'jɔ:z |

Charlie
'tʃɑ:li ‖

I. Der Besitzfall (s-Genitiv)

nur auf Personen, Tiere und in Ausnahme auf Länder

Der Besitzfall antwortet auf die Frage *whose?* wessen Er wird gebildet:

1. **Shirley's** sister [-iz] **my wife's** brother [-fs]	Shirleys Schwester der Bruder meiner Frau	1. in der **Einzahl** durch Auslassungszeichen + *s*
2. my **parents'** house [-ts] our **neighbours'** dog [-əz] Aber: the **children's** noise [-nz]	das Haus meiner Eltern der Hund unserer Nachbarn	2. in der **Mehrzahl** nur durch Auslassungszeichen (wenn die Mehrzahl auf *-s* endet).

II. Die Wortstellung

	Satzgegenstand	Satzaussage	Ergänzung
	We	hear	the trains.
Every minute	we	hear	the trains.
As our garden runs down to the railway,	we	hear	the trains.

Die Wortstellung (Reihenfolge der Satzglieder) ist im Englischen strenger als im Deutschen.
Sie ist immer: Satzgegenstand — Satzaussage — Ergänzung.
Sie darf auch nicht geändert werden, wenn eine Umstandsbestimmung oder ein Nebensatz vorausgeht. Vgl. dagegen das Deutsche!

III. Die Stellung von *always, often, never, sometimes*

She **always** talks about new clothes. She **often** plays the piano. He **never** waters the flowers.	*Always, never, often, sometimes* stehen vor der Satzaussage. *Sometimes* kann auch am Satzanfang oder Satzende stehen. (Their dog howls sometimes.)

Aber: Nach *to be* erfolgt Nachstellung wie im Deutschen: He is never bored.
We are often at home.

IV. Die Zahlen 13—100

13	thirteen	['θə:'ti:n]	**21**	twenty-one ['twenti'wʌn]	**30**	thirty	['θə:ti]
14	fourteen	['fɔ:'ti:n]	**22**	twenty-two	**40**	**forty**	['fɔ:ti]
15	**fifteen**	['fif'ti:n]	**23**	twenty-three	**50**	**fifty**	['fifti]
16	sixteen	['siks'ti:n]	**24**	twenty-four	**60**	sixty	['siksti]
17	seventeen	['sevn'ti:n]	**25**	twenty-five	**70**	seventy	['sevnti]
18	**eighteen**	['ei'ti:n]	**26**	twenty-six	**80**	**eighty**	['eiti]
19	nineteen	['nain'ti:n]	**27**	twenty-seven	**90**	ninety	['nainti]
20	twenty	['twenti]	**28**	twenty-eight	**100**	one (a) hundred	['wʌn'hʌndrəd]
			29	twenty-nine			

I. *Whose?* 1. Whose home is in Greenleaf Road? 2. Whose parents live in the same road? 3. Whose husband is Charlie? 4. Whose brother is the landlord? 5. Whose house is in Bromley? 6. Whose uncle is Uncle Henry? 7. Whose dog howls sometimes? 8. Whose grandmother lives near Hyde Park? 9. Whose car is round the corner?

II. Wandle die Sätze um

Bsp.: The visitors' dog is in the garden.
Their dog is in the garden.

1. *The boy's* mother is not at home. 2. Where are *the children's* parents? 3. *That lady's* brother is our landlord. 4. Is *your friend's* house near the railway? 5. *Aunt Sarah's* cakes are always very good. 6. Is *Uncle Henry's* letter interesting? 7. *Mrs Walker's* baby is ill.

III. Setze das Wort in Klammern an die richtige Stelle

a) *Bsp.:* Charlie goes to the pictures in the evening (never).
Charlie never goes to the pictures in the evening.

1. Mr and Mrs Turner call on Charlie in the evening (often). 2. Mrs Turner and Shirley talk about clothes (always). 3. Charlie and Mr Turner go out for a drink (often). 4. The men have plenty of drinks in the kitchen (always). 5. When they go back to the sitting-room, Shirley plays the piano (sometimes). 6. Mr Turner takes his car when he calls on Charlie (never).

b) "Home, Sweet Home!"

1. Mr Brown is bored at home (sometimes). 2. His wife is in the garden after tea (often). 3. The TV-programme is boring (always). 4. The evening paper is interesting (not always). 5. The neighbours are entertaining (never). 6. The dog is ill (often).

8 Charlie's New Home

It is a Saturday afternoon. Shirley and Charlie are having tea in their sitting-room. The windows are open.

Charlie: I like our new home, Shirley.

Shirley: I know, I like it, too. (Suddenly there is a loud noise from the railway.)

Charlie: Listen! A train is coming.

Shirley: No, it's going.

Charlie: Never mind! They come and go every minute. Pass the cheese and biscuits, please. I'm enjoying my tea.

Shirley: I always enjoy my tea on Saturdays. Have another cup. (Again there is a loud noise from the railway.) The furniture is shaking. What's happening?

Charlie: Two trains are passing. They always pass at this time.

Shirley: Oh yes, they usually meet here. (Charlie is sitting with his head in his hands.) What are you doing, Charlie?

Charlie: I'm waiting.

Shirley: You're waiting for what?

Charlie: I'm waiting for the next train.

Shirley: Oh no, Charlie, please! (She gets up, goes to the piano and begins to play.)

Charlie: Why are you playing the piano now?

Shirley: I often play the piano. I never hear the trains then.

Charlie: So the trains sometimes get on your nerves, too?

Shirley: No, Charlie, the trains never get on my nerves, but you're getting on my nerves.

Charlie: Why?

Shirley: You're sitting there with your head in your hands and you're waiting for the next train. (Shirley begins to play.)

Charlie: What are you playing?

Shirley: I'm playing, "Oh, how lovely is the night". (Suddenly a dog howls outside.)

Neighbour's voice: Stop that noise, Wolf. I'm sorry, Shirley, but Wolf loves it when you play the piano. That's why he howls. What about a drink, you two? Are you coming over?

The music stops. Shirley and Charlie leave the house and go to join their neighbour.

Die einfache Form (ordinary form) steht	**Die Verlaufsform** (continuous form) steht
1. wenn etwas immer so ist:	wenn ein Vorgang in seinem Verlauf geschildert wird (dt. häufig: gerade):
My grandma **lives** in London. The garden **runs down** to the railway.	Shirley **is staying** with her parents this week. Now they **are running** down the street.
2. wenn sich Vorgänge wiederholen (z. B. nach Zeitangaben wie *always*, *often*, *never*, *sometimes*, *every day*):	
She often **plays** the piano. They always **have** tea in the afternoon.	Listen, Shirley **is playing** the piano. Look, they **are having** tea.
3. wenn verschiedene Vorgänge aufeinander folgen oder plötzlich auftreten:	
She **gets** up, **goes** to the piano and **begins** to play. Suddenly a dog **howls.**	She **is writing** letters and **listening** to the radio.
4. bei Vorgängen, die nur einen Augenblick dauern:	
Mr Turner **opens** his eyes. He **turns on** the hot water.	Now she **is opening** the door. Listen, a train **is coming.**

Merke: Meist **nicht** in der Verlaufsform stehen: to have, to hear, to know, to like, to love, to say, to stop, to think, to want

Merke: **to have** im Sinne von nehmen, essen, trinken, hat die Verlaufsform, wenn die Handlung gerade im Gange ist.

Übungen

I. Their New Home

Bsp.: Shirley and Charlie/to have tea in their sitting-room. They always ... Shirley and Charlie are having tea in their sitting-room. They always have tea in their sitting-room.

1. Look, Charlie/to enjoy his cheese and biscuits. He always ... 2. Listen, a neighbour/to play the piano. She often ... 3. At the same time a dog/to howl outside. It usually ... when it hears the piano. 4. Two trains/to pass now. Two trains always ... at this time. 5. The trains often/to get on Charlie's nerves. They never ... on Shirley's nerves. 6. Now Charlie/to wait for the next train. He always ...

II. Answer: 1. Where are Shirley and Charlie having tea? 2. Why is there a loud noise suddenly? 3. What happens when two trains pass at the same time? 4. Why has Charlie his head in his hands? 5. What is Shirley playing on the piano? 6. Why is the dog howling?

III. Bilde Fragen in der Verlaufsform

Bsp.: You/to paint the bath red? Are you painting the bath red?

1. The bus/to come round the corner? 2. A lot of people/to wait at the bus stop? 3. You/to go to the office now? 4. Your friend/to talk about new clothes in front of that shop? 5. Mr Brown/to read an interesting book? 6. He/to write a letter to his parents?

IV. A Letter *(Continuous form or ordinary form?)*

1. Dear Dudley, I (to write) this letter on a Saturday afternoon. 2. Shirley (to water) the flowers in the garden. 3. My parents (to play) with the dog in the kitchen and my sister (to play) the piano in the sitting-room. 4. "Home, sweet home!" I always (to say). 5. What I (to want) to tell you is this: our new house is full of noises. 6. The trains (to come and to go) every minute. The windows (to shake), the table (to shake), my hands always (to shake) when a train (to pass). 7. I (to hear) the trains in the sitting-room, I (to hear) them in the lavatory, I (to hear) them in bed. 8. Now I (to know) why the rent is cheap. 9. I must stop now. Shirley (to come) in. 10. She (to like) our new home. 11. So I (to say) nothing about the noise. All the best, Charlie.

V. Übersetze: 1. Herr Brown ist 44, seine Frau 35. 2. Sie haben ein Haus in Wimbledon. 3. Frau Browns Schwester besucht sie gerade *(to call on them)*[1] mit einem jungen Mann. 4. Sie alle sitzen im Wohnzimmer und trinken Tee. 5. Herr Brown und der junge Mann sprechen über Autos, die Damen *(ladies)* über neue Hüte. 6. Herr Brown mag den jungen Mann. 7. Er wohnt in der gleichen Straße wie die Browns. 8. Der junge Mann verbringt jede freie Minute mit Frau Browns Schwester. 9. Er liebt sie und sie liebt ihn.

[1] Wörter in runden Klammern sind Übersetzungshilfen.

3-5046

9 The Big Store

Do you know Harrods ? When you are in London, go and see this big store. Do you want a haircut ? The big store can provide it. Does a lady want to buy a monkey ? Does a sportsman want a motorboat ? The big store can provide everything.

Do you wish to bring your dog along ? There's a dogs' waiting-room on the ground floor. There your dog can wait until you come back. You don't like to leave it with other dogs ? Well then, you must carry it.

Do you know who the most important customer is ? It is the Queen. Does she shop at Harrods ? Of course she does. What can you do to pass the time ? You can go to the restaurant or take a golf lesson. Golf is better for your figure.

Do you want to get married ? The big store provides the wedding dress, the flowers, the hairdresser, the wine and waiters, the cake, the cars with drivers, in fact everything.

Can it provide the bride ? Look around — use your eyes ! Perhaps your future wife is among the many pretty assistants in the various departments.

You can't go to the store because it's too far ? Never mind ! You can order by phone. Phone the order department even after midnight, and you can have your bacon in time for breakfast.

Do you know that the funeral department even has its own coffin factory ? Yes, the big store can provide everything.

An English Lesson

Good evening, ladies and gentlemen.
I'm your new teacher.
Let's begin to read.
Start at the top (at the bottom, at line 3) of page 3.
Read the last sentence again.
Speak louder, please.
Repeat the last word. All together, please.
Yes, that's difficult to pronounce.
Go on. Stop.
Now translate the first paragraph.
Come to the blackboard, please, Mr N.
Take the chalk.
Write the new words on the blackboard.
Is the first word correct (right) ?
No, it is wrong. (There is a mistake in it.)
Who knows how to spell the word ?
Now look at the picture on page 16 and answer my questions.
Take out your exercise-books.
Write the answers in your exercise-books.
Who knows the answer ?

I. Die Wortstellung im Aussagesatz mit *can, can't (= cannot), must*

Satzgegenstand (Subjekt)	*can, can't, must* (Hilfsverb)	Satzaussage (Vollverb)	Ergänzung (Objekt)	
You	**can (can't)**	**buy** kaufen	**wine**	*He can (can't) — he must* erhält kein *s* in der 3. Person Einzahl! Vergleichen Sie die Wortstellung im Deutschen.
He	**must**	**buy**	**wine**	
She	**can't (cannot)**	**buy**	**wine**	He must buy wine. Er muß Wein kaufen.

II. Der Fragesatz mit *can, can't, must*

Hilfsverb	Subjekt	Vollverb	Objekt	
Can	**you**	**buy**	**wine?**	Im Fragesatz mit *can, can't, must* bleibt die Wortstellung des Aussagesatzes Subjekt — Vollverb — Objekt. Vergleiche dagegen das Deutsche:
Can't	**he**	**carry**	**your dog?**	
Must	**he**	**have**	**a haircut?**	Kann er nicht deinen Hund tragen?

III. Die Frage mit *to do*

Frage	Verneinte Frage
Do I/you/we/they know her? Kenne ich sie?	**Don't I/you/we/they know her?**
Does he/she/it know her?	**Doesn't he/she/it know her?**

IV. Der Fragesatz

Hilfszeitwort (Hilfsverb)	Satzgegenstand (Subjekt)	Vollzeitwort (Vollverb)	Ergänzung (Objekt)	
Do	**you**	**buy**	**wine?**	Die Frage entsteht durch Voranstellung von *do* vor der Aussage. (Wörtl. Tust du kaufen Wein? Wo tust du kaufen Wein?)
Where do	**they**	**buy**	**wine?**	
Why do	**we**	**buy**	**wine?**	*to do* wird verwendet zur Bildung von Fragen bei Vollverben.
Does	**he**	**buy**	**wine?**	**Merke**: Bei der 3. Person Einzahl wird die Frage mit *does* gebildet. Beachte den Wegfall des *s* beim Vollverb.
Does	**she**	**buy**	**wine?**	

I. Satzbautafel *Bilde Fragen und beantworte sie*

Ex.: Do you play tennis? — Yes, I do. — No, I don't.

Do (Does)	you	play tennis?
	your friend	drive a car?
	your sisters	like wine?
	Miss Smith	want to get married?

II. Verwandle die Sätze in Fragen

1. This shop sells stamps. 2. Your parents know my grandmother. 3. Aunt Sarah reads every evening. 4. She goes to bed after midnight. 5. Uncle Henry spends every free minute in the garden. 6. They go to church every Sunday.

III. Ask: *Where?* or *When?*

1. The customers leave their dogs *in the dogs' waiting-room.* 2. Their children pass the time *in the children's playroom.* 3. Many customers phone the store *in the evening.* 4. Uncle Henry takes golf lessons *at Harrods.* — 5. Shirley plays the piano *after tea.* 6. She writes letters *in the evening.*

IV. Bilde Fragen

a) mit *must*

Ex.: to get up at seven — Must he get up at seven?

1. to have breakfast at eight 2. to water the flowers in the garden 3. to hang up the curtains 4. to nail down the carpets 5. to go to the shops 6. to carry the furniture 7. to play golf. 8. to paint the house

b) Bilde die obigen Fragen jetzt mit *to do*

Ex.: to get up at seven — Does he get up at seven?

V. Translate: 1. Diese junge Dame will heiraten. Wo kauft sie ihr Brautkleid? Im *(at)* großen Kaufhaus. 2. Wo kauft sie den Kuchen? Im großen Kaufhaus. 3. Wer ist der zukünftige Mann? Ich habe keine Ahnung. 4. Was kann das Kaufhaus besorgen? Alles von einem Haarschnitt bis zu einer Beerdigung.

10 At the Marriage Agency

Mrs Baker opens the door to the waiting-room and calls: "Next, please." A young woman enters the office of the Wimbledon Marriage Agency.

Young woman: My name is Betty Brown. I want ...

Mrs Baker: Don't tell me what you want. I know ... Tell me your age.

Betty Brown: I'm twenty-five. But I don't know why ...

Mrs Baker: Don't be in a hurry. We've plenty of time. Don't hesitate to answer all my questions. I want to test you. Do you dislike pop music?

Betty Brown: No, I don't dislike pop music. I love it.

Mrs Baker: Do you like to dance?

Betty Brown: Yes, I do. But I don't often dance because I haven't much time.

Mrs Baker: Do you often watch television?

Betty Brown: No, I don't. There's seldom a good programme on.

Mrs Baker: Do you hate classical music?

Betty Brown: No, I don't hate classical music, but I prefer pop.

Mrs Baker: Do you do a lot of sports?

Betty Brown: No, I don't do a lot of sports. I just play tennis and I swim a bit.

Mrs Baker: Do you find it easy to talk to strangers at parties?

Betty Brown: I don't find it difficult to talk to strangers, but I rarely go to parties.

Mrs Baker: Do you think that romantic love is necessary for a successful marriage?

Betty Brown: I don't know.

Mrs Baker: Don't be silly. Of course you know.

Betty Brown: Many people say that romantic love doesn't last long.

Mrs Baker: Don't believe that. It can last a long time with the right man. Are you often bad-tempered?

Betty Brown: I'm only bad-tempered when I don't get my early morning tea.

Mrs Baker: Who makes the early morning tea, your mother, your father, your brother or your sister?

Betty Brown: My husband makes it.

Mrs Baker: Your husband? What can I do for you, Mrs Brown? This is a marriage agency.

Betty Brown: I know, Mrs Baker. The rent for your office is overdue. My husband wants to know whether he can have the money soon.

Die Verneinung mit *to do*

I. Formen

Verneinung: **I do not** play	ich spiele nicht	
I do not (don't) play	you do not (don't) play	he does not (doesn't) play
we do not (don't) play	you do not (don't) play	they do not (don't) play

II. Die Verneinung im Aussagesatz

I **do not**	like	to leave my dog here.	Die Verneinung wird mit *to do* gebildet.
Perhaps you **don't**	want	to go to the store.	
The store **does not**	provide	the bride.	
Aber: The store cannot	provide	the bride.	Aber: *to do* steht nicht bei den Hilfszeitwörtern.
The children are not	playing	in the playroom.	
Cake is not		good for your figure.	

III. Die verneinte Befehlsform

Don't believe that.	Glauben Sie das nicht (glaube das nicht, glaubt das nicht)!	Die verneinte Befehlsform wird mit *don't (do not)* gebildet, auch bei *to have* und *to be.*
Don't be silly.	Seien Sie nicht töricht!	
Don't have a bath after breakfast.	Nimm kein Bad nach dem Frühstück.	

Übungen

I. Questions on the text: 1. What does Mrs Baker say when Betty Brown enters her office? 2. Why doesn't Betty dance very often? 3. Why doesn't she like television? 4. What does she think of romantic love? 5. Why does Betty call on Mrs Baker?

II. Verneine die Sätze:

a) 1. Betty Brown is in a hurry. 2. She hesitates to answer Mrs Baker's questions. 3. She dislikes pop music. 4. She likes to dance. 5. She watches television every day. 6. She hates classical music. 7. She prefers pop. 8. She does a lot of sports. 9. She plays tennis. 10. She finds it easy to talk to strangers. 11. She thinks that romantic love is necessary for a successful marriage. 12. She gets early morning tea in bed. 13. Mrs Baker pays the rent.

b) *Stelle verneinte Fragen zu den obigen Sätzen*

Ex.: Isn't Betty Brown in a hurry?
Doesn't she hesitate ...?

III. Answer the questions

Ex.: What does the boss say when an assistant reads the papers in the shop? — Don't read the papers, please.

What does the boss (your brother, Mrs Brown, Bill, Sally) say when:

1. a typist phones her friends from the office? 2. Your sister plays the piano when television is on? 3. Mr Brown goes to the cinema without his wife? 4. Sally is sad? 5. Sally wants to take a taxi when there is a bus? 6. Bill is bad-tempered?

IV. What they do and what they don't do

Ex.: They go to a snack-bar, but they ... (don't) go to a restaurant.

1. Shirley buys stockings at the big store, but she ... food there. 2. They believe in marriage, but they ... in romantic love. 3. Charlie hears the trains, but he ... the neighbours' dog. 4. Shirley dislikes classical music, but she ... pop music. 5. She talks to her neighbours, but she ... to strangers. 6. Charlie makes early morning tea, but he ... the beds.

V. Translate: In der Heiratsvermittlung 1. Auf dem Tisch im Wartezimmer ist *(there is)* ein Buch: Marriage. 2. Es beginnt: Kauf keinen teuren Wagen ohne deine Frau. 3. Sei nicht traurig, wenn sie Klavier spielt. 4. Sage nicht, daß romantische Liebe nicht lange dauert. 5. Lauf nicht weg, wenn deine Frau singt *(to sing)*. 6. Lies nicht die Zeitung beim Frühstück *(at breakfast)*. 7. Sieh nicht fern, wenn sie einen Ausgehabend will. 8. Sei nicht schwierig, wenn sie schlecht gelaunt ist. 9. Sage nicht, daß du die Frau des Nachbarn magst. 10. Gehe nicht zu Partys ohne deine Frau. 11. Sage nicht, daß andere Frauen hübsch sind.

11 A Week at the Seaside

Monday: August Bank Holiday. It is the Smith family's first day at Brighton. They arrive at their guest-house near the station. The landlady welcomes them with a smile. For dinner they have soup, meat, potatoes, vegetables, and then peaches. Freddie, the son, finds a fly in the soup. He makes a face and passes a remark about flies in the food. The landlady blushes and tries to change the subject. "Do you have eggs and bacon for breakfast?" she asks. Only Sheila, the eighteen-year-old daughter, wants to have tomatoes instead, because she is slimming.

Tuesday: The weather is fine. After breakfast the family hurries to the beach. Freddie takes his camera. The Smiths sit in their new swimsuits on the pebbles (Brighton has no sands). "What about a photograph with the sea in the background?" Freddie says. "We have got plenty of time for that," Sheila replies. "Wait until we are brown." But Freddie takes no notice. They all put on a happy smile. After that they all bathe in the sea.

Wednesday: Rain, nothing but rain. They send their friends picture postcards of Brighton's sunny beach.

Thursday: Three more ladies arrive at the guest-house. The weather clears up.

Friday: Beauty competition on the pier. Has Sheila got a chance? She looks beautiful with her fair hair and slim figure. The judges watch the beauty parade. Miss Lily Pond, the film star, gives out the prizes. Number three wins. Sheila is Miss Brighton.

Saturday: The Smiths are the Mayor's guests! A band is playing on the pier.

Sunday: At the station Freddie buys a paper. Sheila's picture is on the front page. They buy twenty copies.

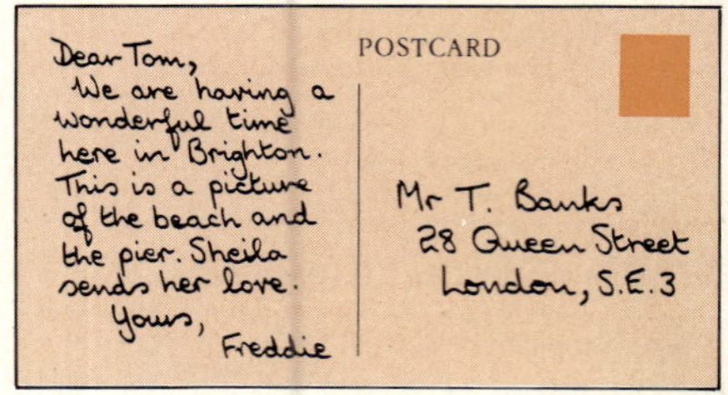

Meals

What meals do the English have?

They have a large *breakfast* in the morning: cornflakes or porridge with milk and sugar, eggs and bacon, toast or bread and butter, and marmalade. And what do they drink? Tea.

Many people have a *cup of coffee* at 11 o'clock.

They have *lunch* about 1 o'clock: usually meat, potatoes, vegetables and a sweet.

And what do they have in the afternoon? *Tea*, of course: several cups of tea, bread and butter with jam, and cakes or biscuits.

In the evening some people have *dinner*, but most people have only a light *supper*.

I. Besonderheiten der Mehrzahlbildung I (Pluralbildung)

1. a) a dress — two **dresses** [ˈdresiz] that peach — those **peaches** a box — two **boxes** b) his face — their faces [ˈfeis**iz**] a prize — two prizes the judge — the judges Beachte: house [haus]— houses [ˈhauziz]	1. Das Mehrzahl-*s* der Hauptwörter muß stets hörbar sein. Daher hängen Hauptwörter, die auf Zischlaute [s, z, ʃ, ʒ] enden, in der Aussprache [-iz] an. In der Schreibung wird ***-es*** angehängt (a), wenn nicht schon die Einzahl auf stummes *-e* endet (b).
2. a lady — two **ladies** a copy — twenty **copies** a fly — many **flies** Aber: a day — two days	2. ***-y*** wird in der Mehrzahl zu ***-ies***, wenn ein Mitlaut vorausgeht.

II. Besonderheiten der 3. Person Einzahl (Singular) des Zeitwortes (Verbs)

1. a) to pass — he **passes** to blush — she **blushes** b) to change — he changes [ˈtʃeindʒ**iz**]	Für die Bildung der 3. Person Einzahl des Zeitworts gelten dieselben Regeln wie für die Mehrzahlbildung des Hauptwortes (s. I oben)
2. to reply — she re**plies** to hurry — he hur**ries** Aber: to buy — he buys	

III. Frage und Verneinung von *to have* — *to have got*

1. **Do** you **have** (= take) a bath every evening? Nimmst du ...? **Do** you **have** eggs and bacon for breakfast? Essen Sie (immer) Eier und Speck zum F.? We **don't have** soup every day. Wir essen nicht jeden Tag Suppe. **Do** you often **have** a drink in the evening? Trinken Sie oft etwas ...?	1. Frage und Verneinung von *to have* werden **mit to do** gebildet, wenn *to have* die Bedeutung eines Vollzeitwortes hat (z. B. „essen, trinken, nehmen").
2. We **have got** plenty of time. Wir haben ... **Has** Sheila **got** a chance? Hat Sheila...? Yes, she has. I **haven't got** a camera. habe keinen Fotoapp. How many brothers and sisters **have you got?** Wieviele Geschwister haben Sie?	2. In der Umgangssprache wird statt des einfachen *to have* haben oft ***to have got*** haben verwendet. In der Kurzantwort entfällt *got.*

I. Give answers: 1. When do the Smiths arrive at Brighton? 2. Is their guest-house near the beach? 3. What do they have for dinner? 4. Why does Freddy make a face? 5. What does the landlady ask the family? 6. Why does Sheila want to have tomatoes for breakfast? 7. What does the family do after breakfast on Tuesday? 8. What does Sheila reply when Freddy wants to take a photograph? 9. What does the family do on Wednesday? 10. Why is Thursday a good day?

II. Setze die Wörter in Klammern in die Mehrzahl

On the last weekend in August many Londoners leave their (house), (office) and (factory) and go to Brighton. (Family) with (child), (boy) and (girl), young (lady) in their best (dress) arrive in (train), (car) and (bus). Brighton's (guest-house) are full. The (landlady) smile. — On Monday evening the visitors go back to London with brown (face).

III. *To have got* for *to have*

Ex.: Has Sheila blue eyes? — Has Sheila *got* blue eyes? Yes, she has *got* blue eyes./No, ...

1. Have the Browns a new car? Yes, ... 2. Has the Turners' house a nice garden? Yes, ... 3. Have the Smiths a child? No, ... 4. Have the Turners plenty of money? Yes, ... 5. Has your sister a dog? No, ...

IV. Translate: 1. Die Familie Smith verbringt (gerade) eine Woche in Brighton. 2. Wenn das Wetter schön ist, gehen sie zum Strand. 3. Frau Smith nimmt einen Korb mit Obst, Keksen und Kuchen [mit][1]. 4. „Hast du deinen Fotoapparat, Freddie?" fragt Sheila. 5. Sie sieht sehr schön aus in ihrem neuen Badeanzug. 6. Sie ist sehr schlank und hat schönes blondes Haar. 7. Sheila gewinnt den Schönheitswettbewerb.

[1] Wörter in eckigen Klammern bleiben unübersetzt

12 Christmas in England

It is Christmas Eve. The members of the Schmitz family in Cologne are unpacking their presents under the Christmas tree. One of the parcels is from England. Karla Schmitz passes it to her father. It is from his friend George Taylor. Herr Schmitz opens the parcel and shows the present to his wife. It is a tape. They put it on the tape-recorder and soon they hear George's voice: "Hello, Karl, hello, Gertrud, hello, Karla! This is George speaking. A merry Christmas to you all. Thank you for your letter, Karl. In Germany you don't seem to know much about Christmas in England, so let me tell you something about it.

Our walls are covered with Christmas cards, and the postman brings us more every day. Some people get hundreds of them. We show them to our friends when they call on us.

I am dreaming of a white Christmas, but the weather is too mild for snow. We do have Christmas trees, but we don't light them until Christmas Day. Christmas Eve is just an ordinary evening: the shops are open until the normal closing time. Only the carol singers in the streets remind us that it is Christmas Eve.

On Christmas morning we receive our presents, go to church, and then have the traditional Christmas dinner with turkey and Christmas pudding. We wear paper hats, the houses look bright with balloons and mistletoe. Marilyn never forgets to hang up the mistletoe. It hangs from the lamp in the sitting-room, and if a lady steps under it, she gets a kiss. Often a hopeful young man waits until the mouse runs into the trap. The lady cannot refuse. Sometimes the mouse is in the trap, and everybody looks away.

Well, friends, Christmas is the season of joy, love, kindness and friendship. If we have quarrels, we should kiss and make it up; if we have no quarrels, we can kiss, too.

And now I send you our best wishes for a merry Christmas and a happy New Year.

Good-bye, and good luck.

Charlotte, Marilyn and George."

Conversation in the Plane

He: We must fasten our seat belts.
She: I always feel nervous before take-off.
He: Do you? Flying is very safe nowadays. What about a drink?
She: Just a small whisky, then. I don't usually drink — or smoke.
He: I only smoke a pipe. Cigarettes are specially bad for your health.
(to the stewardess)
Two neat whiskies, please.
She: That's very kind of you. Do you usually fly when you go to Cologne?
He: Yes, it's so slow by rail. It takes ten hours. Ah, here are the whiskies.
She: Thank you. I feel much better now.
He: Oh, that's good.

Die Beugung (Deklination) des Hauptworts und des persönlichen Fürworts

I. Werfall und Wenfall (Nominativ und Akkusativ)

Werfall Wenfall	1. **Our neighbour** is calling. Can you hear **our neighbour?**	1. haben beim Hauptwort die gleiche Form
Werfall Wenfall	2. **He** (Er) is calling. Can you hear **him** (ihn)**?**	2. beim persönlichen Fürwort verschiedene Form

Formen des persönlichen Fürworts (Personalpronomen)

Werfall	I	you	he	she	it	we	you	they
Wenfall	me mich	you dich	him ihn	her sie	it es	us uns	you euch	them sie

II. Der Wemfall (Dativ)

Der Wemfall wird gewöhnlich mit *to* gebildet: *to me* mir, *to my mother*, meiner Mutter, *to whom?* wem? Bei einigen Zeitwörtern (bes. *to bring, to give, to hand, to pass, to sell, to send, to show, to tell*) gibt es aber zwei Möglichkeiten:

	Wemfall (Dativ)	Wenfall (Akkusativ)	Der Wemfall kann stehen
1. I send The postman brings	**you** **Mr Schmitz**	our best wishes. a small parcel.	1. **ohne** *to* direkt hinter dem Zeitwort (Stellungs-Wemfall, unbetont)
	Wenfall	Wemfall mit *to*	
2. He shows Karla passes	the parcel it	**to his wife.** **to her father.**	2. **mit** *to* hinter dem Wenfall (*to*-Wemfall, betont)

Merke: Das Wichtigere — das, wonach gefragt ist oder worauf es ankommt — steht hinten.

III. Der Wesfall (Genitiv)

1. **Mr Taylor's** tape-recorder **our neighbours'** dog Beachte: George's [ˈdʒɔːdʒiz] voice		1. Der **Wesfall mit *'s*** (vgl. L 7, I) gibt den Besitzer an (Besitzfall) und steht hauptsächlich bei Personen. — Beachte die Aussprache nach Zischlauten!
2. the season **of** joy one **of** the parcels	die Zeit der Freude eines der Päckchen	2. Der **Wesfall mit *of*** steht hauptsächlich bei Sachen.

I. Questions on the Text: 1. What are the members of the Schmitz family doing? 2. What's in the parcel from England? 3. What does George Taylor tell the Schmitz family about Christmas cards? 4. Why can't the Taylors have a white Christmas? 5. What reminds the Taylors that it's Christmas Eve? 6. What do the Taylors do on Christmas morning? 7. What hangs from the lamp in the sitting-room? 8. What should people do when they have quarrels?

II. Setze die fehlenden Fürwörter ein: 1. That lady is our new neighbour. Don't you know ...? 2. The carol singers are in the street. Can you hear ...? 3. Where is my grey jacket? I cannot find ... 4. Uncle Henry is ill. I must go and see ... 5. Here are some flowers for ... 6. Can I go with ...? Please wait for ... 7. Aunt Sarah writes very often. I receive a letter from ... every week.

III. Wemfall mit oder ohne *to*? 1. Before Christmas the postman brings ... us lots of Christmas cards. 2. Do you send presents ... all your friends? 3. No, but I send ... them all Christmas cards. 4. This is a beautiful Christmas card. I must show it ... my guests. 5. Give my love ... your parents. 6. Can you pass this picture ... Mr Turner, please? 7. And can you also hand ... him this parcel?

IV. Translate: 1. Vor Weihnachten schicken wir unseren Freunden Weihnachtskarten. 2. Wir senden ihnen unsere besten Wünsche für ein fröhliches Weihnachten. 3. Euch allen ein glückliches neues Jahr! 4. Am Heiligen Abend zünden wir den Weihnachtsbaum an. 5. Die Engländer *(the English)* hängen Luftballons und Mistelzweig[e] in ihren Zimmern auf. 6. Was essen sie zum Mittagessen am 1. Weihnachtsfeiertag? Das traditionelle Weihnachtsessen ist Truthahn und Weihnachtspudding. 7. Am nächsten Tag besuchen sie ihre Freunde.

13 Landing at Dover

The Belgian boat steams into Dover Harbour. The passengers are on deck with their luggage. A few minutes later the porters come on board. All leave the boat by the gangway. A policeman calls: "British subjects to the right, foreigners to the left." The British subjects show their passports and go straight to the customs; the foreigners must queue at the Passport Control. Several immigration officers are sitting behind high desks. They are asking the passengers questions.

Now it is Signora Capone's turn.

Immigration Officer: Your passport, please, madam. Thank you. Where is your landing card?

Signora Capone: I beg your pardon? What card?

I. O.: Your landing card, madam. Each foreign visitor receives one on the ship.

S. C.: I'm sorry, but I can't find it. What do you want it for?

I. O.: We need it for registration. Well, we must fill up a new card. What is your name, please? — *S. C.:* Capone, Sophia. I am Italian.

I. O.: Where is your place of birth? — *S. C.:* Rome, Italy.

I. O.: What is your date of birth, please, madam?

S. C.: Look in my passport, please.

I. O.: Whom do you want to visit?

S. C.: I have friends in London. Their name is Torelli, and they have a restaurant in Soho.

I. O.: How long do you wish to stay in England, madam?

S. C.: Five days. Who wants to stay long in this climate?

Signora Capone now has to go to the customs hall. Her porter is waiting there with her luggage. "Which of these suitcases are yours?" asks the customs officer. Signora Capone points to two large cases. No, she has nothing to declare, no presents, no cameras, nothing at all. But she must open her luggage. "What's this?" asks the officer, as he finds one gold watch after the other, ten in all. Then he finds eight silver cigarette-cases.

"Will you please come with me?" says the customs officer and takes Signora Capone to the main office.

The boat train to London leaves Dover without the Italian lady.

Porter! Porter!

Porter: Do you want a porter, sir?

Foreign visitor: Yes, please. Will you take my luggage (*Am.* baggage) to the boat train?

P.: Yes, sir. I'll see you at the customs. Here's my number.

F. V.: Get me a corner seat in a non-smoker, please.

P.: I'll do my best, sir. Are you travelling first or second?

F. V.: Second class.

P.: Right, sir!

F. V.: What's the charge for this suitcase?

P.: There's no fixed charge, sir. I leave that to you, sir.

F. V.: Here's 95 pence.

P.: Oh, thanks very much, sir.

I. Die Fragefürwörter

1. **Who** has no landing card? **Whose** passport is this? **To whom** must we show our passports? **Whom** } do you want to visit? **Who**	Wer? Wessen? Wem? Wen?	***Who*** (*whose* usw.) fragen nach Personen ***Whom*** = Wen wird in der Umgangssprache meistens durch *who* ersetzt.

2. Werfall Wenfall	**What** is in the suitcase? **What** does the officer find?	Was?	***What*** (alleinstehend) fragt nach Sachen
3.	**What card** must she show? **What luggage** have you got? **What articles** does the officer find?	Was für (ein,e)?	***What*** vor d. Hauptwort fragt nach einer näheren Bezeichnung der Art

Merke: What is your name? Wie heißen Sie?
What is your age? Wie alt sind Sie?
What colour is your car? Was für eine Farbe hat Ihr Wagen?

4. **Which passengers** go to the right? **Which porter** has your suitcase, sir? **Which** of these suitcases are yours? **Which** is your suitcase, madam?	Welche(r, s)?	***Which*** (vor d. Hauptwort u. alleinstehend) fragt nach Personen und Sachen aus einer begrenzten Anzahl.

II. Der Gebrauch von *to do* in der Frage mit Fragewort

Ergänzung		Satzgegenstand	Vollzeitw. d. Satzaussage		
		Who	wants	to stay here?	Die Frage wird **ohne *to do*** gebildet, wenn das Fragewort selbst Satzgegenstand oder Teil des Satzgegenstandes ist.
		What	makes	her so sad?	
		Which lady	comes	from Italy?	
Aber: What	does	the officer	find?		
Which lady	does	the officer	take	to the office?	

III. Die Nachstellung des Verhältniswortes (Präposition) im Fragesatz

What do you want it **for?**	Wozu...?	In der Umgangssprache tritt das Verhältniswort im Fragesatz ans Satzende.
What are you waiting **for?**	Worauf ...?	
Where do you come **from?**	Woher...?	

I. Give answers: 1. Which harbour does the boat arrive at? 2. To whom do the passengers give their luggage on the boat? 3. Which passengers don't have to queue at the Passport Control? 4. There are immigration officers and customs officers. To which of them must the passengers show their passports, to which their luggage? 5. Whose friends live in Soho? 6. What articles must the passengers declare? 7. Which train leaves Dover without Signora Capone?

II. *Who* or *what?* Frage nach den *schräggedruckten* Wörtern
Ex.: A Belgian boat enters Dover Harbour.
What enters Dover Harbour?
1. *The passengers* are on deck. 2. *Several immigration officers* are sitting behind desks. 3. They are asking the passengers *questions*. 4. Signora Capone shows *her passport*. 5. She must show *her landing card* to the immigration officer. 6. She wants to visit *friends* in Soho. 7. The customs officer finds *ten gold watches*. 8. *The boat train* leaves Dover without the Italian lady.

III. Stelle Fragen mit *whose* und beantworte sie
Ex.: This is a beautiful house. (Charlie)
Whose house is it? It's Charlie's.
1. This is a nice garden. (Mrs Brown) 2. This is an Italian passport. (Signora Capone) 3. This is a big suitcase. (Mr Taylor) 4. These are expensive gold watches. (Mrs Turner) 5. These are lovely children. (our neighbour) 6. These are wonderful picture postcards. (Father)

IV. Translate: 1. Wie heißen Sie? 2. Wie alt sind Sie? 3. Woher kommen Sie? 4. Wen wollen Sie besuchen? 5. Welcher Gepäckträger hat Ihr Gepäck? 6. Wie viele Koffer haben Sie? 7. In Ihrem großen Koffer sind (!) mehrere goldene Uhren. Wozu brauchen Sie sie? 8. Wollen Sie sie verkaufen?

14

The Ideal Husband

Dick and Mary are a young married couple. They have a small furnished flat in the town of Rochester. This is a day in Dick's life.

Seven o'clock. The alarm clock rings. Time for Dick to get up. He jumps out of bed, rushes to the bathroom, washes, shaves and dresses. At ten minutes past seven Mary gets her cup of tea and a bunch of roses from the garden.

At half past seven breakfast is ready. Dick puts the tray with a pot of tea, two boiled eggs, bread and several pieces of toast, butter, marmalade, a bottle of milk and a bowl of sugar beside Mary's bed. He has breakfast with her.

At a quarter to eight breakfast is finished. Dick takes the tray to the kitchen and washes up the dishes: plates, cups, saucers, glasses, knives, forks, spoons and the tea-pot. At five minutes to eight the kitchen is tidy.

At eight o'clock Dick turns on the radio in the bedroom. Then he cleans a pair of shoes for Mary. Mary is reading the morning paper. Dick says: "What are you doing this morning, darling?" Mary says: "I'm waiting for our new cleaner."

The church clock strikes eight. Dick looks at his watch. "It is five past eight," he says. "My watch is right; I always set it by the radio. The church clock is five minutes slow. I'm catching the train to town in twenty-five minutes."

"Are we meeting in town tonight, Dick?" — "Yes, darling, at 7 o'clock at the Café Royal for dinner, is that O. K.?" — "Are we going to have wine, too?" — "Of course, darling." — "Fine, don't be late." — "Good-bye, darling, don't forget to take your umbrella. It's going to rain. I'm off now."

Don't you think Dick is an ideal husband?

What's the Time?

It's (a) quarter past one.
It's ten to seven.
It's half past eleven.
Can you tell me the right time, please?
What's the time by your watch?
I haven't got the right time.
My watch is fast.
The clock is five minutes slow.
I must put it right.
My watch has stopped.
I must wind it up.
There's something wrong with it.

Women's Clothes

A woman wears
a dress
a skirt and blouse or jumper
a suit (skirt and jacket)
and nylon stockings or tights underneath.

In summer she wears
a cotton or woollen dress,
often with a cardigan.

On rainy days she wears
a raincoat,

in winter
a coat with a silk or woolen scarf,
gloves
and a hat.

I. Die Verlaufsform II drückt aus siehe L 8

What **are** you **doing** this morning? Was machst du, was hast du vor? We **are meeting** in town tonight. Wir treffen uns, wollen uns treffen **Are** we **going to have** wine, too? Trinken wir (dann) auch Wein?	daß etwas **beabsichtigt oder geplant** ist. Dabei kann statt der gewöhnlichen Verlaufsform auch eine Umschreibung mit *to be going to* stehen.

Merke: *to go* und *to come* bilden das Futur nur mit der gewöhnlichen Verlaufsform, nicht mit *to be going to.*
Die gewöhnliche Verlaufsform steht meist mit einer Zeitangabe:
We are taking a taxi tonight.

II. Die Uhrzeit I

4 o'clock — 10 minutes **past** 4 — half **past** 4 — 25 minutes **to** 5 — a quarter **to** 5

What's the time? It is	4.0 four o'clock		4.35 twenty-five (minutes)	
	4.05 five (minutes)	**past** four	4.45 a quarter	**to** five
	4.15 a quarter		4.48 twelve minutes	
	4.30 half		4.57 three minutes	

Beachte: a) Die 1. bis 30. Minute bezieht man mit *past* auf die vorhergehende volle Stunde, die 31. bis 59. Minute mit *to* auf die folgende.
b) *o'clock* steht nur bei der vollen Stunde.
c) Das Wort *minutes* kann bei Zeitangaben mit 5, 10, 20, 25 Minuten wegbleiben.

Merke: *dt.* 12 Uhr = *engl.* noon — a quarter of an hour — eine Viertelstunde
dt. 24 Uhr = *engl.* midnight — half an hour — eine halbe Stunde
three quarters of an hour — eine Dreiviertelstunde

III. Besonderer Gebrauch des Wesfalls mit *of* (Genitiv)

1. a cup of tea eine Tasse Tee — a bowl of sugar a pair of shoes — lots of people	1. nach Mengenangaben
2. the City of Oxford die Stadt Oxford the town of Rochester	2. nach einigen geographischen Begriffen

I. At what time ...? 1. At what time does your alarm clock ring? 2. When does your bus (train) go? 3. When do you arrive at your office (shop, factory)? 4. When do you come home? 5. When does your English lesson begin? 6. When do the shops open in the morning? 7. How long are they open in the evening?

II. Forme die Sätze nach folgendem Beispiel um:
Ex.: I often work in the garden. (this evening)
I *am working* in the garden this evening.
I *am going to work* in the g. this evening.
1. My parents always take their holiday in August. (this year) 2. I often spend my holidays in Italy. (next year) 3. Do you meet your friend every Sunday? (next Sunday) 4. We sometimes have dinner at the Café Royal. (tonight) 5. We visit our grandparents every Christmas. (at Christmas)

III. *To bring* (herbringen) **or *to take*** (hin-, wegbringen)**?**
1. Before Christmas the postman ... us Christmas cards. 2. I must ... this parcel to the restaurant. 3. Our neighbour is ill. Let us ... him some flowers. 4. My husband often ... me flowers. 5. I haven't got my car. Can you ... me to the theatre this evening?

IV. Translate: 1. Es ist zehn Minuten nach sechs. 2. Bill kommt [2]vom Büro [1]nach Hause. 3. Er wäscht und rasiert sich. 4. „Wohin gehst (!) du heute abend?" fragt seine Mutter. 5. „Ich gehe (!) ins Theater." 6. Nach einer halben Stunde ist Bill fertig. 7. Er schaut auf seine Uhr. Es ist 20 vor sieben. Geht seine Uhr richtig? 8. Er schaltet das Radio ein und zündet eine Zigarette an. 9. Um $^3/_4$7 Uhr stellt seine Mutter ein Tablett mit Tee, Brot, Butter und Käse auf den Tisch. 10. Aber Bill hat keine Zeit. Er muß [2]um sieben Uhr [1]Sally treffen.

[1] Die kleinen Ziffern geben die Reihenfolge der Satzglieder im Englischen an.

15 Under the Roofs of London

"What you need is a good boarding-house," said the old gentleman opposite me in the boat train to London. "Go to 83 Warwick Terrace. Or was it 38? No, I'm sure it was 83. Very central, near Paddington Station. You can't miss it. Nice little woman — a young widow, you know — good food, TV and all the rest. I stayed there two years ago." I at once had a vision of a warm-hearted widow with a comfortable home, of evenings with party games and laughter.

At Victoria Station I decided to take the Tube to Paddington. When I arrived there twenty minutes later, I turned to the right and then to the left and suddenly was in the London of Queen Victoria's days. Large grey houses, all alike, recalled the time when the rich middle class lived there. Warwick Terrace was a broad street. Some of the houses had notices in their windows 'Bed and breakfast' or 'Rooms to let'. The district was now the dormitory of thousands of clerks and of white, black and yellow students.

I looked for number 83, but did not find it. There was no such number in the street. Was there a number 38? Yes, there it was! I knocked, waited, and a cleaner opened the door. I entered the narrow hall, full of hope. My spirits dropped at the sight of the thin old landlady with orange-coloured hair. She welcomed me with a smile. Yes, she had a room free on the top floor. "My terms are £ 65 a week for bed, breakfast and dinner," she said. "Would you like to see the room?" I nodded and carried my luggage behind her up the stairs into a dark room under the roof with a very small window. "Make yourself at home," she smiled. I did not like the room, but I handed her sixty-five pounds for one week.

This is my third week in that dark room: no cards, no games, no laughter, no warm-hearted young widow! Every time I step into the street I think of the old gentleman in the train, and I wonder which of these houses has the nice little woman inside.

Booking a Room

Kensington Gardens Hotel,
Kensington Gardens Sq.,
London, W.2

Please reserve for me a single room with hot and cold running water for the night of May 17/18th. Kindly confirm.
Mary Bird

Have you a double room free for tonight?
Yes, there is one on the third floor, a quiet room at the back.
What's the charge, please?
£ 35 with breakfast, sir. — Thank you.
Here is your key, room No. 37. The lift is on the right. The porter will show you up.
Thank you. Will you please call me at 7 o'clock?
(The service is not always included in the bill. Visitors leave a tip in the room and also give a tip to the porter.)

I. Die Vergangenheit von *to have, to be, to do* (Präteritum)

to have		to be		to do	
I had	ich hatte	I was [wɔz]	ich war	I did	ich tat
you had	du hattest	you were [wə:]	du warst	you did	du tatest
he had	er hatte	he was	er war	he did	er tat
we had	wir hatten	we were	wir waren	we did	wir taten
you had	ihr hattet	you were	ihr wart	you did	ihr tatet
they had	sie hatten	they were	sie waren	they did	sie taten
I had not (hadn't) etc.		I was not (wasn't) you were not (weren't), etc.		I did not (didn't) etc.	

II. Das regelmäßige Zeitwort: Vergangenheit (1. Vergangenheit, Präteritum)

Past Tense

Formen (gebildet aus der Grundform + Endung *-ed*)

Beispiel: **to open — opened**		1. Aussprache der Endung *-ed*:	
I opened	ich öffnete	a) followed [-əud]	[d] nach stimmhaften Lauten
you opened	du öffnetest	turned [-nd]	
he opened	er öffnete	b) looked [-kt]	[t] nach stimmlosen Lauten
we opened	wir öffneten	fetched [-tʃt]	
you opened	ihr öffnetet	c) needed ['ni:did]	[id] nach *d* und *t*
they opened	sie öffneten	waited ['weitid]	

to close — I closed a) to arrive — I **arrived** b) to drop — I **dropped** to nod — I **nodded** c) to try — I **tried** Aber: to play — I played	2. Besonderheiten in der Schreibung: a) stummes End-*e* fällt weg b) nach einfachem, kurzem, betontem Selbstlaut wird der Endmitlaut verdoppelt c) *-y* wird zu *-ie-*, wenn ein Mitlaut vorangeht

Frage und Verneinung

Did the car **stop** at the traffic lights? Hielt...? The car **did not stop** at the traffic lights. hielt nicht **Didn't** the car **stop** at the traffic lights? Hielt...nicht?	Frage und Verneinung werden mit *did* gebildet.

Merke: Did he find the house? — Yes, *he did.* Ja. — No, *he didn't.* Nein.

I. Bilde die Vergangenheit von: he wants, they marry, I stay, you step, it reminds, he shaves, they rub, she fetches, you reply, she cries, she says, I do, you have, they are, it is, I am, we don't, he hasn't.

II. Holidays at Brighton. Mr and Mrs White are a young married couple. They are on holiday at Brighton. Their room at the guest-house is cheap. Mr White jumps out of bed at half past seven. He washes, shaves and dresses in fifteen minutes. They hurry to the beach after breakfast and stay there until tea-time. When they arrive at their guest-house in the evening, the landlady welcomes them with a smile. Mr and Mrs White like her food. After dinner they play party games. They are very happy.

a) *Erzähle in der Vergangenheit:* Last (letztes) year Mr and Mrs White were on holiday ...

b) *Erzähle in der verneinten Vergangenheit:* Mr and Mrs White are a young married couple. Last year they were on holiday at Brighton. Their room at the guest-house was *not* ... Mr White did *not* ...

c) *Stelle Fragen in der Vergangenheit:* Were Mr and Mrs White a young married couple?

III. Suche den Gegensatz zu: a *broad* street, a *large* house, a *thick* book, a *poor* man, to *pack* a suitcase, he *puts on* his boots, to *miss* the train.

IV. Translate: 1. Als ich auf [dem] Viktoria-Bahnhof ankam, rief ich einen Gepäckträger. 2. Er trug mein Gepäck zu einem Taxi. 3. Das Taxi bog nach rechts ab, dann nach links, und 10 Minuten später hielt es vor einem großen grauen Haus. 4. Es war eine Pension. 5. Der Flur war eng und dunkel. 6. Mein Zimmer war im obersten Stockwerk. 7. Es war nicht sehr behaglich. 8. Die Wirtin sagte: „Machen Sie sich's bequem." 9. Nach zwei Wochen packte ich meinen Koffer und sagte auf Wiedersehen. 10. Voller Hoffnung klopfte ich an die nächste Tür.

16 He Says It the English Way

An Englishman does not like to show his feelings. To show feelings is un-English. That is what the schoolboy learns at school, that is what he practises in later life. Here is a letter from a lonely husband to his wife.

Tree Tops, July 3rd

My dear Ann,

It is now two weeks since you went away. At home everything has gone well. Of course Peter, the dog, has missed you all the time. The buttons of my shirts have all gone, but don't worry. I needn't sew them on. The shirts are all dirty, anyway. We have not starved. Mary is a wonderful cook. We have had tinned tomato soup, corned beef, tinned peas and tinned fruit for lunch and supper every day.

Last Monday, when I went into the garage, I noticed that I had forgotten to turn off the headlights of the car. They had been on all the weekend, and the battery was flat. Yesterday Harrods sent the bill for your evening dress. It was 400 pounds, but the dress is lovely. I hope it fits. By the way, Bill kicked a football through the butcher's window and broke it, so I gave him a good hiding (Bill, not the butcher).

Aunt Lily has been here every evening to keep me company. Her idea of this is to sit by the fire and make a face because she does not like the TV programme. The cat has had her kittens in the best armchair in the sitting-room and is the proud mother of five children.

Father gave me some rum for my cold. The bottle is empty now. I made rum punch for Aunt Lily to cheer her up. She drank three glasses. Later I phoned for a taxi because she could not walk home. This morning she phoned me. She thanked me for a wonderful evening. She is coming again tonight. Well, everything is fine here.

Love from us all,

Jack

PS: The burglars were here last night. They stole your fur coat.

At the Restaurant

Waiter: Have you seen the menu, madam (sir)?

Customer: No, I haven't seen it yet. *(Waiter hands customer the menu)* Thank you. Could you help me? I've forgotten my glasses.

Waiter: Certainly, madam (sir). We have an excellent three-course dinner.

Customer: I'm not very hungry. I'd like something light.

Waiter: What about a breast of chicken?

Customer: Fine! I haven't had chicken for a long time.

Waiter: And perhaps a small sausage? It gives a nice taste to the chicken.

Customer: Yes, I think so.

Waiter: What vegetables, madam (sir)?

Customer: Potatoes and peas, please.

Waiter: And what sweet, madam (sir)? Have you chosen one yet?

Customer: No, not yet. I'll do that afterwards.

I. Das Mittelwort der Vergangenheit (Partizip Perfekt)

Grundform	Vergangenheit	Mittelwort d. Vergangenheit	
to open öffnen	**opened** öffnete	**opened** geöffnet	Bei den regelmäßigen Zeitwörtern wird das Mittelwort der Vergangenheit wie die Vergangenheit durch Anhängen von *-ed* gebildet (vgl. L 13, II).
to try versuchen	**tried** versuchte	**tried** versucht	

II. Die unregelmäßigen Zeitwörter

to come kommen	**came** kam	**come** gekommen	Neben den regelmäßigen Zeitwörtern gibt es, wie im Dt., eine Reihe unregelmäßiger Zeitwörter. (Weitere solche Zeitwörter sind im Wörterverzeichnis aufgeführt.)
to give geben	**gave** gab	**given** gegeben	
to send schicken	**sent** schickte	**sent** geschickt	

III. Die vollendete Gegenwart und die vollendete Vergangenheit

Vollendete Gegenwart (2. Vergangenheit, Perfekt)		**Vollendete Vergangenheit** (3. Vergangenheit, Plusquamperfekt)	
I have waited	ich habe gewartet	I had waited	ich hatte gewartet
you have waited	du hast gewartet	you had waited	du hattest gewartet
he has waited	er hat gewartet	he had waited	er hatte gewartet
we have waited	wir haben gewartet	we had waited	wir hatten gewartet
you have waited	ihr habt gewartet	you had waited	ihr hattet gewartet
they have waited	sie haben gewartet	they had waited	sie hatten gewartet
Ebenso alle anderen Zeitwörter, z. B.:		Ebenso alle anderen Zeitwörter, z. B.:	
I have seen	ich habe gesehen	I had seen	ich hatte gesehen
I have come	ich bin (!) gekommen	I had come	ich war (!) gekommen
I have been	ich bin (!) gewesen	I had been	ich war (!) gewesen

Merke: Have you broken the glass? — Yes, *I have.* Ja. — No, *I haven't.* Nein.

Beachte: 1. Im Englischen werden vollendete Gegenwart und vollendete Vergangenheit aller Zeitwörter mit *to have* gebildet (im Gegens. z. Dt.).
2. Bei Zeitbest. der Vergangenh. wie *yesterday, last night, two years ago* darf im Engl. nur die Vergangenheit (Präteritum), nie. die vollend. Gegenwart (Perfekt) stehen: Yesterday Harrods **sent** the bill for ... *dt.:* schickte *od.* hat geschickt.

I. Bilde die Vergangenheit: I forget, we sit, they send, you are, he goes, she says, you give, it has, we learn, I make, they sit, he keeps, you break, she steals, we come, you see, we choose
Bilde nun die vollend. Gegenwart und die vollend. Vergangenheit

II. Setze folgenden Brief in die Vergangenheit
Beginne mit: Yesterday Mary went to ...
Dear Ann, 1. Mary often goes to the cinema. 2. I send Bill to bed at 8 o'clock. 3. Aunt Lily is often here in the evening. 4. She keeps me company. 5. I make her a cup of tea and give her a glass of rum punch. 6. She sits by the fire and makes a face. 7. I show her pictures of our last holiday. 8. She often forgets the time and does not go before midnight. 9. I am always very tired, but I say nothing. — Love, Jack.

III. Gebrauche die vollendete Gegenwart
Ex.: The battery is flat, because the headlights (to be on all the weekend). — The battery is flat, because the headlights *have been on* all the weekend.
1. Jack gives his son a good hiding, because (to break the butcher's window) 2. Jack needs a glass of whisky, because Harrods (to send the bill for the evening dress) 3. Aunt Lily cannot walk home, because (to have too much rum punch) 4. On Sunday Jack goes out to dinner, because (to have the same lunch every day) 5. Bill and Mary are happy, because their mother (to come back) 6. Ann is sad, because the burglars (to steal her fur coat)
Setze die Sätze nun in die Vergangenheit
Ex.: The battery *was* flat, because the headlights *had been on* all the weekend.

IV. Translate: 1. Lieber Jack! Ich habe Deinen Brief erhalten. 2. Es tut mir leid, daß Du eine Erkältung gehabt hast. 3. Sind die Kätzchen nett? Sind sie noch in dem Sessel im Wohnzimmer? 4. Habt Ihr der Katze [2]jeden Tag [1]ihre Milch gegeben? 5. Hast Du mein Abendkleid Tante Lily gezeigt? Gefällt es ihr? 6. Ich habe ihr eine Ansichtskarte geschickt. Hat sie sie erhalten? 7. Ich habe wunderbares Wetter gehabt. 8. Jeden Tag nach [dem] Frühstück gehe ich zum Strand. 9. Es sind viele nette Leute hier. Herzliche Grüße von Ann.

17 Betting, a National Amusement

There are over 15,000 betting shops in Great Britain. One of the reasons why the English love betting is that it is a way to make money and avoid taxes at the same time. People make and lose fortunes this way. They spend about £ 1,100 million a year on horse-racing alone.

The Derby is the great event on the race-course. It takes place at Epsom, a town of seventy-one thousand inhabitants, south of London. In 1780 Lord Derby founded this classic race for three-year-old horses. The race-course stretches over one and a half miles (2,400 metres). Fifty-five million people live in Great Britain, millions of them watch the Derby on TV, and there are over a hundred-thousand people at the race-course on Derby Day.

Every year, on the first Wednesday in June, thousands of London office employees are absent in the afternoon. Nobody asks where they are. First, because everybody knows, secondly because the boss has gone to Epsom, too.

It was half past three on Derby Day. The Smiths had watched the race on television and knew the result. Mr Smith was happy. His horse was first and he had won £ 200. Mrs Smith was pleased, too. Her horse was third, and she had won £ 20. Only their twenty-year-old son, Freddie made a face. His horse was fifth. He asked his father to lend him a few pounds.

"I'm afraid I can't," said Mr Smith. "It's the second time this month that you've asked me for money. You always bet and you always lose. You've no luck. If you must bet, then bet with me. At least the money stays in the family. You can have a bet once a month." — "Make it twice a month, Dad," said Freddie. "And let's begin with our first bet now. I bet you ten pounds that you aren't going to shave off your beard this week." — "Well," replied Mr Smith. "I could shave off my beard in a few minutes and you've lost your ten pounds." — "Don't make me laugh," said Freddie. "You're much too proud of your beard for that. I tell you, you're going to pay me ten pounds within the week." — "I'm going to teach you a lesson, young man," said his father. "Just wait and see." — On the sixth day, when Freddie came home from the office, he saw that his father's beard had gone. — "Here's your ten pounds, Dad," said Freddie with a happy smile. "You've won the bet." — "I hope you've learnt your lesson," said Mr Smith. "I told you that you always lose. It serves you right." — "Don't say that," answered Freddie. "I had a bet with Mum that you were going to shave off your beard within a week. Now I've won fifteen pounds."

At the Village Shop

(A gentleman has entered the shop.)

Good morning, sir. Can I help you?

How much are these picture postcards, please? (How much do they cost?)

The coloured cards are 35 pence, the black-and-white cards 30 pence.

These two, please. Do you sell stamps?

Certainly, sir. For home or abroad?

What's the postage for abroad?

You need a 21 pence stamp for a postcard, and a 21 pence stamp for a letter. Anything else I can do for you, sir?

Yes, I want some envelopes and writing-paper, a box of matches and a packet of twenty cigarettes. — What brand, sir?

Players, please. Then I want a cake of soap, an electric razor, a tube of tooth-paste and a bar of chocolate.

Anything else, sir? — No, thank you, that's all.

Shall I wrap it up for you? — Yes, please.

(The shop assistant puts the things in a plastic bag. The gentleman pays and leaves the shop.)

1/2 = one half   1/4 = one quarter, one fourth   1/6 one sixth
3/2 = three half   3/4 = three quarters, three fourths   5/7 five sevenths
3/8 three eighths

I. Die Grundzahlen über 100 (Vgl. L 4, IV u. L 7, IV)

100	a (one) hundred ['hʌndrəd]	**100,000**	a (one) hundred thousand
101	a (one) hundred and one	**1,000,000**	a (one) million ['miljən]
200	two hundred	**1,000,000,000**	a thousand million eine Milliarde amerik.: a billion
744	seven hundred and forty-four		
1,000	a (one) thousand ['θauzənd]	**5,349,612**	five million three hundred and forty-nine thousand six hundred and twelve
1,001	a (one) thousand and one		
2,000	two thousand		

Beachte: a) Kommas bei Zahlen von vier und mehr Stellen!
b) *three million people: million* ohne *-s*, wenn Benennung oder kleinere Zahl (s. Kästchen) folgt
millions of people: million mit *-s*, wenn *of* folgt
c) Bei Jahreszahlen steht im fortlaufenden Text immer *in:* **in** 1975

II. Die Ordnungszahlen

1st	the first [fə:st]	**20th**	the **twentieth** ['twentiiθ]
2nd	the second ['sekənd]	**21st**	the twenty-first
3rd	the third [θə:d]	**22nd**	the twenty-second
4th	the fourth [fɔ:θ]	**23rd**	the twenty-third
5th	the **fifth** [fifθ]	**30th**	the thirtieth ['θə:tiiθ]
6th	the sixth [siksθ]	**40th**	the fortieth
7th	the seventh ['sevnθ]	**50th**	the fiftieth
8th	the **eighth** [eitθ]	**60th**	the sixtieth
9th	the **ninth** [nainθ]	**70th**	the seventieth
10th	the tenth [tenθ]	**80th**	the eightieth
11th	the eleventh [i'levnθ]	**90th**	the ninetieth
12th	the **twelfth** [twelfθ]	**100th**	the hundredth ['hʌndrədθ]
13th	the thirteenth	**101st**	the hundred and first
14th	the fourteenth	**102nd**	the hundred and second
15th	the fifteenth	**200th**	the two hundredth
16th	the sixteenth	**1,000th**	the thousandth
17th	the seventeenth	**6,543rd**	the six thousand five hundred and forty-third
18th	the eighteenth		
19th	the nineteenth		

Beachte: Herrschernamen werden geschrieben: Elizabeth II, Henry VIII (ohne Punkt), gesprochen: Elizabeth the Second, Henry the Eighth.

III. Die Wiederholungszahlen

once	einmal	twice	zweimal	three times	dreimal	four times	viermal etc.

I.

Town	Miles from London	Inhabitants
Greater London	—	7,345,000
Birmingham ['bə:miŋəm]	110	1,008,000
Glasgow ['glɑ:sgəu]	394	862,000
Liverpool ['livəpu:l]	197	591,000
Manchester ['mæntʃistə]	184	535,000
Leeds [li:dz]	190	500,000

Read: Birmingham is 110 miles from London. It has 1,008,000 inhabitants, etc.

II. Beantworte die Fragen in ganzen Sätzen

Ex.: How often does the Derby take place? (1x a year)
The Derby takes place once a year.

1. How often does Shirley play the piano? (2x a day) 2. How often did Aunt Lily keep Jack company? (7x a week) 3. How often did Jack phone his wife? (1x a week) 4. How often do the Smiths go to Brighton? (20x a year) 5. How often does the Queen shop at Harrods? (2x a month)

III. Beantworte die Fragen in ganzen Sätzen

Ex.: Did you see the Derby? (on TV)
Yes, I saw it on TV.

1. When did the race take place? (on the first Wednesday in June) 2. When did the race begin? (at three o'clock) 3. Did an Italian horse win the race? (No, an English horse) 4. Did you lose a lot of money? (five pounds) 5. When did you come to England? (four weeks ago) 6. Where did you learn English? (at school)

IV. Translate: 1. Herr Turner ist ein Angestellter in einem Londoner Büro. 2. Am ersten Mittwoch im Juni war niemand im Büro. 3. Einige der Angestellten waren nach Epsom gegangen, andere waren nach Hause gegangen, um das Rennen im Fernsehen zu beobachten. 4. Jedermann wußte, warum sie fehlten. Der Chef sagte nichts.

Datum: I was born on the twenty-sixth of December in nineteen (hundred and) fifty-nine / his birthday is on the on December the twenty

18 A Ticket to Washington

"I'm flying to Washington tomorrow," said Mr Scott, a New York businessman, to his secretary. "Please call the airline and book a return flight for me. I must be in Washington before 11 a.m." "When do you want to be back in New York?" asked Miss Baker. "On April 3rd, let's say about 3 p.m.," answered Mr Scott. He finished his cigarette and then he added, "Are there any telegrams?" "No, there aren't any," replied Miss Baker. "After you've booked my seat on the plane, come into my office again," said Mr Scott. "I want to dictate some letters."

Miss Baker dialled the number of the airline, 9734066, and made the necessary arrangements for the flight. Then she went back into her boss's office.

The date was March 31st, 1973. While Mr Scott was on his way to the airport, he noticed that his flight tickets were missing. He returned to his office. "Have you seen my tickets anywhere?" he asked his secretary. "No, I haven't," replied Miss Baker. "Have you any idea where you left them?" As Mr Scott could not find them, he hurried out of the office. It was not possible to get a seat on another plane. Therefore he took the train for his trip to Washington.

During his stay in Washington Mr Scott was so busy that he did not read any newspapers or watch television. He stayed two extra days, for, like other tourists, he hoped to see the President and the White House. On April 5th, Mr Scott travelled back to New York by plane. He had seen the White House, but he had not seen the President. He reached New York at 15.45 hours. As he was rather tired, he took a taxi and drove straight home. Some children were playing on the grass in front of his house. They immediately stopped their game and stared at him.

"Anything wrong with me?" asked Mr Scott. The children did not answer, but ran into the house next door. While he stood there, an old lady came out of the house and looked at him with her mouth wide open.

"Good afternoon, Mrs Miller," said Scott. "Something must be wrong, but I haven't got any idea what it can be."

"Well, I can tell you," answered Mrs Miller. "Your plane crashed after take-off. The police found tickets with your name on them in the pocket of one of the dead passengers. A policeman informed your wife of your death."

Mr Scott was very surprised. He took a deep breath and finally said, "Somebody must have found or stolen my tickets. So I went to Washington by train. I was born lucky. Have you got any idea where my wife is?"

"She's gone to your funeral," said Mrs Miller.

In a Railway Carriage

1st passenger: Excuse me, is this anybody's seat?

2nd passenger: I'm afraid so, but the corner seat is not occupied.

1st p.: I nearly missed the train. Does this train stop at Leamington Spa?

2nd p.: No, it doesn't. First stop is Birmingham.

1st p.: Are you sure? I've got to change at Leamington for Stratford-upon-Avon.

Ticket-collector: Tickets, please. — I'm sorry, sir, but your ticket only takes you to Leamington. You must pay the difference.

1st p.: How much is it?

T.-c.: The return fare from Leamington to Birmingham is £ 8.25.

1st p.: Here you are.

T.-c.: Departure from Birmingham to Leamington at 13.00 hours, and a connection to Stratford at 14.25. Arrival at Stratford at 14.55.

1st p.: Thank you very much.

T.-c.: That's all right, sir.

I. Das Datum (Date)

Months Monate	January	['dʒænjuəri]	May	[mei]	September	[sep'tembə]	
	February	['februəri]	June	[dʒu:n]	October	[ɔk'təubə]	
	March	[mɑ:tʃ]	July	[dʒu'lai]	November	[nəu'vembə]	
	April	['eiprəl]	August	['ɔ:gəst]	December	[di'sembə]	
Seasons Jahreszeiten	spring	[spriŋ]	Frühling	summer	['sʌmə]	Sommer	
	autumn	['ɔ:təm]	Herbst	winter	['wintə]	Winter	
Geschrieben:	15(th) March, 1974 =		gesprochen:	the fifteenth of March, 1974			
	March 15(th), 1974			March the fifteenth, 1974			

Merke: a week 8 Tage — 3 months ein Vierteljahr — 9 months ein Dreivierteljahr
a fortnight, two weeks 14 Tage — 6 months ein halbes Jahr — 18 months eineinhalb Jahre

II. Die Uhrzeit II (Vgl. L 14, II)

Im Englischen rechnet man gewöhnlich nur bis 12 Uhr. Zur Kennzeichnung gebraucht man, wenn notwendig, a.m. und p.m. Auf Bahnhöfen und Flughäfen rechnet man bis 24 Uhr.

This store is open from **9.30 a.m.** (*read:* nine thirty a.m.) until **6.45 p.m.** (*read:* six forty-five p.m.) Departure 1645 Arrival 1805 (*read:* sixteen forty-five — eighteen-o-five)	***a.m.*** ['ei'em] (von *lat.* ante meridiem) = vormittags für 0—12 Uhr ***p.m.*** ['pi:'em] (von *lat.* post meridiem) = nachmittags für 12—24 Uhr

III. *some — any*

1. Here are **some** letters for you. einige Briefe	1. *Some* und seine Zusammensetzungen können nur im bejahten Satz stehen.
2. Are there **any** letters for me? Sind (irgendwelche) Briefe ... da? There are**n't any** letters for you. keine B.	2. Im verneinten Satz und in der Frage stehen *any* und seine Zusammensetzungen. (*Any* bleibt im Dt. oft unübersetzt.)

Zusammensetzungen: somebody, anybody, something, anything, somewhere

IV. *while — during*

She had tea **while** she was at the office.	*while* leitet Nebensätze ein,
It was cold **during** the night.	*during* steht vor einem Hauptwort als Verhältniswort.

I. The Date
Ex.: Today is Wednesday, 12th October.
1. What is the date tomorrow (the day after tomorrow)? 2. What was the date yesterday (the day before yesterday, last Sunday)? 3. When is Christmas Day, Christmas Eve, New Year's Day? 4. When is (was) Easter, Whitsun this year?

II. Months and Seasons 1. April is the fourth month of the year. Which month of the year is: February, July, October, May, August, November? 2. Which months have 30 days, which have 31? 3. When does spring, summer, autumn, winter begin?

III. *Some* or *any*? 1. Have you got ... first-class seats for February 23rd? Yes, there are still ... seats. 2. Are there ... foreign passengers on the plane? Yes, ... German businessmen. 3. The stewardess ['stju:ədis] gives the passengers ... thing to read. She is sorry that she hasn't got ... German papers. 4. ... body says, "I cannot find my coat. Does ... body know where it is?" 5. Have you got ... thing to declare? I have only got ... presents.

IV. Translate: Ich habe den Zug um 15.15 nach London versäumt. 2. Wann fährt der nächste Zug ab, bitte? — Um 15.58, meine Dame. 3. Wann kommt er in Paddington an? — Um 17.22 Uhr. 4. Hält der Zug unterwegs *(on the way)*? — Ja, er hält zweimal. 5. Eine Rückfahrkarte nach London, bitte. 6. Erster oder zweiter Klasse? 7. Zweiter, bitte. Was ist der Rückfahrtpreis? 8. Zwei Pfund neunzig. 9. Kann ich einen Sitzplatz reservieren für den *(on the)* Zug um 9.35 nach Manchester am 13. März? 10. Sicherlich, meine Dame. Wie ist Ihr Name? 11. Von welchem Bahnsteig fährt der Zug um 15.58 nach London ab, bitte?

19

A Sunday in Hyde Park

All over the world parks are for people who want to go for a walk. Hyde Park in London is more: on weekdays a playground for children, on Sundays the playground of democracy. Political and non-political speakers of all kinds make speeches on soap-boxes. You hear opposite opinions six yards apart, and nobody minds, not even the policeman. A practical lesson in tolerance.

What has that tall fellow got to say? Let's go and listen to him.

"Yes, my friends, I've been in prison eleven times, and this in six different countries, and I would still be a sinner, if I had not started a new life. I was a hopeless drinker, until one night I had a dream.

My dear old mother said to me:

'Bill, my son,' she said, 'you won't drink from now on. Very soon the world will come to an end. There will be another terrible war, the last war. Disease will follow. Men will die in the big flood and the devil's government will rule the world.'

I awoke, and a great light had come upon me. I've never drunk a drop of alcohol since. I founded the Doomsday Brotherhood League. I hope you'll join it before it's too late.

Everybody can become a member of the league for fifty pence a year. We should be happy to welcome you to our brotherhood.

If you've seen the red light, you'll follow me, and I'm sure you'll find happiness and peace. We'll help you in your fight against sin, we'll show you the path to a new and pure life."

Asking the Way

"Excuse me, can you tell me where the nearest Underground station is?"
"Sorry, I'm a stranger here myself."
"Could you please tell me the way to Waterloo Station?"
"If you go down this street, you'll find it on your right."
"What is the quickest way to Hyde Park Corner?"
"Follow this road, take the second turning on the left, and turn right at the traffic lights."
"How far is it?" — "About twenty-five minutes, I'd say. You'd better take a bus. If you take the bus, you won't lose your way."
"What number, please?" — "Take the No. 24 bus, then change onto a No. 52 at Victoria."
"How long will it take me?" — "Only ten minutes by bus. The bus stop is round the corner."
"Will you tell me when we get to Victoria Station, please?"
"Thank you very much." — "Thank you so much." — "That's very kind of you."
"Not at all." — "Don't mention it." — "That's all right."

I. Die Zukunft (Futur)

ich werde finden	Kurzform
I **will** find you **will** find he **will** find we **will** find you **will** find they **will** find	I'll [ail] find you'll [ju:l] find he'll [hi:l] find we'll [wi:l] find you'll [ju:l] find they'll [ðeil] find
Verneinte Form	Kurzform
I will not find	I won't find
Frageform	**Fragend-verneinte F.**
will you find?	will you not find? won't you find?

II. Die Bedingungsform (Konditional)

ich würde finden	Kurzform
I **would** find you **would** find he **would** find we **would** find you **would** find they **would** find	I'd [aid] find you'd [ju:d] find he'd [hi:d] find we'd [wi:d] find you'd [ju:d] find they'd [ðeid] find
Verneinte Form	Kurzform
I would not find	I wouldn't ['wudnt] find
Frageform	**Fragend-verneinte F.**
would you find?	would you not find? wouldn't you find?

Merke: Nach persönlichen Fürwörtern steht meist die Kurzform: I'll come tomorrow. In der ersten Person Einzahl und Mehrzahl kann statt 'will' *I shall, we shall* gebraucht werden, statt 'would' *I should, we should*, statt 'won't' *I shan't, we shan't.*

III. Der Gebrauch der Zukunft

	Die Zukunft steht i. Gegens. z. Dt.
1. I hope you'**ll join** the league. ..., Sie treten bei I'm sure that you'**ll find** peace. ..., daß Sie Frieden finden	1. nach *to hope* hoffen, *to fear, to be afraid* fürchten, *to think, to be sure*
2. If you take this bus, you'**ll be** at Hyde Park in ten minutes. ... sind Sie in 10 Minuten in Hyde Park	2. im Hauptsatz zu einem *if*-Satz

IV. Die Stellung der Orts- und Zeitbestimmung

Im Engl. ist das Zeitwort mit seiner Ergänzung so eng verbunden, daß sich kein anderes Satzglied dazwischenschieben darf.

	Zeitw. + Ergänz.			
I	heard	a speech	**in Hyde Park.**	Daher stehen Orts- und Zeitbestimmung gewöhnlich **am Satzende.**
I	see	you	**tomorrow.**	
This man	has been —		**in prison** × **eleven times.** elfmal im Gefängnis	Treffen beide Bestimmungen am Satzende zusammen, so gilt: **Ort vor Zeit.**

Die Stellung am Satzanfang (wie im Dt.) ist im Engl. seltener: *One night* I had a dream.

I. Wie heißen die vollen Formen von I'd, they'll, he won't, we wouldn't, she'd, I'll, we won't, she'll, we'll, won't you, wouldn't he, we'd?

II. a) What will you *(your family, your friends)* **do next Sunday?** (I, we, my parents, my sister, my friends — to get up at 9 o'clock, to have breakfast late, to go to church, to have dinner, to go for a walk, to listen to the radio, to go to the cinema)

b) What would you *(your family etc.)* **do** *if you lived in London*? (to have bacon and eggs for breakfast, to take a bus to Hyde Park, to go to Brighton for the weekend, to watch TV)

III. Setze die Sätze sinngemäß in die Zukunft
Beginne mit den Ausdrücken in Klammern
Ex.: Did you enjoy your Sunday morning in Hyde Park? (I am sure)
I am sure you will enjoy ...
1. We heard many different opinions. (I am sure, Do you think?) 2. Were there any political speakers? (Do you think? I hope) 3. Did the policeman stop them? (I don't think) 4. Did many people join the Brotherhood League? (The speaker hopes) 5. Nobody wanted to start a new life. (I fear)

IV. Translate: 1. Wenn Sie an einem Sonntagmorgen zum Hyde Park gehen, finden (!) Sie dort viele Menschen. 2. Manche von ihnen machen (gerade) einen Spaziergang, manche hören (gerade) den Rednern zu. 3. Sie können Redner aller Art sehen. Sie halten Reden gegen [den] Krieg, gegen [die] Demokratie und sogar gegen die britische Regierung. 4. „Schließen Sie sich uns an", sagt einer der Redner, „und Sie werden Glück und Frieden finden. 5. Wenn Sie ein Trinker sind, werden Sie von jetzt an nicht [mehr] trinken. 6. Wenn Sie ein Sünder sind, werden Sie morgen ein neues Leben beginnen. 7. Wenn Sie uns in unserem Kampf gegen [den] Alkohol und [die] Sünde helfen (!), helfen (!) wir [auch] Ihnen."

20 Teaching English

In Britain, as in most other European countries, household help is scarce. So girls from the Continent are welcome, if they are prepared to look after children, help in the household or work at a hospital. In special evening classes they learn the English language.

Mr Walker enters the classroom. "Good evening, ladies and gentlemen. Last week we learnt some irregular verbs. You haven't forgotten them, have you? Who can tell me the tenses of *to eat*?" A big Dutch girl puts up her hand and says: "To eat, ate, eaten." — "You are Miss Vandenberg, aren't you? Now, what did you eat for lunch today?" — "Flesh," she says. "No, Miss Vandenberg, that's wrong. You ought to know that. Flesh is what you've got on your body. You eat meat; please remember, eat and meat, it rhymes, it's easy. You see the difference, don't you?"

Miss V. says she thinks she does, but her *th* is not correct, she pronounces *think* like *sink*. She has to repeat it until she is able to pronounce *th*.

Then Mr Walker draws some animals on the blackboard, an ox, a calf, a sheep and a pig. "Who knows what kind of animal this is?" He points to the ox. One of the students thinks it is a cow, but Mr Walker points out that his drawing must be an ox and not a cow. Then he takes the chalk and draws a direct line from the ox to a steak, and explains that this is beef. The calf, which some students take for a goat, others for a donkey, gets a line that points to a cutlet, and Mr Walker tells them that this is veal. He also tells them that sheep becomes mutton, and that pig becomes pork when prepared for food.

"Please, sir, could you tell us the reason for these different words?" asks a young Austrian. "You see," Mr Walker tells them, "ox, calf, sheep and pig are old Germanic words. In 1066 the Normans conquered England. They spoke French, and they were the masters. When they sat down at the table, they told their Anglo-Saxon servants in French what they wanted to eat. Beef, veal, mutton, pork are words of French origin. Now you will be able to understand why English is a mixture of old Germanic and French words, won't you?"

We Attend Evening Classes

Is everybody present?
No, Mr Curry is absent.
What's the matter with him?
He is ill.
You ought not to speak so fast.
Your pronunciation of the word 'to conquer' is not correct (is wrong).
You must not make that mistake again.
Don't you know the meaning of the word?
Please look it up in your dictionaries.
Do you know a similar word?
We need not translate this paragraph.
May I go on with the text?
I'm sorry, I didn't want to interrupt you.
Collect the textbooks, please.

I. Die unvollständigen Hilfszeitwörter I (Hilfsverben)

1. haben in der 3. Pers. Einzahl kein *-s*: he *can*, she *may*, it *must*, he *ought to*
2. werden in Frage und Verneinung nicht mit *to do* umschrieben: *Can* you come? — I *could not* come. — You *need not* help me.
3. haben a) keine Grundform (kein *to*), b) kein Mittelwort.
   Sie können daher keine Zukunft (dt. „ich werde nicht kommen können") und keine vollendete Gegenwart und Vergangenheit (dt. „ich habe nicht kommen können") bilden. In diesen Zeiten müssen andere Zeitwörter mit ähnl. Bedeutung als Ersatz an ihre Stelle treten.

Hilfszeitwort		Verneinung	Kurzform	Ersatzzeitwort
I can **I could**	ich kann 1. ich konnte 2. ich könnte	cannot could not	can't couldn't	**to be able to** können
may I?	darf ich?	must not darf nicht	mustn't [mʌsnt]	**to be allowed to** dürfen
I must	ich muß	need not muß nicht, brauche nicht zu	needn't	**to have to** müssen
shall I? **I should** **I ought to**	soll ich? ich sollte ich sollte	shall I not? should not ought not to	shan't I? shouldn't oughtn't to	
[I will not [I would not	ich will nicht] ich wollte nicht]	*Will* kommt im Sinne von „wollen" nur selten und dann hauptsächlich verneint vor. Daher am besten in allen Zeiten immer das Ersatzzeitwort verwenden!		**to want to** wollen

Beispiele: **Could** you please tell us the reason? Könnten Sie uns bitte ...?
Now you **will be able to** understand this better. Sie werden ... verstehen können.
The students **were not allowed to** smoke in the classroom. durften nicht rauchen
Mr Walker **will have to** explain this word. wird ... erklären müssen
I have always **wanted to** ask you about that. habe immer fragen wollen

II. Kurzfrage zur Wiedergabe des dt. „nicht wahr?"

a) You **are** Miss V., **aren't you?** nicht wahr? She **sees** the difference, **doesn't she?** b) You **haven't** forgotten them, **have you?** The students **don't** understand everything, **do they?**	Das Hilfszeitwort des Vordersatzes wird wiederholt. Ein Vollzeitwort wird in der Frage durch *to do* ersetzt. Beachte: a) Vordersatz bejaht — Frage verneint b) Vordersatz verneint — Frage bejaht

I. Can you ...?

Ex.: Can you speak French? (English)
No, I can't, but I'll soon be able to speak English.

1. Can you play golf? (tennis) 2. Can she write business letters in English? (in French) 3. Can she ask for a meal in Italian? (in German) 4. Can you answer the phone in English? (Dutch) 5. Can you read French newspapers? (English newspapers)

II. *Must, must not* or *need not*

1. When you eat at a hotel, you ... choose an expensive meal, but you ... pay the bill. 2. When you take a taxi, you ... tell the driver where you want to go and you ... forget to pay the fare. 3. If you want to go to the theatre, you ... wear your best suit, but you ... forget to buy a ticket. 4. If you dance with a girl, you ... be nice to her, but you ... tell her that you want to marry her. 5. When you are in England, you ... drink tea all the time, but you ... speak English.

III. *You may* or *you mustn't*

Ex.: drink alcohol/be a drinker. — *You may* drink alcohol, *but you mustn't* be a drinker.

1. speak to strangers/believe everything they say 2. drive a car/drive too fast 3. like money/steal it 4. be bad-tempered/show it 5. go to the races/lose all your money

IV. *Ought to, should*

Ex.: Why don't you take an umbrella when it rains?
a) You *ought to take* an umbrella when it rains.
b) You *should take* an umbrella when it rains.

1. Why don't you go to the theatre when you're in London? 2. Why don't you watch TV when you're bored? 3. Why don't you take a hot bath when you are ill? 4. Why don't you attend evening classes if you want to learn French? 5. Why don't you spend your weekends at the seaside?

21 Alone Among Millions

> Wanted: Lady's companion, London. Apply Box K 31.

This advertisement in the personal column of the *Sunday Times* had started it all. Ingrid Müller, a German girl of 22, was now a companion to an old lady, Mrs Bunby. Ingrid took her out in her wheel chair to the park near by, read to her, looked after the dog and cats, and was very unhappy.

Like thousands of German girls, Ingrid had come to England to learn the language. Although Mrs Bunby treated her well, Ingrid was terribly homesick. She obviously missed the company of other young people.

One day she heard of the *International Friendship League*, with its head office in London and branches all over Britain. The League's aim was to promote friendship between young people of all nations. Ingrid wrote to the League, and a few days later she got an invitation to a dance at the IFL's Youth Hostel. She accepted it gladly.

As Ingrid slowly entered the dance hall, a 'Paul Jones' was already in full swing. The ladies formed an inner circle, the gentlemen a ring around them; the two circles were moving in opposite directions to the tune of a march. Soon Ingrid was in the midst of it. As the music suddenly changed to a slow waltz, each gentleman turned to the lady just opposite him and danced with her until the march tune began again. Then they quickly formed circles as before. This went on for some time.

"Haven't we met before?" asked a young Frenchman happily when he stood in front of Ingrid for the third time.

"Perhaps," smiled Ingrid. "Listen, my favourite tune," said the young man, "they are playing *I'll see you again.*" Ingrid laughed. "I know the song myself," she said. "It's called *Beware of the tall, dark stranger.*" But she was very happy.

Ingrid is no longer homesick! She works hard, and she does it willingly — and all the week she looks forward to Saturday evening or Sunday, to the next social, excursion or discussion.

A Date

Are you free at the week-end?
Have you anything on next Saturday?
How about going for a walk on Saturday afternoon or to a dance on Saturday evening?
That would be nice.
That's a good idea.
(That's very nice of you, but I'm afraid I won't have time.)
Where can I meet you?
Can I pick you up with my car?
Let's say at half past seven outside Woolworths. Would that be all right?
Are you on the phone? Can I ring you up again on Friday?
Certainly. My number is 377 5079.
Thank you. See you on Saturday.

Das Umstandswort (Adverb)

Im Dt. haben Eigenschaftswort u. Umstandswort dieselbe Form, im Engl. verschiedene Formen:

Eigenschaftswort: Der Filmstar ist **schön.** — The film star is **beautiful.**
Umstandswort: Der Filmstar singt **schön.** — The film star sings **beautifully.**

I. Bildung des Umstandswortes (Adverb)

1. Normalfall	quick — **quickly**	Eigenschaftswort + ***-ly***
2. Besonderheit der Schreibung	terrible — terri**bly** happy — happ**ily**	*-le* fällt weg *-y* (nach Mitlaut) wird *-i-*
3. Ausnahme	good — well	He dances well er tanzt gut
4. Bleiben als Umstandswörter unverändert:	hard, fast, straight early daily, long, far, late die Worte, die die Zeit bezeichnen	He works hard and fast. He gets up late and can't walk straight. The postman comes daily. You won't have to wait long, for he comes early.

Merke: *very* sehr bei Eigenschafts- und Umstandswörtern: He plays very well.
very much sehr bei Zeitwörtern: I like him very much.

II. Stellung des Umstandswortes

Das Umstandswort kann ein Eigenschaftswort oder ein anderes Umstandswort bestimmen und wird dann wie im Dt. diesem vorangestellt:
She is *terribly* homesick. — She sings *very* beautifully.
Im allgemeinen aber bestimmt das Umstandswort ein Zeitwort:

		Hilfs-zeitw.		(Voll-) Zeitwort	+ Ergänzung	
1.	Ingrid		**slowly**	entered	the dance hall.	
	They		**quickly**	formed	circles.	
	Ingrid	had	**gladly**	accepted	the invitation.	
2.	She	had		accepted	it	**gladly.**
	Ingrid			does	her work	**willingly.**
	The Frenchman			laughed	—	**happily.**

Das Zeitwort und seine Ergänzung sind so eng miteinander verbunden, daß sich das Umstandswort nicht dazwischenschieben darf (vgl. dagegen das Deutsche!).
Das Umstandswort steht daher
1. unmittelbar **vor dem (Voll-)Zeitwort**
2. (wenn es betont ist) **hinter** der Gruppe **Zeitwort + Ergänzung.**

I. Wie heißen die Umstandswörter zu: hard, happy, good, easy, comfortable, fast, beautiful, early?

II. Setze die Umstandswörter ***nach folgendem Muster ein:***
Ex.: The speaker answered every question (willingly).
The speaker *willingly* answered every question.
1. The teacher welcomed the new students (warmly). 2. Then he dictated a few sentences (slowly). 3. One student repeated the tenses of ten irregular verbs (proudly). 4. You will find more irregular verbs in your books (easily). 5. A girl put up her hand (slowly). 6. The teacher had forgotten her name (suddenly). 7. He looked at his list of names (quickly).

III. Setze Umstandswörter ein
Ex.: The Austrian's English was excellent. He spoke English *excellently.*
1. Mrs Bunby was a kind woman. She welcomed Ingrid ...
2. The old lady was a quiet person (ˈpə:sn]. She always spoke ...
3. The weather had been wonderful. It had been ... warm.
4. The Frenchman was proud of his car. He ... showed it to Mrs Bunby. 5. Mr Scott was a busy man. He worked ... from morning until evening. 6. They had to leave their houses at an early hour. They always left ... 7. There were special evening classes for foreigners. They were ... interesting for foreigners.
8. Mr Walker drew a straight line from the ox to the cutlet. He then walked ... back to his seat.

IV. Translate: Liebe Karla! 1. Ich habe kein Heimweh mehr. 2. Gestern abend war ich bei *(at)* einem Tanz, wo ich einige sehr nette Leute kennenlernte. 3. Als ich ankam, war ein Marschwalzer in vollem Gang. 4. Ich stand ²einige Zeit ¹am Eingang; dann betrat ich langsam den Saal. 5. Nach ein paar Minuten wechselte der Marsch plötzlich in einen langsamen Walzer über. 6. Ein Franzose kam auf mich zu *(to come up to)*. 7. Ich sagte: „Ich kenne diesen Tanz nicht." Aber er antwortete: „Sie werden ihn schnell lernen." 8. Als der Marsch wieder begann, mußten die Damen und Herren Kreise bilden und in entgegengesetzte Richtung(en) marschieren. 9. Der Franzose tanzte ²dreimal ¹mit mir. Er tanzt sehr gut. — Ingrid.

22 Safety Last

"I bought this car second-hand from a car-dealer in Warren Street. I paid £900 in cash, and now this beauty belongs to me, including new tyres and a new engine. Get in, Marjorie, we're going for a drive."

Bill pressed the starter, put the car into bottom gear, and off they went. A few minutes later they had left the town behind them. While the car was speeding along a narrow country road, Bill looked at the speedometer. The needle was pointing to 70 miles an hour. Bill was proud. "Look, Marjorie, we're driving at top speed." They were driving over the mountains and through the valleys of the Lake District.

But Marjorie was not enjoying Bill's efforts as a racing driver.

"Be careful, Bill," she said. "Why must you men always drive at top speed?"

"Now you're trying to spoil my fun," Bill replied. "Don't you like to be master of distance and time?"

"No, I don't, Bill. If there's a crash, it will be your fault. A puncture, and we shall run into a tree. Slow down, Bill, please — or I shall never come with you again. It's not safe. You seem to love speed more than you love me."

"Don't worry, Marjorie, the brakes are good. Look! We're getting near a village. The speed limit is 30. Is that better?" And he changed into second gear.

Three miles beyond the village, when Bill was preparing for a new speed record, the car suddenly slowed down and then stopped. Several times he tried the starter. The engine would not start. "Don't worry, Marjorie," said Bill. "It's probably a loose wire. I can repair it." He climbed out, lifted the bonnet and, with the air of an expert, turned a few screws. But still the engine would not start.

Finally they had to push the car to the nearest garage. There the mechanic looked at the engine, then at the petrol and said to Bill, "How many gallons, sir? She needs juice. The tank is empty. Filling-station outside."

The German Word *fahren*

to go *irgendwohin fahren* (ganz allgemein; gleichgültig mit welchem Verkehrsmittel)

I must go to London tomorrow.
Are you going by bus or by train?
I always go there by car.
Where are you going for your holidays?
Does this train (bus) go to Brighton?
Can I go there by car?

to drive *Auto fahren*

Can you drive?
Don't drive so fast.
Shall we walk or drive?

to run (von Fahrzeugen)

a) = *laufen*
This car runs very well.
b) = *verkehren*
Does this bus run daily?

to leave *abfahren*

When does the next train leave?
The next train leaves at four o'clock.

A Breakdown

Have you had a breakdown? (Has your car broken down?) Or have you had an accident?
We bumped (crashed) into another car.
We've a flat tyre.
We're out of petrol. We must get some from the nearest filling-station.
Thank Heaven it was nothing serious.
Can I give you a lift? — Thank you.
Will you please drop me at the garage?
Shall I pick you up again on the way back?

I. Die Steigerung des Eigenschafts- und Umstandswortes

Es gibt zwei Arten der Steigerung: 1. die germanische auf *-er, -est,*
2. die romanische mit *more, most.*

1. Auf *-er, -est* werden gesteigert

a) great fast b) heavy simple	greater faster heavier simpler	greatest fastest heaviest simplest	a) alle einsilbigen Eigenschafts- und Umstandswörter b) manche zweisilbigen Eigenschaftswörter (bes. die auf *-y* und *-le*)
Besonderheiten in der Schreibung:			Besonderheiten in der Aussprache:
large big easy	larg-er bigger easier	larg-est biggest easiest	long longer ['lɔŋgə] longest ['lɔŋgist] young younger ['jʌŋgə] youngest ['jʌŋgist]

2. Mit *more, most* werden gesteigert

a) important awful	more important more awful	most important most awful	a) alle drei- u. mehrsilbigen Eigenschaftswörter sowie manche zweisilbigen (s. 1 b)
b) confused boring	more confused more boring	most confused most boring	b) die Mittelwörter
c) slowly	more slowly	most slowly	c) die Umstandswörter auf *-ly*

3. Unregelmäßige Steigerung

good, well	gut	better	best
bad(ly)	schlecht, schlimm	worse [wə:s]	worst [wə:st]
much, many	viel(e)	more	most
little	wenig	less	least

Merke: *most* people (cars, etc.) die meisten Leute (Wagen, usw.)

4. Doppelformen

late	spät	later	last latest	letzter neuester
near	nahe	nearer	nearest next	(Entfernung) (Reihenfolge)
far	weit	farther further[1] [ə:]	farthest furthest [ə:]	

[1] 1. = weiter (Entfernung), 2. = ein weiterer, weitere, z. B. *further questions*

II. Vergleiche im Satz

Rhona turned **as** white **as** a sheet. She was **not so** elegant **as** the others. She was **not as** elegant **as** the others. She was **more** superstitious **than** most people.	**as . . . as** (eben)so ... wie **not so . . . as** } nicht so ... wie **not as . . . as** } **. . . than** ... als (nach Steigerungsform)
Merke: He was **most** astonished. She is **no longer** superstitious.	**most . . .** (ohne Vergleich) äußerst, höchst **no longer** nicht mehr

I. Steigere: comfortable, fine, sunny, advanced, far, interesting, thin, lucky, terrible, bad, long, expensive; quickly, badly, well, entertaining

II. Which is more?

Ex.: expensive — second-hand car — new car
a) Which is more expensive, a second-hand car or a new car?
b) A new car is more expensive than a second-hand car.

1. interesting — book about London — visit to London 2. exciting — dance with your brother — dance with a stranger 3. comfortable — office-chair — armchair at home 4. beautiful — short hair — long hair 5. terrible — to be alone among millions — to be in a dormitory with five other people 6. entertaining — to go to the theatre — to go to the cinema 7. difficult — to speak English — to write English

III. Suche Sätze, die das Gegenteil ausdrücken

1. December 21st is the shortest day of the year. 2. January is the coldest month. 3. Luxemburg ['lʌksəmbə:g] is one of the smallest countries in the world. 4. The best time for a holiday at the seaside is July or August. 5. The longest route [ru:t] from London to Glasgow is by water.

IV. Translate: 1. Am 13. Mai bewarb sich Rhona um eine Stelle bei der ältesten und bedeutendsten Firma (in) der Stadt. 2. Als sie das Büro betrat, warteten schon drei Bewerberinnen. 3. Eine der Damen war älter als Rhona. Sie trug ein äußerst elegantes Kleid. 4. Rhona war in Verlegenheit, weil ihr Kleid mit Flecken bedeckt war. 5. Es war schlimmer als der schlimmste Traum! 6. Rhona entschuldigte sich und verschwand. 7. Zehn Minuten später kam sie zurück und verkündete: „Ich habe die Stelle bekommen." 8. Die elegante Dame wurde kreidebleich. 9. Für Rhona war es ein glücklicher Tag.

24 A Murder has been Planned

"I'm going to be operated on early in the morning," said Roy Bilk to the night nurse. "I hope I won't be cut up too much by the doctors."

"Well, you must try to sleep now. Don't worry about the operation. It has been done hundreds of times already and your stomach trouble will be cured afterwards. Good night."

With these words the nurse turned off the light and left the patient's room.

As soon as she had gone, Bilk threw back the sheet and blankets, rushed to the cupboard to get his clothes and dressed hastily. He put his hat and coat on. However, he did not bother about his false teeth in the glass of water beside his bed. Then he climbed out of the window into the yard. He could do this without the help of a ladder as his room was on the ground floor. Nobody saw him leave the hospital. If everything went well, he would be back in less than half an hour.

He rushed through the empty streets and in exactly seven minutes he reached the road where he lived. The time was ten past eleven. There was no moon. His wife was already in bed, for there were no lights on in the house. He crossed the road, took his key and quietly opened the front door. His dog was lying in its basket and greeted him with a friendly movement of its tail. Bilk gave it a sign to be silent and to remain where it was. Then he went up the stairs to his wife's bedroom. She loved fresh air, and for this reason her bedroom door was kept open. Her regular breathing could be heard. She was fast asleep.

The street lamps gave plenty of artificial light, so that everything in the room could be seen clearly. Bilk crept to the small wooden table beside her bed where, as usual, there was a glass of milk. It hadn't been touched yet. With his leather gloves on, Bilk took a small bottle out of his pocket, poured the contents, a clear liquid, into the glass and disappeared from the room as quietly as he had come. At the bottom of the stairs the dog received a friendly touch on the head and was warned to keep quiet. Carefully Bilk closed the front door behind him and stepped into the road. He felt as light as a feather.

On his way back to the hospital Bilk threw the bottle away so that it shouldn't be found on him. He noted with satisfaction that the window of his room had not been shut during his absence. He had been away for seventeen minutes. Back in bed he rang for a drink. He did this on purpose to have an alibi. (to be continued)

FOR

1. Ziel, Zweck
She *sailed for* Germany yesterday.
I am *leaving for* New York tomorrow.
He *shouted for* help.
She is *applying for* a job.
He *asked* me *for* some money.
What are you *looking for*?
We must *send for* the doctor.
What do you want the book *for*? (Wozu ...?)
She flew back *for* the funeral.
He has married her *for* her money.

2. Zeitraum
They had been at the hotel *for two days*.
I waited at the bus stop *for half an hour*.
The music went on *for some time*.

I. Die Leideform I (Passiv)

Formen (gebildet aus *to be* + Mittelwort der Vergangenheit)

Gegenwart	I	am	watched	ich werde	beobachtet	
Vergangenheit	I	was	watched	ich wurde	beobachtet	
Vollendete Gegenwart	I have	been	watched	ich bin	beobachtet	worden
Vollendete Vergangenheit	I had	been	watched	ich war	beobachtet	worden
Zukunft	I will	be	watched	ich werde	beobachtet	werden
Bedingungsform	I would	be	watched	ich würde	beobachtet	werden
Grundform	to	be	watched	beobachtet werden		

Tatform und Leideform (Aktiv und Passiv)

	Satzgegenstand	Satzaussage	Ergänzung	Ortsbestimmung o. ä.
Tat-form	The nurse Die Schwester	brought brachte	the tea den Tee	to his bedside. an sein Bett.
Leide-form	The tea Der Tee	**was brought** wurde		to his bedside (by the nurse). (von d. Schwester) an sein Bett gebracht.

Die Wenfall-Ergänzung wird in der Leideform zum Satzgegenstand.
Die Satzstellung **Satzgegenstand — ganze Satzaussage** bleibt erhalten.
Soll in der Leideform die handelnde Person genannt werden, so wird sie mit *by* angefügt. z. B. The tea was brought to his bedside *by the nurse.*

II. Zeitwörter mit Wenfall-Ergänzung (Akkusativ-Objekt)

Tat-form	The doctors **helped the patient.** halfen dem Patienten At first nobody **believed him.** glaubte ihm	Mehrere engl. Zeitwörter haben im Ggs. zu den entspr. dt. Zeitwörtern eine **Wenfall-Ergänzung** (s. Liste unten)
Leide-form	The patient **was helped** by the doctors. Dem Patienten wurde ... geholfen At first he **was not believed.** wurde ihm nicht geglaubt; glaubte man ihm nicht	Diese Zeitwörter können auch in die persönliche Leideform gesetzt werden. (Wiedergabe im Dt. mit unpersönl. Leideform „es wird..." oder mit „man")

to approach	s.o.	sich jdm. nähern	to meet	s.o.	jdm. begegnen
to believe	s.o.	jdm. glauben	to remember	s.o.	sich an jdn. erinnern
to follow	s.o.	jdm. folgen	to thank	s.o.	jdm. danken
to help	s.o.	jdm. helfen	to trust	s.o.	jdm. (ver)trauen
to join	s.o.	sich jdm. anschließen			

I. Verwandle in die Leideform (Verwende *by* nur in den Sätzen, wo es in Klammern angegeben ist)
1. Several people saw the accident. (by) 2. A policeman lifted the dead man into a police car. 3. They took the dead man to the nearest hospital. 4.The policeman asked some questions. (by) 5. The taxi driver gave some details. 6. They found the man's luggage in the street. 7. They opened his luggage. 8. They found his name and phone number in his suitcase. 9. They informed his wife of the accident. 10. His wife will order the coffin from Harrods.

II. Setze die Sätze *a) in die vollendete Gegenwart, b) in die vollendete Vergangenheit, c) in die Zukunft*
1. The invitation was accepted. 2. Several speeches were made. 3. Two films were shown. 4. The prizes were given out. 5. A lot of cake was eaten. 6. The guests were taken home by taxis. — 7. We were prepared for the examination. 8. The text was read twice. 9. The difficult words were explained. 10. Long sentences were repeated.

III. Translate:
a) 1. Ein Mann wurde ins nächste Krankenhaus gebracht. *(to take)* 2. Er war von einem Taxifahrer auf *(in)* der Straße gefunden worden. 3. Das linke Bein war gebrochen. 4. Er mußte operiert werden. 5. Ihm wurde von den Ärzten geholfen. 6. Drei Wochen später wurde er auf *(at)* dem Rennplatz gesehen.
b) 1. Ein Mord war geplant worden. 2. Bilk wurde nicht gesehen, als er das Krankenhaus verließ. 3. Er wurde nicht beobachtet, als er die Haustür öffnete. 4. Der Hund wurde ermahnt, sich ruhig zu verhalten. 5. Das Atmen von Mrs Bilk konnte gehört werden. 6. Der Inhalt einer kleinen Flasche wurde in ein Glas Milch gegossen. 7. Die Haustür wurde wieder geschlossen. 8. Würde Mrs Bilk sterben? 9. Niemand konnte diese Frage beantworten.

25 The Proof

After his operation Bilk was unconscious for some time. A lorry in the yard woke him up. Somehow he felt that he was not alone. He turned his head and saw a man with a sërious expression on his face. Bilk guessed immediately that the person was a police-inspector. He said his name was Brown and he had bad news for Bilk. Somebody had attempted to murder Mrs Bilk.

"Is she dead?" asked Bilk anxiously. "Has the house been robbed?"

"Fortunately not," answered the inspector. "Your wife is alive."

He informed Bilk that robbery was out of the question since the jewels in the drawer had not been touched. He added that he had come to make some inquiries and to get more details.

Bilk replied that he was quite ready to answer any questions. He wondered whether the police were on his track, but he was not in the least nervous.

The inspector then said that Bilk had talked while unconscious.

"What you said was plain enough," he continued. "You spoke of a glass of milk and a bottle of poison. The milk at your wife's bedside actually contained enough poison to kill a horse. You tried to poison her."

"How could I?" replied Bilk calmly. "I came into hospital yesterday for my stomach operation and haven't left it since. Besides, I couldn't hurt a fly." There was nothing strange in his manner. He could lie without shame.

"You spoke of a bottle filled with poison," insisted the inspector.

"My wife takes a lot of dangerous medicine, she suffers from bad nerves. So it shouldn't be surprising if I spoke about it in my sleep. I suggest that she put the stuff in her milk. By the way, how was the poison discovered?"

The inspector told Bilk that the cat had jumped onto the table and had knocked over the milk beside Mrs Bilk's bed. The animal had drunk some of the milk and within seconds lay stiff. Mrs Bilk had rung up the police. The liquid had immediately been examined. There was no doubt that it contained poison.

The inspector had hardly finished talking when a scratching noise was heard outside Bilk's window. He went to look and saw a little dog with its front legs up against the wall. In its teeth it was carrying a bottle. The inspector pulled the animal into the room. Full of joy it sprang onto its master's bed, where it laid down the bottle and cheerfully looked up for praise.

"Do you mind if I take this bottle for a thorough examination?" asked the inspector. He paused and then added sharply, "We needn't discuss the case any longer".

Bilk tried to say something, but the words stuck in his throat. Twenty-four hours later he was arrested for attempted murder.

How are you?

I'm very well, thanks. I'm feeling fine.
I'm not up to the mark.
I'm afraid I'm seriously ill.
I'm unwell. I feel rather weak.
I sweated heavily. I must have a temperature.
I couldn't go to sleep for a long time.
What's wrong with you?
What's the matter with you?
That fish didn't agree with me.
I'm going to be sick. My ear aches.
You have a headache. Take these pills.
Are you feeling better now?
It's done me good. I must have caught a cold.
Yes, I have a bad cold.
You must see a doctor (send for the doctor).
I'm doing quite well.

I. Besonderheiten der Mehrzahlbildung II (Pluralbildung) (Vgl. L 2, I u. 11, I)

1. Einz.: **-f(e)** — Mehrz.: **-ves**			3. Unregelmäßig			5. Immer in der Mehrz. stehen	
knife	— kni**ves**	Messer	foot	— feet	Fuß	a) clothes[1]	Kleidung
life	— li**ves**	Leben	tooth	— teeth	Zahn	contents	Inhalt
wife	— wi**ves**	(Ehe-)Frau	goose	— geese	Gans	goods	Waren
leaf	— lea**ves**	Blatt	mouse	— mice	Maus	stairs	Treppe
thief	— thie**ves**	Dieb	man	— men	Mann	b) trousers	lange Hosen
calf	— cal**ves**	Kalb	woman	— women	Frau	shorts	kurze Hosen
wolf	— wol**ves**	Wolf	child	— children	Kind	pyjamas[2]	Schlafanzug
2. Einz.: -o — Mehrz.: -oes			**4. Ein- u. Mehrz. gleich**			braces	Hosenträger
hero	— her**oes**	Held	fish	Fisch; Fische		scissors[3]	Schere
Negro	— Negr**oes**	Neger	sheep	Schaf; Schafe		spectacles	Brille
potato	— potat**oes**	Kartoffel	deer	Hirsch(e); Rotwild		glasses	Brille
tomato	— tomat**oes**	Tomate				lungs	Lunge

[1] clothes [kləuðz] — [2] pyjamas [pə'dʒɑ:məz] — [3] scissors ['sizəz]

Merke zu 5. a): Das Zeitwort steht in der Mehrzahl, z. B. The contents *are* bad. Der Inhalt *ist* schlecht.
zu 5. b): *a pair of* scissors (glasses etc.) *eine* Schere (Brille usw.)

II. Die nichtwörtliche (indirekte) Rede

1. Im Dt. steht in der nichtwörtl. Rede die Möglichkeitsform, im Engl. die Wirklichkeitsform: Er sagt, sein Name *sei* Brown. — He says his name *is* Brown.
2. Im Dt. wird in der nichtwörtl. Rede im allgemeinen die Zeit der wörtl. Rede beibehalten; im Engl. dagegen werden die Zeiten verändert, wenn die nichtwörtl. Rede eingeleitet wird durch ein Zeitwort in der Vergangenheit (z. B. said, replied):

Wörtliche Rede		Nichtwörtliche Rede			
The doctor said,		The doctor said (that)			
a) "She **is**	my patient."	she	**was**	his patient.	sei
b) "I **have** not **seen**	her since."	he	**had** not **seen**	her since.	habe gesehen
c) "I **gave**	her some tablets."	he	**had given**	her some tablets.	habe gegeben
d) "A holiday **will do**	you good."	a. h.	**would do**	her good.	werde tun

Dabei werden:			
Gegenwart	zu	Vergangenheit	(Beispiel a)
vollend. Gegenwart	zu	vollend. Vergangenheit	(Beispiel b)
Vergangenheit	zu	vollend. Vergangenheit	(Beispiel c)
Zukunft	zu	Bedingungsform	(Beispiel d)

Beachte: Vor der nichtwörtl. Rede steht **kein Komma.**

I. Setze in die Mehrzahl
a) lorry, inquiry, distance, factory, key, boy, face, branch, touch; b) wolf, hero, leaf, potato, piano, photo; c) mouse, sheep, fish, tooth, policeman, woman, foot, child

II. Was ist gemeint? (Vgl. Gramm. I,5)
1. ... are worn in bed. 2. ... are worn for sports. 3. ... are used to keep trousers up. 4. ... are worn by people with bad eyes. 5. Dressmakers have several pairs of ... 6. Trousers, shirts and ties are men's ... 7. A pair of glasses, a knife, and a key were the ... of Mr Bilk's pockets.

III. Verwandle in nichtwörtliche Rede: 1. The inspector said, "There's some liquid at the bottom of the glass." 2. He added, "I have come to make some inquiries." 3. Mrs Bilk said, "I always trusted my husband." 4. She told the police, "He went to hospital in the afternoon." 5. The inspector informed Mrs Bilk, "Your husband will be arrested." 6. She answered, "I'll visit him in prison."

IV. Verwandle in wörtliche Rede: 1. The patient said that she could not sleep at night. 2. She said that she suffered from headaches. 3. The doctor told her that cigarettes were poison for her. 4. He said that too much tea was bad for her health. 5. Then he said that he would give her some medicine. 6. He also informed her that she would soon need glasses.

V. Translate: 1. Herr Bilk war ganz gut gelaunt, als er ins Krankenhaus zurückkam. 2. Er hoffte, daß der Inhalt der Flasche seine Frau töten würde. 3. Er hatte keine Ahnung, daß die Katze das Glas Milch umwerfen und die Flüssigkeit trinken würde. 4. Die Polizei würde glauben, daß seine Frau zu viel Medizin genommen hätte. 5. Er hatte den Mord lange vorher geplant und genug Gift gesammelt, um ein Pferd zu töten. 6. Er hatte ein ausgezeichnetes Alibi und war bald fest eingeschlafen.

26 The Man who was Waiting for his Wife

The great city of London is full of surprises. One day I felt hungry and entered a restaurant near Piccadilly to have lunch. At a small table a man was sitting with a sad, but honest face. After some minutes he addressed me, "Excuse me, sir, you look so kind. May I tell you what is worrying me?"

"Certainly! What can I do for you?"

"May I introduce myself? My name is White, Captain John White. You see, I'm waiting for my wife. I can't imagine what has happened to her."

"Well, women are often late."

"That's true," said the man, "but I've been waiting for over three hours. I don't want to make a fool of myself here, so allow me to explain what has happened. I had had a good meal, and when I had waited for about an hour, I decided to go. Then I discovered that I had forgotten my wallet and hadn't a penny in my pocket. It was impossible for me to pay the bill myself, so I had to wait for my wife after all. I ordered a pot of tea. Later I had a piece of cake, and now a cup of coffee. If I tell the waitress now that I can't pay, she'll call the manager, and nobody will believe my story."

"Don't worry!" I said. "I'll pay the bill for you. Take my card. You can send me the money when you get home." The man's expression suddenly changed and he looked very happy. He called the waitress. The bill amounted to £1.55. When the waitress had gone, I told him, "The next time you have lunch at a restaurant, don't forget to take some money with you". — "It's really very kind of you," said the man. "Thank you so much." He rose, and we parted.

Some weeks later I had lunch at another restaurant. As I went in I heard a familiar voice, "Excuse me, sir, you look so kind. May I ..." It was my Piccadilly friend who was telling his story to someone else. At once I knew that I had been tricked and went straight to his table. But the man remembered me, too. In no time he had disappeared. Was he ashamed of himself?

MENU

£ 9.25 **LUNCHEON** £ 9.25

Cream of Tomato Soup

Choice of: —
Grilled Sausages & Spaghetti
Roast Lamb & Mint Sauce
Roast Beef & Yorkshire Pudding

Vegetables

Roast, Boiled or Chipped Potatoes
Spring Cabbage · Green Peas

Sweets

Vanilla Ice-cream
Cheese & Biscuits

Cup of Tea 30p · Cup of Coffee 35p

IN — ON — AT (örtlich)

IN *(Grundbedeutung: in einem Raum)*

to be *in* a house, *in* a room
Besonderheiten: *in* the street auf der Straße
in the picture auf dem Bild
in the country auf dem Land

ON *(Grundbedeutung: auf einer Fläche)*

an actress *on* the stage, to sit *on* a chair,
a fly *on* the wall, a word *on* the blackboard
My room is *on* the first floor. im 1. Stock
They are *on* the way to America.

AT *(Grundbedeutung: an einem Punkt)*

We met *at* the corner.
We stayed the night *at* a hotel (youth hostel).
I saw him *at* the station (post-office, customs).
The Derby takes place *at* Epsom.
Bill is not *at* home, he is *at* school.

Das Fürwort (Pronomen) mit *-self*

Formen

I introduce **myself**	ich stelle mich vor	we introduce **ourselves**	wir stellen uns vor
you introduce **yourself**	du stellst dich vor	you introduce **yourselves**	ihr stellt euch vor
he introduces **himself**	er stellt sich vor	they introduce **themselves**	sie stellen sich vor
she introduces **herself**	sie stellt sich vor	**Grundform:**	
it — **itself**	es — sich	to introduce **oneself**	sich vorstellen

Gebrauch

1. May **I** introduce **myself?** Darf ich mich . . . ? **He** did not want to make a fool of **himself.** wollte sich nicht lächerlich machen	Das Fürwort mit *-self* steht 1. **rückbezüglich** (reflexiv): es bezieht sich auf den Satzgegenstand zurück
2. It was impossible for **me** to pay the bill **myself.** selbst Will **you** call the waitress **yourself,** or shall I? Wollen Sie selbst Why don't you speak to **the manager himself?** mit dem Geschäftsführer selbst	2. **verstärkend** zur Hervorhebung von Haupt- und Fürwörtern; dt. „selbst"

Beachte:

1. The two men looked at **each other** in silence. sahen sich (einander) . . . an	1. Dt. „einander, sich (gegenseitig)" = ***each other*** oder ***one another***
2. His expression **changed.** wandelte sich We **parted.** Wir trennten uns. The waitress **withdrew.** zog sich zurück	2. Den meisten deutschen rückbezüglichen Zeitwörtern entspricht im Engl. ein nicht rückbezügl. Zeitwort (s. Liste unten)

to afford [ə'fɔ:d]	sich leisten	to inquire	sich erkundigen
to be afraid of	sich fürchten vor	to join	sich anschließen
to amount to	sich belaufen auf	to look forward to	sich freuen auf
to apply for	sich bewerben um	to meet	sich treffen
to approach	sich nähern	to mix in	sich einmischen
to change	sich (ver)ändern	to move	sich bewegen
to complain of, about	sich beklagen über	to open	sich öffnen
to deal with [di:l]	sich befassen mit	to quarrel	sich streiten
to decide	sich entscheiden	to refuse	sich weigern
to depend on [di'pend]	sich verlassen auf	to remember	sich erinnern
to feel (well)	sich (wohl) fühlen	to rise	sich erheben
to happen	sich ereignen	to sit down	sich setzen
to hurry	sich beeilen	to take care of [kɛə]	sich kümmern um
to imagine	sich einbilden, sich vorstellen	to wonder	sich wundern, sich fragen
to improve	sich verbessern	to worry about	sich Sorgen machen um

I. Setze Fürwörter mit *-self* ein: 1. Although my mother has two daughters, she always makes the tea . . . 2. Did you make this cake . . . ? 3. Did you speak to the secretary or to the managing director . . . ? 4. My parents send me some money every month, although they haven't got much . . . 5. I am not going to tell you the story, children. Read it . . . 6. I can't give you these stamps, because my sons collect them . . . 7. We painted this room . . .

II. A Letter
(-self, -selves* or *each other / one another?)

Dear Ann,
I must tell you about Peter. We saw . . . for the first time in front of a theatre box-office. We looked at . . . and he smiled. I had to smile to . . ., although I hated . . . for it. He was confused . . . when he suggested that I should accept his friend's ticket. Later, when we knew . . . better, he told me that he had tricked me with the ticket, because he wanted to spend the evening with a pretty girl. We love . . . very much and see . . . every day. He's got a nice little flat all by . . . *(für sich ganz allein).* He does everything . . . He cooks his meals . . ., he cleans the rooms . . ., he washes up . . . He says that unmarried Germans do all these things . . .

Love,
Rhona

III. Translate: Im Flugzeug nach London 1. Die Dame setzte sich neben mich in einen der engen Sitze. 2. Ich konnte sehen, daß sie sich fürchtete. 3. „Ich fliege zum ersten Mal," sagte sie. „Unglücke ereignen sich so leicht." 4. „Machen Sie sich keine Sorgen," sagte ich. „Sie können sich auf dieses Flugzeug verlassen. ‚Sicherheit zuerst' ist das Motto der Gesellschaft." 5. Eine Stewardess *(stewardess)* beeilte sich, uns Zeitungen zu bringen. Einige Minuten später starteten wir *(to take off).*

27 Journey's End

400 years ago English ships delivered the first African slaves to the white sugar-planters in the West Indies. The slave-trade continued until 1833, when throughout the British Empire the Negroes became free.

One day in 1977, John Baker, the great-grandson of a former Negro slave, landed at Liverpool. A clever boy, he had attended the grammar school at Kingston (Jamaica) and had decided to study physics at London University. At night he used to work as a liftboy in a big West End hotel.

In England there are plenty of Negroes who earn the same wages as their white colleagues. You see them as bus conductors, lorry drivers, porters, waiters and waitresses, as nurses and as students. But where they are hardly found is in the higher professions. A Negro doctor in London is as rare as a five-pound note in a church collection.

When John Baker had passed his examinations, for which he had worked hard, he began to look for a position as a physicist. He applied for dozens of posts with private firms, but the answer was always the same: "We're sorry, but the position has been filled." Everybody was most polite. Nobody explained to him the reason for his lack of success. But John Baker knew: a barrier stood between him and his career. It was his colour.

At last, almost in despair, he applied for a government post. The British Government offered him a job in the London social welfare service. This was not the profession which he had studied for. Should he refuse?

Then he saw an advertisement in the newspaper. The Federal Government of Nigeria offered positions as instructors to science graduates. Somebody suggested to him that he should apply. Nigeria, whose political independence had been proclaimed, belonged to the Commonwealth, just like Jamaica. English was the language which was common to them all. Baker applied for a position and got it. He was also appointed professor of physics at Lagos University.

When he landed in Africa, John Baker, a free und educated man, ended the journey which his ancestor had started as a slave four centuries before.

Identification

Surname (in block letters):	SMITH
Christian names:	Vera Rose
Maiden name:	Maier
Single or married:	married
Date of birth:	April 16th, 1937
Place of birth:	Vienna, Austria
Sex:	female
Occupation:	interpreter
Nationality:	British
Nationality at birth:	Austrian
Permanent address:	12 Raymond Road, London, S. W. 19
No. of passport:	840666
Place of issue:	London
Signature:	Vera R. Smith

What do you say

a) *when you want to get past someone in a bus?*
Excuse me.
when you speak to a stranger in the street?
Excuse me, can you tell me the way to ...?
Excuse me, do you know where the ... is?

b) *when you have stepped on someone's foot?*
Sorry. I am (so) sorry.
Sorry, I didn't mean it.
I beg your pardon.

c) *when you didn't catch what someone said?*
I beg your pardon?
Sorry? What did you say?

d) *when you want to smoke?*
Do you mind if I smoke (mind my smoking)?
Answer: Not at all. Please do.
I'd rather you didn't.

I. Die bezüglichen Fürwörter *who* und *which* (Relativpronomen)

Bsp.: Der Mann, *der in London keine Stelle fand*, stammte aus Jamaika.
Ein Satz, der ein Hauptwort näher erläutert, heißt Beifügungssatz (Relativsatz). Er wird eingeleitet durch ein bezügl. Fürwort (dt. „der, welcher").

Formen

Werfall	**who**	der, die, das	**which**	der, die das
Wesfall (Besitzf.)	**whose**		**of which, whose**	
Wemfall	**to whom**		**to which**	
Wenfall	**whom**		**which**	
(mit Verhältnisw.)	about (of, from, etc.) **whom**		about (of, from, etc.) **which**	

1. There are plenty of Negroes **who** earn the same wages as... John Baker, **whose** great-grandfather had been a slave, was now a student at London University. All the Negroes **whom** he knew wanted to stay in England.	1. *who* bezieht sich auf Personen
2. English was the language **which** was common to them all. When he had passed his examinations, **for which** he had worked hard, he looked for a position.	2. *which* bezieht sich auf Sachen u. Tiere
Beachte: His journey ended in the country **which** his ancestor had come **from.** von dem ... gekommen war	Ein Verhältniswort tritt im Beifügungssatz oft hinter das Zeitwort (vgl. L 13, III)

II. Zeitwörter mit Wen- u. Wemfallergänzung (Akk.- u. Dativobjekt)

1. The British	Government	offered	**him**	a job.
The Nigerian	Government	offered	positions	**to science graduates.**
2. a)		Nobody explained	the reason	**to John Baker.**
b)		Nobody explained	**to him**	the reason for this.

1. Der Wemfall steht — je nach seiner Stellung (vgl. L 12, II) — **mit oder ohne *to*** nach

to bring bringen	to offer (an)bieten	to sell verkaufen	to tell sagen, erzählen
to give geben	to pass (weiter)reichen	to send schicken	
to hand (über)reichen	to pay zahlen	to show zeigen	

2. Der Wemfall muß **immer mit *to*** stehen nach

to add s.th. to	hinzufügen	to explain s.th. to	erklären
to announce s.th. to	verkündigen, bekanntgeben	to introduce s.o. to	vorstellen
to deliver s.th. to	zustellen, liefern	to suggest s.th. to	vorschlagen
to dictate s.th. to	diktieren	to say s.th. to	sagen

Stellung im Satz: Gewöhnlich wird der Wemfall nachgestellt (a); ist jedoch der Wenfall wichtiger oder viel länger, so tritt dieser ans Satzende (b).

I. Connect the sentences with a relative pronoun

Ex.: The plane took John Baker to Africa. *It* was British.
The plane, *which* took John Baker to Africa, was British.

1. Lagos University had 6,000 students. *Its* buildings lay outside the city. 2. The private houses were beautiful. *They* were built for science graduates. 3. English was used for teaching. *It* was common to all instructors. 4. The barrier had gone. *It* had stood between Baker and his career in England. 5. Thus ended a long journey. *It* had been started by Baker's ancestor four centuries before. 6. Baker lives in a rich country. *Its* goods are sold all over the world. 7. Nigeria belongs to the Commonwealth. *Her* political independence was proclaimed in 1960.

II. Put the preposition after the verb

Ex.: The taxi for which we were waiting didn't arrive.
The taxi *which we were waiting for* didn't arrive.

1. The woman about whom we are talking is his wife. 2. The case with which we are dealing is interesting. 3. The headaches from which we are suffering are not normal. 4. The girl with whom he used to dance went to New York. 5. The secretary upon whom he depended so much has left. 6. The holidays to which we had looked forward were spoilt by bad weather. 7. The picture at which we are looking is by Picasso. 8. The dog of which you are afraid is not dangerous. 9. The book for which I was looking was under my bed. 10. The man to whom I spoke said he was the managing director.

III. Setze die Wenfall-Ergänzung (Akkusativobjekt) unmittelbar hinter das Zeitwort

Ex.: Rhona brought the manager the letters.
Rhona brought *the letters to the manager*.

1. The waiter handed the customer the bill. 2. The nurse gave the patient some medicine. 3. The physicist showed the staff-manager his certificates. 4. The gentleman offered the lady a cigarette. 5. The landlady passed her guest the milk and sugar. 6. The assistant sold the lady a pair of pink pyjamas.

28 The World Food Crisis

"The only way to stop the rise in prices is to have a price freeze," Mrs Brown told her husband, who was reading the paper at the kitchen table. Mrs Brown had just come back from the shops and was very angry. Though her husband, who was an engineer, had just received an increase in salary, she had no more money left than before, because the price of food, especially bread and meat, had gone up, too.

Mr Brown looked up from his paper and said calmly, "That won't solve the problem, dear. Food prices will continue to rise whether we like it or not. The cause, which lies outside Britain, is the increasing world population."

"Why don't they increase food production, too?" asked Mrs Brown. "All I know is that your increases in salary don't make any difference at all."

"So far we've never had to go hungry," replied her husband. "Do you realize that two thirds of the world's population haven't got enough to eat? You are lucky that you live in a country rich enough to produce or buy the necessary food for its people. But the developing countries in Asia, Africa and South America haven't got the means to feed their growing populations."

"You still haven't answered the question I asked you. Why isn't it possible to increase the food production of countries in which people are starving?" said Mrs Brown.

"There has been an increase in food production, particularly in India," replied her husband, "but the Indian farmers couldn't keep pace with the population explosion. The rains that India needs for her living failed to come for several years, and then great floods followed, sweeping away valuable land. Afterwards, millions of people were starving."

"One answer to the problem could be either birth control or new food resources, or both," said Mrs Brown.

"Easier said than done," replied her husband. "Only those countries that have modern industry can provide the necessary food for their people."

"Isn't there anything that could be done for the developing nations?"

"Well, the United Nations Organization, with the help of wealthier states like the members of the European Community, the USA and Japan, does something, but it's not enough."

"Since we in Britain aren't directly affected by the food shortage the Third World suffers from, why do prices go up here?" asked Mrs Brown.

"It's a question of supply and demand," replied her husband. "The present world shortage of food sends up the prices we have to pay for our bread and meat. However, as long as we can buy the food we need, we shouldn't worry about ourselves, even if prices go up. We should feel sorry for those who were born to be hungry."

Der Beifügungssatz (Relativsatz)

Im Engl. unterscheidet man notwendige und nicht notwendige Beifügungssätze:

Notwendig: The lady *who has just arrived* is my sister's friend.
Nicht notwendig: The Queen, *who has just arrived,* is wearing a pink hat.

Der nicht notwendige Beifügungssatz könnte wegbleiben, ohne daß der Hauptsatz in seinem Sinn unvollständig oder entstellt würde. Der notwendige Beifügungssatz dagegen könnte nicht wegbleiben. — Vor und hinter dem notwendigen Beifügungssatz steht kein Komma!

1. Her husband, **who** was an engineer, had just received an increase in salary.	1. Im **nicht notwendigen** Beifügungssatz stehen: ***who*** für Personen ***which*** für Sachen (u. Tiere)
2. a) In Asia there are millions of people **who (that)** are starving. The rains **that (which)** India needs for her daily bread didn't come.	2. Im **notwendigen** Beifügungssatz a) stehen ***who*** oder ***that*** für Personen ***which*** oder ***that*** für Sachen (u. Tiere)
b) The film **(that) we went to** last Monday was most entertaining. Do you remember the lady **(that) you gave** your address to?	b) **kann** das bezügliche Fürwort im Wenfall weggelassen werden; das Verhältniswort muß in diedem Fall hinter das Zeitwort treten.
Aber: It was the greatest population explosion **that** had ever taken place.	*Aber:* Das bezügl. Fürwort im Werfall darf nicht weggelassen werden.
c) She said I was too late, **which** made me very angry! The policeman showed us the way to the station, **which** was very kind of him.	c) der sich auf den gesamten Inhalt eines vorhergehenden Satzes bezieht, steht ***which***

Beachte: 1. *That* hat für Wer- und Wenfall dieselbe Form. Mit Verhältniswörtern kann es nicht verbunden werden.
2. *That* steht fast immer nach a) *much, many, little, few, all, every, any, no, something, everything, anything, nothing* b) *the first, the last, the only.*

Statt *at which, in which, on which* etc. steht

3. a) He visited the town *where* he was born. Is this the house *where* you live?	a) bei Ortsangaben *where*
b) Summer is a time *when* farmers are busy.	b) bei Zeitangaben *when*

I. Wo sind bezügliche Fürwörter notwendig?

1. What was the name of the young couple ... we met at the seaside? 2. Do you remember the French people ... were at our guest-house? 3. This is the swimsuit ... I bought in Brighton. 4. The photograph ... was lying on the table has disappeared. 5. What was the game ... they played at the party last night? 6. I didn't like the film ... we saw at the cinema yesterday. 7. The film ... was shown on TV was much better. 8. Is this the telegram ... has just arrived?

II. Verwandle in die normale Umgangssprache

Ex.: Is this the picture of which you are so proud?
Is this the picture you are so proud *of*?

1. The party of which I dreamt was held in a large house. 2. The visitors for whom you are waiting won't be here before five o'clock. 3. The only person to whom these children will listen is their grandfather. 4. What was the subject about which we were talking last time? 5. Do you remember the English customs about which I told you? 6. All the jobs for which he applied had already been filled. 7. Toothache is one of the troubles of which she always complains.

III. Translate

1. Die Bevölkerungsexplosion ist einer der Gründe, warum es eine Lebensmittelknappheit auf *(in)* der Welt gibt. 2. Die Länder, die leiden, sind besonders die Entwicklungsländer. 3. Aber auch die reicheren Nationen fühlen die Knappheit, die sich in steigenden Lebensmittelpreisen zeigt. 4. Das Brot, das die Hausfrau *(housewife)* kauft, ist teurer. 5.Das Futter, mit dem die Tiere gefüttert werden ist auch teurer. 6. Das ist ein Grund für die hohen Fleischpreise. 7. Die Erhöhung der Lebensmittelproduktion, die überall stattfand, konnte mit der wachsenden Bevölkerung nicht Schritt halten.

29 The Problem of Automation

Fred Jones is a dockworker in the Port of London. Mary, his wife, a cleaner in an office building half a mile from their home. They have two sons, both pupils at a comprehensive school.

Five mornings a week Mr Jones drives to the docks in his car, which, like their TV set, washing-machine and furniture, has been bought on hire-purchase. Once a year the whole family flies to Spain to spend two happy weeks in the sunshine. They need not save, for they enjoy social security.

One evening Fred Jones came home looking as if he had lost a pound and found a penny. "What's the trouble?" asked Mary.

"It's those containers that are causing the trouble," replied Fred. "Ever since they appeared, our jobs have been threatened. It makes my blood boil."

"Can't you do anything about it?" asked Mary.

"We're going to strike," replied her husband. "We must stop those lorries. The sooner the better. They roll in and out of the docks with the containers while we look on. They call it progress! All they really want is to save labour costs! Do you realize that the number of dockworkers has dropped from 65,000 to 42,000 in seven years?"

"Those who don't work get unemployment pay, don't they?" said Mary. "So we needn't worry if that happened to us."

"That's not the point," said Fred. "That side of the problem isn't troubling me. They're offering £ 22,500 to those who are willing to leave the docks. It's a large sum. But my job is to load and unload ships, and I don't want to be retrained. At my age one's too old to go to school and learn a new job."

The problem the dockworkers have to face is automation. In the USA, where automation is most advanced, unemployment has been quite a problem for years. One computer can do the work of a thousand clerks. Millions have to look for new jobs. The consequences of this development must be studied carefully. Could a four-day-week of 35 hours in certain industries be the answer?

Employers, unions and the State will have to consider the problem.

Weights and Measures

The smallest amount of beer you can order in an English pub is half a pint.

The smallest amount of petrol you can ask for at a filling-station in Britain is a gallon.

The heaviest baby ever born in Britain was a 20 pound 2 ounce boy (20 lb. 2 oz.).

The tallest man of all time was an American. As an adult his height was 8 feet 10 inches (8 ft. 10 ins.).

The heaviest man known in medical literature was an American born in 1798. He weighed 71 stone 6 pounds, or nearly 10 hundredweight (cwt.).

The world's largest office building is the World Trade Center in New York. Its two towers stand side by side and provide room for 50,000 office workers, the number of people in an average town.

The longest suspension bridge in the world is the Verrazano Bridge in New York. It is 4,260 feet in length. Next comes the Golden Gate Bridge in San Francisco. It is 90 feet wide and is only 20 yards shorter than the Verrazano Bridge. It is 220 feet above sea level.

I. Das unbestimmte Geschlechtswort (unbest. Artikel) — Gebrauch

1. Mary is **a cleaner.** Mary ist Putzfrau. Is that gentleman **an American?** I am **a Catholic.** Ich bin Katholik.	1. steht abweichend vom Dt. bei Bezeichnungen für Beruf, Staatsangehörigkeit und Religion
2. They earn £ 180 **a week.** in der Woche Once **a year** they fly to Spain. im Jahr These peaches cost 40 p **a piece.** pro Stück	2. steht in der Bedeutung *je, pro* bei Zeit-, Maß- und Gewichtsangaben
3. **half a mile** eine halbe Meile **rather a large sum** eine ziemlich große Summe **such an event** ein solches Ereignis **What a mistake!** Welcher Fehler!	3. wird nachgestellt bei *half, quite, rather, such, what!* (im Ausruf)

Beachte zu 3.: Das unbest. Geschlechtswort wird auch bei Eigenschaftswörtern nachgestellt, die mit *as ... as, too, how* oder *however* verbunden sind:
He is **as good a football-player as** his brother.
It is **too long a story** to tell.

II. Englisches Geld (English Money)

1. Münzen (coins)		2. Banknoten (bank-notes)
1p a penny	10p ten pence	£1 a pound (= 100 pence)
2p two pence	20p twenty pence	£5 five pounds
5p five pence	50p fifty pence	£50 fifty pounds

Beachte: Geldbeträge
£ 5.99 five pound(s) ninety-nine (pence)
£ 3.09 three pound(s) nine (pence)
£ 1,920 one thousand nine hundred and twenty pounds

III. Englische Maße und Gewichte (Weights and Measures)

1 inch (in., ins.)		= 2,54 cm	1 yard (yd., yds.)	= 3 feet	= 91,5 cm
1 foot (ft.)	= 12 ins.	= 30,5 cm	1 mile (m.)	= 1,760 yds.	= 1,6 km
1 ounce (oz., ozs.)		= 28 g	1 hundredweight (cwt.)	= 112 lbs.	= 51 kg
1 pound (lb., lbs.)	= 16 ozs.	= 454 g	1 ton	= 2240 lbs.	= 1016 kg
1 pint (pt.)	= 0.568 litres (l.)		1 gallon (gal.)	= 4.546 litres	

I. How many times . . . ?

Ex.: a week/you go to evening classes?/three
How many times a week do you go to evening classes? — I go to evening classes three times a week.

1. a year/the Browns go on holiday?/twice 2. a day/English people drink tea?/four 3. a month/the cinema programme change?/six 4. a day/you take your medicine?/three 5. a year/you go to the dentist?/once

II. How much . . . ?

Ex.: do the Taylors earn together? (£180 — week)
How much do the Taylors earn together? — They earn £ 180 a week.

1. do those peaches cost? (40p — piece) 2. do these buttons cost? (30p — dozen) 3. did John Baker earn as a liftboy? (£ 100 — week) 4. does beer cost in an English pub? (80p — pint) 5. does petrol cost? (41p — litre).

III. Translate: 1. Fred und Mary arbeiten fünf Tage in der Woche. Fred ist Dockarbeiter, Mary Putzfrau. 2. Fred fährt *(to go by)* [3]mit dem Wagen [1]zur [2]Arbeit *(work)*. 3. Es ist ein recht guter Wagen. Er kostete 1.100 Pfund. 4. Sie mußten die Summe nicht sofort bezahlen. Sie kauften den Wagen auf Abzahlung. 5. Die Miete für ihr Haus beträgt nur 8,50 Pfund in der Woche. 6. Beide Söhne *(Both their sons)* besuchen eine Gesamtschule. 7. Einmal im Jahr fliegt die ganze Familie nach Spanien, um ihre Ferien im Sonnenschein zu verbringen. 8. Aber Fred macht sich Sorgen *(to worry about)* wegen der Container. Die Zahl der Dockarbeiter ist in sieben Jahren von 65.000 auf 42.000 gefallen. 9. Obwohl die Regierung £ 22.500 denjenigen anbietet, die die Docks verlassen wollen, will Fred ein solches Angebot *(offer)* nicht annehmen.

30

The Open Window

"My aunt will be back in a few minutes, Mr Nuttle," said a young lady of sixteen, "she is at the baker's, the butcher's or the chemist's. Meanwhile, perhaps you would like to take off your coat." Mr Nuttle had come to the small village because his nerves were bad. As he had no friends of his own there, his sister had given him a letter of introduction to the Sappleton family so that he should not feel too lonely. "Do you know many people round here?" asked the niece. "Not a soul," Nuttle replied. "Then you know nothing about my aunt," the girl said. "Only her name and address," admitted the visitor, "she is a friend of my sister's." He followed the girl into the library.

"Poor Aunt! Her illness began three years ago on this very day," said the girl. "You may wonder why we keep that French window open on this wet October afternoon. Out through that window, three years ago, her husband and two young brothers of his went off to go shooting. They never came back. Their bodies were never found. Poor Aunt always thinks that they will come back. That is why that window is kept open. She has often told me how they went out, her husband with his white raincoat over his shoulder, his two brothers and their little brown dog. Sometimes on dull evenings like this one gets a creepy feeling that they will walk through that window." She had tears in her eyes. She took out her handkerchief and blew her nose.

At that moment the aunt appeared. "I hope you don't mind the open window," she said, "my husband and his brothers will be home soon, and they always come this way. They have been out for wild duck today." To Nuttle's discomfort she talked all the time of the shooting prospects for the winter and all the time her eyes were fixed on the window and the wood beyond.

"Here they are at last," she cried. "Just in time for tea!" Nuttle trembled and looked at the niece. The girl was staring out through the open window with fright in her eyes. Nuttle turned in his seat.

In the darkness three figures were walking across the garden towards the window. They carried guns under their arms and one of them had a white raincoat over his shoulder. A brown dog followed. Nuttle quickly took his hat and coat and, without warning, he was through the hall and the front garden.

"Sorry we are late, my dear," said Mr Sappleton, "but on the way back we called at the vicar's. I borrowed a few books of his. By the way, who was that funny man?" — "A Mr Nuttle," said his wife. "He ran away without a word. One might think he had seen a ghost." The niece said nothing. Jokes of that kind were a hobby of hers.

Paying a Visit

Is Mr Gordon at home?
Yes, sir, he is. Please come in.
May I introduce you to my wife?
Herr Heinz Schmidt, a German friend of mine.
How do you do? — How do you do?
I hope I'm not disturbing you.
Not at all. We are glad to see you.
Do sit down.
Will you have a cigarette? — Thank you.
Tea will be ready soon.
How do you like London? — I love it.
Oh, I'm glad to hear that.
I'm afraid I must go now.
Come again whenever you like.
You are always welcome.
I do appreciate that.
Thank you very much for a delightful evening.
Give my regards to your daughter.

I. Besonderer Gebrauch des Wesfalls mit *-s* (Genitiv) (Vgl. L 7, I u. 12, III)

1. We are going **to the vicar's** (house). zum Pfarrer Mother is **at the Browns'** (house). bei Brauns My aunt is **at the baker's** (shop). beim Bäcker Our marriage took place **at St. Mary's** (church).	Das zum Wesfall gehörige Hauptwort **bleibt weg,** wenn es 1. selbstverständlich ist (z. B. *shop, house, church*)
2. Our garden is larger than **our neighbour's.**	2. kurz zuvor genannt wurde

Merke: She is a friend **of my sister's.** Sie ist eine Freundin meiner Schwester.
Two brothers **of Mr Sappleton's** went with him. Zwei Brüder von Herrn Sappleton ...

II. Das besitzanzeigende Fürwort II (Possessivpronomen)

Formen: mit Hauptwort				alleinstehend			Grundform
I	carry	**my**	suitcase(s). —	I	carry	**mine.**	One must do **one's** duty. Man muß seine Pflicht tun.
You	carry	**your**	suitcase(s). —	You	carry	**yours.**	to do **one's** duty seine Pflicht tun
He	carries	**his**	suitcase(s). —	He	carries	**his.**	
She	carries	**her**	suitcase(s). —	She	carries	**hers.**	
We	carry	**our**	suitcase(s). —	We	carry	**ours.**	
You	carry	**your**	suitcase(s). —	You	carry	**yours.**	
They	carry	**their**	suitcase(s). —	They	carry	**theirs.**	

1. Das besitzanzeigende Fürwort (mit Hauptwort)

a) He had a raincoat over **his shoulder.** über der Schulter They carried guns under **their arms.**	a) steht immer bei Körperteilen und Kleidungsstücken. (Beachte die „anschauliche Mehrzahl" bei *arms*; dt.: „unter *dem Arm*".)
b) I saw them with **my own eyes.** mit eigenen Augen Aber: My aunt has **a** house **of her own.** We have **no** garden **of our own.**	b) kann verstärkt werden mit *own* eigen Merke aber: ein(e) eigene(r) = *a ... of my own* kein(e) eigene(r) = *no ... of my own*

2. Das alleinstehende besitzanzeigende Fürwort

Your garden is larger than **ours.** als unserer, der unsere Don't get out your cigarettes. Have one of **mine.** von meinen	steht immer ohne Geschlechtswort und wird in der Form nicht verändert, gleichgültig, ob es sich auf ein Hauptwort in der Einzahl oder Mehrzahl bezieht.

Merke: She is a friend **of mine.** Sie ist eine Freundin **von mir.**
Two brothers **of his** went with him. Zwei Brüder **von ihm** gingen mit.

I. Comparisons

Ex.: Mr Brown's house is older than his mother's.
His is older than hers.

1. My car is newer than my friend's. 2. My friend's job is more interesting than my sister's. 3. Mrs Brown's occupation is not so well paid as her husband's. 4. The Browns' holidays were longer than Betty's. 5. Your dress is prettier than your niece's. 6. Our examination papers were more difficult than our friends'.

II. ***A — of — own***

Ex.: This house belongs to my wife.
She has got a house of her own.

1. This gun belongs to my father. 2. The garden belongs to the Taylors. 3. That car belongs to me. 4. This bowl belongs to our dog. 5. This dictionary belongs to my niece.

III. ***Not — a — of own***

Ex.: This TV set doesn't belong to me.
I haven't got a TV set of my own.

1. This washing-machine doesn't belong to us. 2. This passport doesn't belong to that baby. 3. This fur coat doesn't belong to my wife. 4. That dog doesn't belong to me. 5. This office doesn't belong to me.

IV. Translate: 1. Mit dem Hut in der Hand und dem Mantel unter dem Arm rannte Herr Nuttle die Straße entlang. Er ging zur Apotheke. 2. „Hilfe!" schrie er. „Meine Nerven! Bitte geben Sie mir (einige) Tabletten." 3. „Was ist los, mein Herr?" fragte der Apotheker. „Man könnte denken, Sie hätten ein Gespenst gesehen." 4. „Ich habe drei gesehen!" schrie Herr Nuttle. „Herrn Sappleton und zwei Brüder von ihm." 5. „Aber die (sie) sind [doch] nicht tot", lachte der Apotheker. „Ich sah Herrn Sappleton vor ein paar Minuten auf der Straße. Er ist ein Freund von mir."

31 Don't

"When in Rome, do as the Romans do." This is indeed one of the oldest English proverbs. It means that in a foreign country you will feel happier if you behave as everyone else does.

Therefore, when you are in England:

DON'T drive on the right-hand side of the road; if you did, you would land in hospital within five minutes of your arrival.

DON'T shake hands, except when you meet somebody for the first time or when you go away for a long time. But of course you knew, didn't you?

DON'T walk on the inside of the pavement when you are with a lady. If you did, she would hardly think you very polite. Always let her walk on the side where the houses are. You will remember, won't you?

DON'T use your fork like a shovel. Hold it so that the food is pushed on its back. However, you may cut your potatoes with a knife. That's very practical. Don't you think so?

DON'T remain seated in a restaurant or in a café when the lady leaves your table even for a short time. Get up when she comes back and hold the chair for her. You won't forget, will you?

DON'T forget to leave a tip on the table. The service is not always included. For a cup of tea or coffee not less than two pence is expected. For larger bills 10 per cent is plenty. At least let's hope so.

DON'T try to find a pub open in the afternoon before 5.30 or after 11 o'clock in the evening. Fifty-three per cent of the English don't drink alcohol. The licensing hours are a compromise between those who drink and those who object to it.

DON'T only pay for your own drink when you are in company. In England it is the custom to order rounds. This means that a company of five will drink a lot. Do many people lose their driving-licences? We hope not!

DON'T be astonished when in the morning tea is brought to your bedside. It is the custom to be awakened with a hot cup of tea.

DON'T refuse a cup of coffee at bedtime. English coffee won't keep you awake. If you don't like it, don't tell your host!

DON'T complain of draughts. The English love fresh air and cough a lot.

I. Bedingungsform und Bedingungssatz (Konditional und Konditionalsatz)

Erste Bedingungsform: ich würde finden	**Zweite Bedingungsform:** ich hätte gefunden (wörtl.: würde gefunden haben)	
I would find, etc. (s. L 19, II)	I would have found	we would have found
Merke: I would be — ich wäre; I would have — ich hätte	you would have found	you would have found
	he would have found	they would have found

Der Bedingungssatz

1. *if*-Satz: Gegenwart	Hauptsatz: Zukunft
If we **refuse** morning tea, Wenn wir ... ablehnen,	our host **will be** astonished. ist unser Gastgeber erstaunt.
If you **drive** on the right,	you **will land** in hospital within a short time.
2. *if*-Satz: Vergangenheit	Hauptsatz: 1. Bedingungsform
If **we refused** morning tea, Wenn wir ... ablehnten,	our host **would be** astonished. wäre ... erstaunt.
If you **drove** on the right,	you **would land** in hospital within a short time.
3. *if*-Satz: Vollendete Verg.	Hauptsatz: 2. Bedingungsform
If we **had refused** morning tea, Wenn wir ... abgelehnt hätten,	our host **would have been** astonished. wäre ... erstaunt gewesen.
If you **had driven** on the right,	you **would have landed** in hospital within ...

Beachte zu 2.: Im *if*-Satz steht nicht die Bedingungsform, sondern die Vergangenheit!
Merke: if I, you, he, etc. **were** wenn ich wäre, du wärst, er wäre, usw.
Im *if*-Satz steht *were* in allen Personen.

II. Die Wiedergabe von dt. „es" (auf einen vorhergehenden Satz zurückweisend)

1. Ten per cent is plenty. — Let's **hope so.** Hoffen wir's! If you haven't filled up your landing card, please **do so** at once.	1. dt. „es" = engl. *so* nach *to expect* annehmen, *to hope*, *to say*, *to suppose* vermuten, *to think* und oft nach *to do*
2. If you don't like English coffee, don't **tell** your host. Sagen Sie es nicht ... You may cut your potatoes. — I **know.**	2. „es" bleibt unübersetzt nach *to forget*, *to know*, *to remember*, *to tell*, *to try* und oft nach *to do*

Auch im Dt. bleibt „es" manchmal weg: Haben Sie ein Fünfmarkstück? — Ich glaube nicht.
Beachte: I hope not; auch I suppose not, I believe not für I don't suppose so, I don't believe so

I. If I were you ...

Ex.: Don't drive on the right-hand side.
If I were you, I wouldn't drive on the right-hand side.

1. Don't walk in the middle *(Mitte)* of the street. 2. Don't use your fork like a shovel. 3. Don't forget to leave a tip. 4. Don't try to find a pub open at midnight. 5. Don't refuse a cup of coffee at bedtime. 6. Don't complain of draughts.

II. What will you do if ...?

a) *Ex.:* If I go to England, I'll take the car.
If I take the car, I'll be careful.
If I'm careful, I won't land in hospital.

Now go on: 1. If ..., I'll save a lot of money. 2. ..., I'll be able to go to a nice seaside hotel. 3. ..., I'll meet some English people. 4. ..., I'll have some evenings out with them. 5. ..., we'll go to a number of pubs. 6. ..., we'll drink a lot.

b) *Now put the sentences into the past tense*
Ex.: If I went to England, I'd (I would) take the car.
If I took the car, I'd be careful.
If I were careful, I wouldn't land in hospital.

III. Gib kurze Antworten, wenn notwendig verneint

Ex.: Will you be back soon? (to hope, to think, to try, to tell)
I hope so. (I think so. I don't think so. I'll try. I can't tell you.)

1. When is Mary's birthday? (to forget, to remember, to know, to tell) 2. Do you think she will send us an invitation to her party? (to hope, to expect, to think, to suppose) 3. At what time does the train leave? (to forget, to remember, to know, to tell) 4. Can I take my dog with me to England? (to think, to suppose, to expect, to tell, to believe — *alle verneint!*)

32 Stratford-on-Avon

Shakespeare has made this town famous. Standing outside the house where he was born in 1564, we hear most languages of the earth and we see people of all nationalities, drawn here by the world's greatest dramatist, who spent his youth and the last years of his life in Stratford-on-Avon.

Every morning people queue at the box-office of the Royal Shakespeare Theatre, hoping to get a seat for a matinée or evening performance of one of Shakespeare's plays. It is 'house full' from April until the end of the season in November, and the wise man has booked his seat weeks in advance if he does not wish to be disappointed.

Walking through the streets of this pleasant little market town with its half-timbered houses, many dating from the time of Elizabeth I, we are reminded at every step of the great poet.

We see the Grammar School where "the schoolboy with his satchel and shining morning face, creeping like a snail unwillingly to school" *(As You Like It)* learnt "little Latin and less Greek".

Not far from the town we find the cottage of his wife, Anne Hathaway. She was 26 and Shakespeare was 18 when they married. They had three children.

At about the age of twenty-two Shakespeare left his family and went to London, the large city offering better opportunities for an intelligent young man than a small town like Stratford. He became a well-known actor, dramatist and poet, wealthy enough to buy New Place, the finest house in Stratford. About 1610 Shakespeare returned to his native town, where he died six years later at the age of fifty-two.

The poet lies buried in Holy Trinity Church, which is pleasantly situated on the River Avon. On his tombstone he had his own epitaph engraved, cursing the man who should move his bones from the place where they rest.

No other native town of a great poet has been transformed to such an extent into a place of pilgrimage, where not even a hotel room can be obtained unless reserved well beforehand.

What is the secret of Shakespeare's lasting popularity after 360 years? Is it perhaps that Shakespeare, more than anyone else, understood the human heart and human nature, and that human nature does not change?

"He was not of an age, but for all time."

IN — ON — AT (zeitlich)

IN *(Grundbedeutung: innerhalb eines Zeitraumes)*

Shakespeare was born *in* 1564.
I went for a walk *in* the morning (*in* the afternoon, *in* the evening).
Aber (Tageszeit mit näherer Bestimmung):
I saw him *on* Christmas morning.
I'll ring you up *on* Wednesday afternoon.
His letter arrived *on* the evening of May 3rd.

ON *(nur im Sinne von „an einem Tag")*

We are going to Stratford *on* Wednesday (*on* May 18th, *on* the first day of our holidays).
Open to visitors *on* weekdays and *on* Sundays.
Aber: the next day (morning) am nächsten Tag
that day (evening) an jenem Tag

AT *(Grundbedeutung: zu einem Zeitpunkt)*

at four o'clock, *at* ten past eight, *at* midnight
at that moment, *at* the same time
at tea-time (lunch-time, bedtime)
at (the age of) twenty-two
at Christmas, *at* Easter, *at* the weekend
Merke: at night (*aber:* by day)

Der Gebrauch der Mittelwörter (Partizipien)

Formen

Mittelwort der Gegenwart (Partizip Präsens):	opening, giving	(vgl. L 6, I)
Mittelwort der Vergangenheit (Partizip Perfekt):	opened, given	(vgl. L 16, I u. II)
Zur Bezeichnung einer schon vorangegangenen Handlung (Vorzeitigkeit) dienen die zus.ges. Formen:	having opened, having given having been opened (given)	

Gebrauch

A. Die Mittelwörter stehen **satzverkürzend**

1. All the people **queueing** there hope to get tickets. die Menschen, die anstehen The performances **given** at the Royal Shakespeare Theatre are always well attended. Die Vorstellungen, die ... gegeben werden ...	1. an Stelle von **Beifügungssätzen**
2. a) **Standing** outside Sh.'s birth-place, we can hear many languages. Wenn wir ... stehen b) **Having booked** a seat in advance, I did not have to queue. Da ich ... bestellt hatte c) At the age of 22 Shakespeare went to London, **leaving** his family in Stratford. (wobei er ... ließ) Seine Familie ließ er ...	2. an Stelle von **Umstandssätzen** a) der Zeit; dt. wenn, als, nachdem b) des Grundes; dt. da c) der Begleitumstände; dt. meistens neuer Hauptsatz
Beachte: *Shakespeare* went to London, **the large city offering** better opportunities. da die große Stadt ... bot Everywhere *we* can see old houses, **many dating** from the 16th century.	Beachte: Wenn der Satzgegenstand des Mittelwortes nicht mit dem Satzgegenstand des Hauptsatzes übereinstimmt, muß er besonders genannt werden.

Manchmal muß ein Wort wie *while*, *unless* wenn nicht, *if*, *although* dem Mittelwort vorangehen, damit sein Sinn klar wird: Hotel rooms cannot be obtained *unless reserved* in advance.

B. Die Mittelwörter **nach bestimmten Zeitwörtern:**

1. One evening I *watched* dozens of buses **driving** into Stratford. beobachtete, wie ... fuhren Suddenly I *heard* my name **called.** hörte, wie ... gerufen wurde, hörte meinen Namen rufen	1. nach Zeitwörtern der **Wahrnehmung:** to see to watch to hear to feel
2. I can't read this letter. I must *have* it **translated.** muß ihn übersetzen lassen We booked seats and *had* the tickets **sent** to us. ließen uns die Karten schicken	2. (nur Mittelwort der Vergangenheit) nach ***to have*** = „lassen". (In der Umgangssprache steht statt *to have* manchmal *to get.*)

I. Forme die Sätze um; *verwende Mittelwörter*

Ex.: As Shakespeare *hoped* to find better opportunities in London, he left Stratford.
Hoping to find ..., Shakespeare left ...

1. As Stratford-on-Avon *is* the birth-place of William Shakespeare, it draws visitors from all over the world. 2. Shakespeare attended the Stratford Grammar School. He *learnt* 'little Latin and less Greek'. 3. After he *had become* a wealthy man, Shakespeare was able to buy New Place. 4. About 1610 Shakespeare left London. He *had decided* to spend his last years in his native town. 5. When we *stand* in front of Shakespeare's tombstone, we can read the epitaph which he wrote himself.

II. Women in modern Britain

Ex.: When we look at women's careers, we see that men often have better opportunities.
When looking at women's careers, we see ...

1. Even before they hold top positions, men get more money than women. 2. When they go into business or industry, women usually end up as typists or secretaries. 3. After they have been in business for a few years, women often marry and give up their careers. 4. While they look after the household and the children, women seldom fill important positions in politics, business or industry. 5. While they still wait for things to change, women in Britain are beginning to fight for equal opportunities.

III. Füge passende Sätze hinzu (dt. „lassen"):

Ex.: I have an awful toothache.
I must have the tooth pulled out.

1. Your hair is too long. (to cut) 2. My watch has stopped. (to repair) 3. What a lovely dress! Did you make it yourself? No, I ... 4. The goods are too heavy to carry. (to deliver) 5. I don't like the colour of this bath. (to paint pink)

6-5046

33 Starting a New Life in Australia

I. "Yes," said 28-year-old Jane Bird, sitting in the bar on board the 30,000-ton ocean liner QUEEN OF AUSTRALIA. "I'm going to open an ice-cream parlour in Sydney."

Jane was one of the 72,000 British emigrants taking advantage that year of the Australian Government's offer. This offer allowed people to travel to Australia for £ 10, everything included.

"Look," she said, showing a map of Sydney to the man who was sitting beside her. "I'll have my ice-cream parlour in Victoria Street near the harbour." Jane was referring to her business plans.

"Ice-cream always sells where there's plenty of sunshine," said George Grey, also a £ 10 passenger to Australia. "Why didn't you go by plane? It's quicker and the price of the passage is the same as by ship." "Well," replied Jane, "Apart from the comfort of the boat, I chose the sea as it may be my last holiday for years. Besides, you get to know people on board. I'm going to make friends so that I won't leave the ship all by myself."

"You won't have to," said George, taking her hand. "I'll be there, too." "Thank you," said Jane. "Life can be so difficult for a woman alone. I've no relatives in Sydney and I could do with some help."

II. Jane and George opened their ice-cream parlour in the first week of December. It was summer and temperatures ranged from 32° to 36° centigrade at noon. Soon they were supplying their customers with ice-cream, Coca-Cola and other soft drinks as fast as they could fetch them out of the refrigerator. Before the end of the summer they were employing two waitresses. It was on Sunday that they had most customers, for on that day the pubs were closed.

Autumn came and lucky Jane and George already owned a chain of ice-cream parlours on the coast. Success didn't make them blind. Whenever they chose a new place, they carefully studied its possibilities. Was it on the right side of the road? Was there any competition in the neighbourhood? Was the rent reasonable? When did most people pass by, in the morning, in the afternoon or at night? For it was important that there should be crowds of people when the heat was greatest. Thus their business went smoothly and grew steadily. They never regretted that they had left old England with her awful weather and crowded cities. They had emigrated to a country with sunshine and space instead.

Both George and Jane applied for registration as Australian citizens three years after landing in Sydney.

Australia

Australia covers 2,971,081 square miles.
Its capital is Canberra.
The population is about 15 million.
More than three-quarters of the population live in towns.
1 Australian dollar equals about DM 2.53.
No large city gets less than an average of about 5½ hours of sun a day.
About 27 per cent of the work-force of 5 million is employed in factories.
The basic wage averages 200 Australian dollars for a 38-hour-week.
Australia produces about half of all the wool entering the world market.
Australia also has large quantities of metals like iron, zinc and nickel of excellent quality.

Das bestimmte Geschlechtswort (bestimmter Artikel)

A. Ohne Geschlechtswort stehen (oft im Gegensatz zum Dt.)

1. folgende Arten von Hauptwörtern, wenn in **ganz allgemeinem Sinn** gebraucht:	
a) **People** often see Shakespeare's plays. **Most** of them do so regularly. Die meisten … b) **English beer** is not drunk ice-cold. Das engl. Bier c) **Love** is blind. Die Liebe **Life** is short. Das Leben	a) **Hauptwörter in der Mehrzahl** *people* die Leute, die Menschen, man *most* + Hauptw. **die** meisten b) **Stoffnamen** } auch mit **Begriffe** } Eigenschaftswort
2. folgende **Zeitbestimmungen**	
a) **Spring** begins on March 21st. Der Frühling **August** is the holiday month. Der August **Christmas Eve** is a normal working day. b) I'll meet you after **breakfast.** nach dem Frühstück c) **Night** is the time for sleep. Die Nacht	a) **Jahreszeiten,** Monate, Wochentage, Festtage b) **Mahlzeiten** c) **Tageszeiten** in allg. Sinn
3. folgende **Ortsbestimmungen**	
a) My friend lives in **Greenleaf Road.** **Hyde Park** is the playground of democracy. Our train leaves from **Victoria Station.** Aber: Stratford lies on **the Avon.** **The North Sea** is often rough. b) We read Shakespeare **at school.** in der Schule Do you go **to church** every Sunday? in die Kirche Father is ill. He is **in hospital.** im Krankenhaus	a) Namen von **Straßen,** Parks, Bahnhöfen usw., wenn zus.gesetzt mit *Street, Circus, Park, Station* usw. Aber: Flüsse und Meere mit Geschlechtswort b) *school, church, hospital, bed,* wenn nicht nur an das Gebäude (den Gegenstand) gedacht ist
4. **Eigennamen in der Einzahl**	
Poor **Aunt Mary** seems to be ill. Die arme Tante… Good old **Tom** married again. Der gute alte Tom … Merry old **England.** Das gute alte England.	Ohne bestimmten Artikel stehen Eigennamen in der Einzahl, auch in Verbindung mit Eigenschaftswörtern

Aber: Das Geschlechtswort muß stehen, wenn das Hauptwort näher bestimmt ist, bes. durch einen Wesfall mit *of* oder einen Beifügungssatz: Much has been written about **the** life *of Shakespeare.* Do you know **the** people *who have just arrived?*

B. Bestimmtes Geschlechtswort und besitzanzeigendes Fürwort werden nachgestellt

Half the time he is asleep. **All his life** he lived in London.	bei *all* alle, ganz, *half* halb, *both* beide, *double* doppelt, *quite* ganz, durchaus

I. With or without *the*?
1. … work is the key to … success. 2. … money alone does not bring … happiness. 3. At weekends the Queen enjoys … happiness of … family life. 4. … life of a queen is not all sunshine. 5. … breakfast is the first meal of the day. 6. Is … democracy very old in England?

II. Use the definite article where necessary
1. … life of an emigrant in Australia can be disappointing. 2. … most emigrants haven't got much money when they land. 3. … success isn't just waiting for them. 4. For the first week they stay at a government hostel and … non-British emigrant must accept… work which the Australian Government has to offer. 5. Besides, every man arriving in Australia as an emigrant from another country may be called up for … national service in … Australian Army.

III. *In, on,* or *at*? (Vgl. L 32) 1. My parents took me to Stratford … my 15th birthday. 2. That was … a Saturday … August 1978. 3. … the evening we went to the theatre. 4. We did not return to London … the same day, because my father does not like to drive … night. 5. The Shakespeare season begins … spring; this year it began … Easter.

IV. Translate: 1. Für viele Auswanderer, die England verlassen, ist das Leben in Australien nicht immer leicht. 2. Viele kehren nach einem Jahr nach England zurück, aber die meisten von ihnen bleiben in der neuen Welt. 3. Der Dezember liegt im Sommer, aber sonst *(otherwise)* ist das Leben nicht sehr verschieden von dem in Britannien. 4. Alle Einwanderer können sich nach drei Jahren um die australische Staatsangehörigkeit *(nationality)* bewerben.

34 The Boat Race

In late March or early April one of Britain's biggest sporting events takes place. More than 3,000,000 Britons give up their normal Saturday occupation and go to see the Boat Race or take the opportunity of watching it on TV.

"There, old boy, this time you're beaten," John announced to his American friend Joe. "This is something the USA hasn't got."

Joe, who loved telling everybody that everything was bigger and better in America, had to admit that the crowds watching the Boat Race between the Universities of Oxford and Cambridge were larger than any mass meeting in the States.

"It's no use saying I enjoyed watching it," Joe continued, "for I did not. This morning after breakfast I drove to Hammersmith and joined the people going to the river. The weather was wet and cold, and yet, by car, by coach, on bicycles and on foot, people were moving in one direction: to the river. I wanted to go on a bridge, but I gave up trying. They were standing there like sardines in a tin.

At last I succeeded in finding my way to the river bank. There I was in danger of being pushed into the river. Somebody suggested going on a launch. I took his advice. I got cold and wet through. What was the sense in that?

And then they came. Eight strong young men in each boat with a small shouting passenger at the back were rowing like mad as if the devil were behind them. All I could see was over in about three minutes.

Four and a half miles up the River Thames in less than twenty minutes is not bad, but an American child of ten would say, 'Why all the excitement? The two boats should have outboard motors to save time and energy.' I can't help thinking that I could have saved myself the trouble."

In spite of disliking what his friend had said, John didn't show his feelings.

"This might apply to any kind of sport," he said. "You might just as well say that football isn't worth bothering about. And yet, millions of people are interested in it. They don't mind waiting at the gates for hours, they don't object to paying a lot of money to see a match. They find their amusement in watching strength and skill. Sport is a great experience."

What's the Weather like?

There are dark clouds in the sky.
The weather forecast is 'mainly fair'.
The weather seems quite settled.
I hope it will stay fine.
The weather has changed (is dull).
It looks like rain (like a thunderstorm).
It's going to rain in a moment.
It's pouring with rain.
What nasty (awful, ugly) weather!
Today it's foggy (there's a thick fog).
It's snowing. It's freezing.
It's dry but fairly cool.
The sun is shining again.
It's very warm.

Das Gerundium I

Das Gerundium hat dieselbe Form wie das Mittelwort der Gegenwart: *washing*, *singing*. Es hat aber eine andere Bedeutung: es ist die Hauptwortform des Zeitworts, dt. „das Waschen, das Singen". Auch von der Leideform kann ein Gerundium gebildet werden, z. B. *being washed* (wörtl.: „das Gewaschenwerden"). Das Gerundium ist besonders häufig in Überschriften, z. B. *Teaching English*, *Asking the Way*, und in zusammengesetzten Hauptwörtern, z. B. *washing-machine*, *sitting-room*. Im Dt. wird das Gerundium oft durch eine Grundform wiedergegeben.

Wie ein Hauptwort steht das Gerundium

1. **Rowing** is a pleasant sport. Rudern ist . . . *It's no use (no good)* **saying** that I enjoyed it. Es hat keinen Zweck, zu sagen . . .	1. als **Satzgegenstand,** bes. nach einleitendem *it* **is** *no use (no good)* es hat keinen Zweck
2. I did not *enjoy* **watching** the race. Es machte mir keinen Spaß, . . . zuzusehen. People *don't mind* **waiting** for hours. Somebody *suggested* **going** on a launch. At 11 o'clock it *started* **raining (to rain).**	2. als **Ergänzung** nach einer Reihe von Zeitwörtern. Die wichtigsten sind in der folgenden Liste aufgeführt.

a)	to avoid	vermeiden	to love*	lieben, sehr gern tun
	to go on, to continue*	weiterhin (tun), weiter-	to prefer*	vorziehen, lieber tun
	to keep (on)	dauernd (tun)	to hate*	hassen, sehr ungern tun
	to give up	aufgeben	c) I can't help	ich kann nicht umhin
	to have finished	fertig sein mit	I don't mind	ich habe nichts dagegen
	to stop	aufhören	would you mind?	würden Sie bitte?
b)	to enjoy	Spaß, Freude haben an	to remember	sich erinnern an
	I enjoy	es macht mir Spaß	to suggest	vorschlagen
	to like*	lieben, gern tun	to be busy	beschäftigt sein

*nach diesen Zeitwörtern kann statt des Gerundiums auch die Grundform stehen

3. People don't *object to* **getting** wet. haben nichts dagegen, . . . zu werden We took the *opportunity of* **watching** the race on TV. Möglichkeit, . . . zu sehen Joe was *keen on* **talking.** redete gerne	3. nach Zeitwörtern, Haupt- und Eigenschaftswörtern **mit Verhältniswörtern.** Die geläufigsten sind in der folgenden Liste aufgeführt:

a)	to insist on	bestehen auf	opportunity of	Gelegenheit zu,
	to look forward to	sich freuen auf	c) accustomed to	gewohnt an
	to object to	etwas dagegen haben	used to	gewohnt an
	I succeed in	es gelingt mir	to be interested in	Interesse finden an
b)	chance of	Aussicht, zu	keen on	scharf darauf, zu
	difficulty in	Schwierigkeit, zu	to be tired of	etw. satt haben

I. Joe tells another American about the Boat Race

Ex.: I had to smile at all the excitement over a boat race. (I couldn't help)
I couldn't help smiling at all the excitement over a boat race.

1. *You mustn't tell* an Englishman that you don't like the boat race. (It's no use) 2. *I had to laugh* when I saw the two boats moving up the Thames. (I couldn't help) 3. Thousands of people *tried hard to* get a good place. (to be busy) 4. *Why should I inform* everybody that I thought the whole event silly? (It's no good) 5. *Why tell* people that you don't appreciate their amusements? (It's not worth) 6. *I have to think* about it all the time. (I can't help).

II. Ersetze die schräggedruckten Ausdrücke durch die Wörter in Klammern + Gerundium

Ex.: Someone *thought we should go* on a launch (to suggest). — Someone *suggested going* on . . .

1. Oxford *managed to beat* Cambridge last year (to succeed in). 2. *It will be nice to see* you next Sunday (I look forward to). 3. *Please shut* the door (would you mind). 4. I *always read* the newspaper at breakfast (to be accustomed to). 5. *It was not very easy to find* a place on the river bank (I had difficulty in).

III. Translate: 1. Als ich zum erstenmal zum Bootsrennen ging, war ich fünfzehn Jahre alt. 2. Mein Freund und ich ruderten gern, und wir freuten uns darauf, dieses große Sportereignis zu sehen. 3. Ich schlug vor, auf eine Brücke zu gehen, aber die Menschen standen dort schon wie die Heringe. 4. Endlich gelang es uns, das Flußufer zu erreichen, aber die Menschenmenge war so groß, daß keine Aussicht bestand, das Rennen zu sehen. 5. [Am] nächsten Abend gingen wir ins Kino und sahen das ganze Rennen.

35 Sales Psychology

Dear Sirs, May 31st, 19..

On starting as branch manager in the Dover supermarket I soon began to apply some methods which increased sales by 20 per cent. This increase was partly realized by arranging the articles on show differently. Fast sellers like sugar and salt were within easy reach of the public. But why block valuable space on the shelf with goods people will buy in any case? I put the slow sellers like toothbrushes, combs, lipsticks and powder in places where our female customers could not avoid seeing them. I had observed that most people have the habit of looking to the right when walking. So I placed the slow sellers to the right. Also, by building up expensive goods in heaps and advertising them as 'special offers' I made a handsome profit for the company.

Another point of importance was the question of lighting and general effect. I recommended bright lights on all the goods, and records playing soft music. The sound of music produces that free and easy feeling which often makes people spend more than they really intend. I spread the spirit of Christmas spending over the whole year. And I didn't forget the children, for they make their mothers buy all sorts of things, from toys to ices. When I noticed that the sweets, chocolates and nuts were out of sight of the four-year-olds, I had them placed right under their noses and the results were very satisfying.

Then there were the prices. It is a fact, though I have never completely understood why, that prices containing the figure 9 will sell more easily. I put my observation to the test. Our jams marked at 89p were greater favourites than those at 85p. The nuts priced at 99p a pound were sold in no time, while the same nuts priced at 87p were not in demand. As far as prices are concerned, it's just as bad to charge too little as too much. Recently we had some apples. They were in good condition, but extremely ripe. So we were offering them at a very generous price. "As cheap as that?" said a woman to her friend. "Must be something wrong with them." The next day I put the price up, and all the apples were sold by the afternoon. In writing this I wish to draw your attention to the fact that much of the success of a business depends on the skill and responsibility of the branch manager. Yet, for three years I haven't had an increase in salary, which proves that a good salesman has to sell not only goods to his customers but, in addition, his ability to his employers.

I would be grateful if you would give this letter your close attention.

Yours faithfully, John Smith

Private Letters

a) *Anrede*
Dear Jack (Mother, Father), My dear Jack, Dear Mr Brown (Mr and Mrs Brown),

b) *Empfehlungen vor dem eigentl. Briefschluß*
Remember me to your wife (to Mrs Brown). Empfehlen Sie mich Ihrer Frau Gemahlin.
Kind regards to all. Freundl. Grüße an alle.
Give my love to Aunt Sarah (the children). Grüße Tante S. herzlich von mir.

c) *Briefschluß*
Yours sincerely, / Yours very sincerely, } Mit freundlichen (besten) Grüßen
Yours ever, Herzlichst Dein — Yours, Dein

d) *Anschrift*
c/o Brown bei Brown *(bei Untermietern)*

Business Letters

a) *Anrede*
Sir, — Madam, *(Amtsstil)*
Dear Sir, — Dear Madam, — Dear Mr Brown, Dear Sirs, *(an e. Firma; amerik.:* Gentlemen:)
"For the attention of Mr J. Brown" = z. Hdn. von

b) *Beginn*
In reply to (with reference to, referring to) your letter of June 21st.
In Beantwortung Ihres Schreibens (Bezug nehmend auf ...)

c) *Briefschluß*
Yours faithfully, Hochachtungsvoll
Yours truly, Mit verbindlichen Grüßen
Yours sincerely, Mit freundl. (bestem) Gruß

I. Der Gebrauch des Kommas

Während im Deutschen der Gebrauch des Kommas festen Regeln unterworfen ist, hängt er im Englischen vielfach von der Willkür des Schreibenden ab. Jedoch gelten ohne Einschränkung folgende Regeln:

1. Im Gegensatz zum Dt. steht **kein Komma**

a) Please note **that** you can reach Brighton direct from Dover.	a) vor Nebensätzen mit *that*
b) Mr Walker said **(that)** he would come. He asks **at what time** he is expected.	b) vor der nichtwörtl. Rede und nichtwörtl. Frage
c) It is nice **to see** you again.	c) vor der Grundform
d) The telegram **which** has just arrived is from Mr Turner. I found a letter **addressed** to Mr Ball. Who are those children **playing** in our garden?	d) vor u. nach notwendigen Beifügungssätzen (vgl. L 28) und entsprechenden Mittelwortkonstruktionen (vgl. L 32, A 1.)
e) Please ring me up **if** you can't come. I'll wait here **until** I hear from you. Let's have a drink **before** we go to bed.	e) oft vor nachgestellten Umstandssätzen

2. Im Gegensatz zum Dt. **steht ein Komma**

a) Mr Turner said, "I hope to see you again soon."		a) vor der wörtlichen Rede (Doppelpunkt selten)
b) Dear Mr Turner, Yours sincerely,	Dear Mother, Much love, herzliche Grüße	b) nach der Anrede und nach der Schlußformel in Briefen
c) February 6th, 1975		c) im Datum vor der Jahreszahl

II. Das Gerundium II (Vgl. L 34)

1. **On reading** the guide-book you will find that Brighton is ideal for a seaside holiday. Beim Durchlesen des Führers ... Read page 7 of this guide **before booking** a room. bevor Sie ... bestellen	Die Konstruktion **Verhältniswort** + **Gerundium** hat die Bedeutung eines Nebensatzes 1. der Zeit (Verhältniswörter: *before*, *after*, *on* bei)
2. You can reach Brighton direct from Dover **by taking** a bus via Folkestone. indem Sie (wenn Sie) mit dem Bus fahren **Instead of coming** during August you should visit Brighton in June. Anstatt ... zu	2. der Art und Weise (Verhältniswörter: *by* durch, *in* durch, bei, *instead of*, *without*)

35

I. Fill in the prepositions: 1. ... landing at Dover we went through the customs. 2. You can reach Brighton from Dover ... going through London. 3. ... reading the illustrated guide Hans Becker wrote to Mrs Bell. 4. Let us spend our holidays in the country this year ... going to the seaside again. 5. You can get all the information you need ... writing to the Public Relations Office.

II. Form the gerund after prepositions

Ex.: On / to start as a branch manager / John Smith / to begin to apply some new methods. On starting as a branch manager, John Smith began to apply some new methods.

1. Instead of / to block valuable space with fast sellers / he / to place the slow sellers under the eyes of the customers. 2. By / to build up expensive articles in heaps / he / to make a handsome profit. 3. In spite of / to get some articles cheaper / some customers / to buy things they didn't need. 4. By / to have soft music played / John Smith / to produce the Christmas feeling of / to spend freely. 5. In / to place the chocolates and nuts within easy reach of children / Smith / to obtain satisfying results.

III. Translate: Sehr geehrte Herren! Bezugnehmend auf Ihr Schreiben v. 21. März teile ich Ihnen mit *(I should like to inform you)*, daß die Schokolade sich schlecht verkauft. Als *(eine)* britische Staatsangehörige, die vor zwei Monaten aus England kam, konnte ich nicht wissen, daß im Sommer Schokolade ein schlechtgehender Artikel in Australien ist. Diese Ware nimmt eine Menge Raum [ein]. Statt mir diese Ware zu senden, hätten Sie vorschlagen sollen, mehr nicht-alkoholische Getränke zu bestellen. Ich wäre Ihnen dankbar, wenn Sie mindestens 40% der Schokolade zurücknähmen. Indem Sie mir helfen, werden Sie eine Kundin behalten *(to keep)*. Mit freundlichen Grüßen. J. Bird

36 For Whites Only? I

"It's like hell on earth," said a coloured lawyer somewhere in the deep South. He was looking at a restaurant window which bore the notice FOR WHITES ONLY. "Some day our anger is going to explode like a bomb. Our patience won't last for ever. Black society is not going to stand for this any longer."

The bomb exploded — though the explosion was not recognized as such at the time — on the 5th of December, 1955. That was the day Mrs Rosa Parks was arrested in Montgomery, Alabama.

Mrs Parks was a coloured woman, a widow of about fifty. She was waiting at the bus stop. If anyone had reason to be tired after a hard day's work, it was Mrs Parks. She had been on her feet without interruption from 9 a.m. to 4 p.m. in the department store where she was employed. When the bus came that late December afternoon, Mrs Parks got on it as she had done so many times before. One half of the bus — from the front to the middle — was reserved for white people. From the middle to the back the Negroes could sit. Mrs Parks was in the first seat behind the white part. She was glad to have a rest, for her knees were hurting badly. It was the rush hour and the bus filled quickly. Some Negroes and Whites had to stand. Shortly after Mrs Parks had sat down, the white bus driver approached her. "We can't have Niggers sitting while Whites are standing," he said to her and three other Negroes. "Don't be lazy. Get up at once."

"Stop calling me 'Nigger'," she said. "I won't get up for anybody. This is the colored part and I know my rights."

"We'll soon settle that," said the driver. "I'm not going to argue." He left the bus and returned to the scene with a policeman.

"Do be reasonable," said the policeman. "You know the law. You've got to respect the orders of the driver."

"Ask somebody else to get up," replied Mrs Parks. "You can't force me to give up my seat to anyone. That's not right."

"Don't try to teach me what my duties are," said the policeman. "You ought to know better at your age. Come on, you're under arrest for disturbing the peace."

"It's not a crime to sit in a bus," protested Mrs Parks. "You can't treat me like a criminal." In spite of her protests, Rosa Parks was led away by force. She had not the slightest idea that her refusal to meet the bus driver's demand was the beginning of a nation-wide Negro movement for freedom and black power.

At the Post-Office

A book of stamps, please.
This letter to Germany is urgent. Can I send it by air mail?
That's not necessary. All letters to the Continent go by air mail.
I want to send a registered letter. Will it be delivered tomorrow?
I should advise you to send it express.
I want to send this book. Will it be cheaper by parcel post or as printed matter?
I want to send a telegram. (*Am.* wire)
Please fill in this form and hand it in at the next counter.
What is the charge for this telegram, please?
Where is the nearest letter-box?

A Slight Misunderstanding

A sweet, helpless young thing had just bought a postage stamp. "And must I stick it on myself?" she asked.

"Oh, no," said the postal clerk. "It will do more good if you stick it on the envelope."

Einige unbestimmte Fürwörter (indefinite Pronomen)

1. He doesn't eat **much**, but drinks **a lot.** I have **a lot** (**a lot of** work, **a lot of** things) to do. I had **plenty of** time.	1. ***much*** viel u. ***many*** viele werden als Ergänzung im bejahten Satz meistens vermieden. Stattdessen stehen z.B. *a lot (of)* eine Menge, *plenty (of)* (eigentl.: eine Fülle)
2. a) I had saved **some** money. etwas Geld I should like to have **some** bacon. würde gerne (etwas) Speck essen There is **some** in the kitchen. Es ist welcher ... **Some** days later he looked at the book. Einige Tage später I like **something** nice for my tea. b) We haven't got **any** bacon (sausages). Have we got **any** bacon (sausages)? Haben wir Speck (Würste) da? I should like some bacon (sausages), if we have got **any**. wenn wir welche(n) h. If **anyone** comes late, the boss will see him. Wenn jemand zu spät kommt Aber: May I offer you **some** bacon? (das Vorhandensein wird nicht bezweifelt) c) I was prepared to take **any** job. jede beliebige Arbeit **Anyone** will tell you the way. Jeder	2. *Some* und *any* bezeichnen eine unbestimmte Menge oder Anzahl. a) ***some*** und seine Zusammensetzungen (s. unten) werden gebraucht, wenn etwas als wirklich vorhanden betrachtet wird. Sie stehen daher im bejahten Satz. Im Dt. bleibt *some* manchmal unübersetzt. b) ***any*** und seine Zus.setzungen werden gebraucht, wenn das Vorhandensein verneint oder bezweifelt wird. Sie stehen daher im verneinten Satz, in der Frage u. im Bedingungssatz. Merke: *not ... any* (od. *not ... a*) kein *not ... anyone (-body)* niemand *not ... anything* nichts c) ***any*** im bejahten Satz = „jeder (beliebige)". Vgl. dag. *every*, *each* = „jeder (ohne Ausnahme)"
3. a) You must look for **another** job. b) Would you like **another** cup of tea? Can I stay **another** two days? noch 2 T. Aber: My new job was **different from** my work at school. anders als I shall have to look for **someone else.**	3. ***another*** a) „ein anderer" b) „noch ein, (ein) weitere(r)" Aber: [*from* „anders als" (=andersartig) = ***different*** „jemand anderes" = *someone* ***else*** „alles andere" = *everything else*, etc.
4. **One** cannot eat one's cake and have it. (proverb) **You** heard nothing but the word 'patience'.	4. ***One*** man ist im Engl. seltener als im Dt. Statt dessen oft *you*, *we*, *they*, *people* (od. Leideform; vgl. L 39, Beachte)

Alleinstehend (wie Hauptwörter) werden gebraucht:

somebody (-one)	jemand	something	etwas
anybody (-one)	(irgend) jemand	anything	(irgend) etwas
everybody (-one)	jedermann, alle	everything	alles

Umstandswörter:

somewhere	irgendwo(hin)
anywhere	irgendwo(hin)
everywhere	überall(hin)

I. *Much/many* or *a lot (of)*? 1. Do you smoke ...? No, but my wife smokes rather ... 2. Mrs Sim talks quite ..., although she hasn't got ... to say. 3. I have ... friends in London, but I don't know ... people round here. 4. Do you read ... books? Oh yes, ... 5. There are not ... children at our hotel, but I have seen quite ... at the guest-house across the road. 6. It's not ... use listening to that speaker. He talks ... nonsense.

II. *Some* und *any* und ihre Zusammensetzungen

a) 1. Are there any sausages in the kitchen? Yes, there are ... — No, ... 2. Have you any money? Yes, ... — No, ... 3. Do you know anyone who is unable to read or write? Yes, ... — No, ... 4. Have you seen the newspaper anywhere? — Yes, I have seen it ... — No, ... 5. Have you got some tickets for the theatre? No, ... — Yes, ... 6. Do you know anyone who will show us the way to the cinema? Yes, ... — No, ...

b) 1. I should like ... nice for my tea. Have we ... cheese? No, but we have ... bacon. 2. ... has not signed the letter. 3. Have you ... idea why Smith did not sign it? 4. I couldn't get ... sausages today. We shall have to eat ... else. 5. I have ... important letters to write. The children must play ... else.

III. *Not any*

Ex.: There *was no* early morning tea.
There *wasn't any* early morning tea.

1. The guests were offered no drinks with their meals. 2. There was no music in the evening. 3. The landlady allowed no television after 10 p.m. 4. There was no hot water. 5. The windows had no curtains. 6. There were no carpets on the floors. 7. On Sunday there was no breakfast. 8. The guests had no fun, pleasure, or amusement.

37 For Whites Only? II

Twenty-four hours after Mrs Parks' arrest, the Negro leaders were holding a meeting to discuss a plan of action.

"We've been waiting nearly a hundred years for equal rights," said one Negro leader bitterly. "I've lived in Montgomery since I was born, and have always suffered because of my colour. The time has come when we must act."

It was decided to organize a bus boycott for the following Monday. On that day 17,000 Negroes would walk to work. A young Baptist minister, Dr Martin Luther King, took on the task of spreading the news to Montgomery's 50,000 Negro citizens.

The following Sunday the Baptist church was packed. After the other leaders had spoken, Martin Luther King addressed the crowd: "We are here this evening to say to those who have been treating us so badly for so long that we are tired of being segregated and humiliated. We are tired of being kicked about by the brutal feet of oppression. For many years we have shown amazing patience. We have sometimes given our white brothers the impression that we like the way we are treated. But we have come here this evening to be saved from the patience that makes us patient with anything less than freedom and justice ..."

Before he had ended his speech, the angry Negroes were ready to march and fight against the Whites, wherever they met them. It was only King's influence that prevented them from rushing into something so risky. His faith and his religion forbade the use of force. Not only should the black man refuse to shoot his enemy, but he should also refuse to hate him.

On Monday morning the buses driving through the Negro quarters were empty. The Whites reacted sharply. They blamed King and other Negro leaders for the boycott, and put them in prison. But this time the Negroes would not give in. The case was taken to the United States Supreme Court, which decided in favour of the Negroes. The Negro movement had won its first victory. The fight against school segregation followed. King became the driving force of the movement. Battle upon battle was won by peaceful means. In 1964, Martin Luther King received the Nobel Peace Prize. Four years later he was shot and killed by a political enemy.

Many young Negroes, however, have not accepted King's ideals. Especially in the big cities the number of those using force is increasing. Their anger is largely caused by unemployment. Often they are the last hired and the first fired. Most of them are unskilled workers whose jobs have been taken over by machines. Can the USA find an answer to its Negro problem — a problem which is both social and racial? As long as it cannot, it will live with the bomb. The struggle goes on.

Useful Phrases for Business Letters

Thank you for your letter of May 3rd.
Please quote your lowest prices.
In reply to (with reference to, referring to) your inquiry we are glad to inform you that ...
We confirm our telegram as follows: ...
We enclose our catalogue and price-list.
We are sending samples under separate cover.
Your orders will receive our best attention.
The goods will be dispatched tomorrow.
We cannot accept responsibility for any delay.
Our terms of payment are cash without discount within 30 days of date of invoice.
Our goods are payable c.o.d. (cash on delivery).
Your claims will be considered.
I hope we can come to an agreement.

Der Gebrauch der Vergangenheit und vollendeten Gegenwart

I. Die Vergangenheit (Präteritum)

besagt, daß ein Vorgang in der Vergangenheit stattgefunden hat, völlig abgeschlossen ist und zur Gegenwart keine Verbindung hat (Merkwort: „damals"). Die Vergangenheit steht daher:

1. I **spent** £50,000 on advertising *last year*. Ich habe ... ausgegeben. *When* **did** you **open** your bank account? Wann haben Sie ... eröffnet? **Did** you **see** the film *last night* Haben Sie ...?	1. bei **Zeitangaben der Vergangenheit,** wie z.B. *yesterday, last night (week), in 1970, some time ago, then, when I was in England, when?* Im Dt. oft vollend. Gegenwart.
2. On Monday the buses **were** empty. The Whites **reacted** sharply. They **blamed** King.	2. als **Erzählzeit** zur Wiedergabe aufeinanderfolgender Vorgänge (wie im Dt.).

II. Die vollendete Gegenwart (Perfekt)

Formen: Einfache Zeitform: I (you) have written, he has written, etc.
Verlaufsform: I (you) have been writing, he has been writing, etc.

Die vollendete Gegenwart besagt, daß ein Vorgang der Vergangenheit irgendwie mit der Gegenwart in Verbindung steht (Merkwort: „bis heute"). Sie wird daher angewandt:

1. I **have known** this man *for ten years*. Ich kenne ihn (schon) seit zehn Jahren. We **have been treated** badly *for many years*. sind schlecht behandelt worden seit vielen Jahren (bis heute) *How long* **have** we **been waiting** for equal rights? Wie lange warten wir schon auf Gleichberechtigung?	1. wenn ein Vorgang, der in der Vergangenheit begonnen hat, **bis in die Gegenwart hineinreicht;** bes. mit *since* seit (Zeitpunkt), *for* seit (Zeitraum) und *how long?* (In diesen Fällen steht oft die Verlaufsform.) — Im Dt. meistens Gegenwart, oft mit „schon".
2. *Up to now* we **have shown** patience. Bis jetzt haben wir ... We **have started** the boycott *this week*. haben diese Woche begonnen We **have been living** here *since* Easter. Wir wohnen hier seit Ostern	2. wenn etwas **während eines noch laufenden Zeitabschnitts** geschehen ist (Merkwort: „bis jetzt", „schon" od. „noch nie"); oft in Verbindung mit *so far, up to now* bis jetzt, *since ..., for ..., this week (year)*; *not yet* noch nicht, *never*.

Merke als Faustregel: Enthält ein Satz eine Zeitbestimmung der Vergangenheit (s. I, 1. oben), so ist dadurch der Gebrauch der vollendeten Gegenwart von vornherein ausgeschlossen.

37

I. Form sentences

Ex.: to visit Italy (never, two years ago)
I **have** *never* **visited** Italy.
I **visited** Italy *two years ago*.

1. to give up smoking (several times, in 1973, last year) 2. to eat German sausages (often, for tea yesterday, never) 3. not to see the film 'Black Power' (so far, up to now, yet) 4. to have lunch with the Smiths (twice this week, a few days ago, yesterday, often, never, last week) 5. to see a Shakespeare play (when I was in England, not yet, last year, never)

II. *For* or *since*?

1. I have kept a shop ... 1965. 2. We have been married ... twelve years. 3. Shakespeare has been dead ... over three hundred years. 4. I have not seen Jack ... Christmas. 5. Mrs Brown has been in hospital ... five weeks. 6. I have not heard from Mary ... last June.

III. Ask questions and give answers

Ex.: (you/to live in this town) (9 years)
How long have you been living in this town?
I have been living in this town for 9 years.

1. (you/to learn English) (18 months) 2. (you/to attend evening classes) (2 years) 3. (he/to be employed by his present firm) (3 years) 4. (she/to be married) (7 years) 5. (the film/to be on at the Odeon) (5 weeks)

IV. Translate: 1. Am 5. Dezember ist Mrs Parks verhaftet worden. 2. Seit dieser Zeit boykottieren *(to boycott)* wir die Busse. 3. Haben Sie die Rede von Martin Luther King letzten Montag gehört? 4. Seit vielen Jahren zeigen wir [eine] erstaunliche Geduld. 5. Jetzt ist die Zeit gekommen, wo *(when)* wir handeln müssen. 6. Ich kenne King seit fünf Jahren.

38 London Through the Ages

Although London was already a town in the days of the Romans, it was not to become the capital of England until the 12th century. The royal residence and cultural centre in Anglo-Saxon times was Winchester, London remaining a small south-eastern port.

In Shakespeare's age there were two different cities a few miles apart from each other on the left bank of the Thames. One was the City of London, protected by its grey walls, the other, to the south-west of it, the royal City of Westminster, where Parliament used to meet. Small in comparison, it contained the royal palace of Whitehall, Westminster Abbey, where the kings of England have been crowned since William of Normandy, government offices and the houses of some officials. The City of London with its famous castle, the Tower, already had about 100,000 inhabitants. People going from Westminster to London would pass green fields and, perhaps, stop half-way at the village of Charing Cross for a drink when they were thirsty.

Today Charing Cross is one of the busiest parts of this strange mixture of old and new called Greater London, which has a population of 7 million and is not only the capital of the United Kingdom but also the centre of the Commonwealth. Its solid heart, the City, the business centre, has a day population of 550,000 and a night population of only 9,000. London is not only the centre of the nation's commerce and trade, but also the biggest industrial town in England and the largest port. 39 per cent of Britain's exports are sent from the Port of London; its docks stretch 36 miles along the River Thames.

London is also the news centre of Britain. Most national daily papers with a total circulation of twenty-two million copies are printed in London's Fleet Street, with the exception of *The Times*, England's oldest and most serious newspaper, which has its buildings in the shadow of St. Paul's Cathedral.

Millions of Londoners will spend hours daily in local trains, buses and the Underground, taking them from the suburbs into town and back again. They will lunch in crowded restaurants, or may eat their sandwiches in a city office or on the grass in a park. Though everyone wants to get home as quickly as possible in the evening, they will still keep order and discipline in the traffic rush. No one will get out of a queue, nor will anyone lose his temper. This disciplined behaviour is one of London's most striking features.

1 Westminster Abbey **2** The Tower of London **3** St. Paul's Cathedral **4** The Houses of Parliament

I. Einige unvollständige Hilfszeitwörter II (Hilfsverben)

1. a) You **may** be right. kannst recht haben **May** I go now? Darf ich? b) You **might** be right. könntest recht haben	1. a) ***may*** 1. „kann vielleicht, vielleicht" 2. „darf"; Verneinung: *must not* b) ***might*** „könnte vielleicht"
2. a) Many Londoners **will** spend hours daily in trains and buses. verbringen People going from Westminster to London **would** pass green fields. kamen über b) Parliament **used to** meet at Westminster. versammelte sich immer When I lived in London, I **used to** go to work by Underground.	2. a) ***will, would*** drücken oft Wiederholung, Gewohnheit aus. In der Vergangenheit meistens = dt. „pflegte". b) ***used to:*** Wiederholung in der Vergangenheit; dt. meistens Verg.heit mit „immer". (Zu *used to* gibt es keine entspr. Form f. d. Gegenw.!)
3. a) Everyone **wants to** get home as quickly as possible. Jeder will b) Do you **intend to** stay here for ever? Haben Sie vor, wollen Sie What **are** you **going** to do now?	3. Dt. **„wollen"** muß meistens durch Ersatzzeitwörter wiedergegeben werden: a) *to want to* (Wunsch) b) *to intend to, to be going to* (Absicht)
4. We **are to** meet our friends at 10 a.m. sollen London **was not to** become the capital until the 12th century. sollte erst ... werden	4. ***To be to*** = „sollen" (es ist festgelegt, vereinbart, vom Schicksal bestimmt)

Merke: I could have gone (come, stayed, etc.) — ich hätte gehen (kommen, bleiben) können
I should (ought to) have gone — ich hätte gehen sollen
I needn't have gone — ich hätte nicht zu gehen brauchen

II. Besonderer Gebrauch der Hilfszeitwörter

Wo im Dt. als Antwort u. ä. ein einzelnes Wort genügt, muß im Engl. oft das Hilfszeitwort des Vordersatzes wiederholt werden. Ist kein Hilfszeitwort vorhanden, so wird das Vollzeitwort durch *to do* wiederaufgenommen.

1. *Is* the Tower big? — Of course it **is.** Natürlich. *Do* these people understand English? — Most of them **don't.** Die meisten nicht.	Hilfszeitwörter stehen 1. in kurzen Antworten, bes. nach *yes, no* u. ä. Wörtern
2. I *have* lived in London all my life. — **So have I.** Ich auch. My parents *don't* like it here. **Nor (neither) does** my brother. (My brother doesn't either.)	2. nach ***so*** auch ***nor, neither*** / *not ... either* } auch nicht

To do steht ferner a) im bejahten Satz zur Verstärkung: You *do speak* English well. wirkl. gut
b) zum Ausdruck einer dringl. Bitte: *Do come* in. Kommen Sie doch bitte herein!

I. *Can* or *may?* (*can* = I'm able to, *may* = perhaps)
1. . . . you drive? 2. If we don't leave at once, we . . . get into the traffic rush. 3. Who . . . tell me the way to the Tower? 4. During my visit to England I . . . have time to spend a few days in London. 5. I know a good hotel near Victoria Station, but I . . . not find the address at the moment. 6. If you do not book your room in advance, you . . . be disappointed.

II. *Mustn't* or *needn't?* 1. You . . . talk when someone else is speaking. 2. It's only a few minutes to Charing Cross. We . . . take a bus. 3. You . . . go to the post-office for stamps. I have some in my desk. 4. I . . . get up early tomorrow. It's Sunday. 5. Tomorrow is Aunt Mary's birthday. I . . . forget to send her a card. 6. You . . . drink strong coffee just before you go to bed. 7. I must go now. I . . . miss the last bus.

III. Add sentences beginning with *so, nor, neither*
Ex.: The City of London already existed in Shakespeare's age. — *So did* Westminster.

1. Liverpool is a great port. (Hamburg) 2. Germany is not a kingdom. (France) 3. Stratford does not lie on the Thames. (Cambridge) 4. Canada is a member of the Commonwealth. (Australia) 5. I have never eaten French sausages. (my wife) 6. The boy could not read or write. (his brother).

IV. When we lived in London we *used to* . . .
Ex.: I *listened* to the 8 o'clock news every morning.
I used to listen to the 8 o'clock news every morning.

1. On Saturdays we *often went* to the theatre. 2. John *regularly bought* the Daily Mail at the street corner. 3. We *usually had* lunch at a snack-bar in Soho. 4. Mary *always went* by Underground to the City. 5. We *were accustomed to watching* TV with our landlady. 6. I *went* to bed at 11 o'clock.

39 The Channel Tunnel

For more than 170 years building a tunnel under the English Channel has been dreamt of by engineers and politicians. Actually, the hole in the ground dug in 1880 marking the spot where the tunnel was begun on French soil can still be seen. However, in those days soldiers in both the French and English camps protested for military reasons. They feared that the tunnel would be destroyed in time of war. At last an end has been put to fears and hesitation. The tunnel is about to become reality.

If everything goes according to plan, travellers will be carried by trains under the Channel as easily as they now travel by Underground under the Thames. No longer, when thick fog covers southern England, will newspaper headlines report "Continent Isolated!" No longer will there be stories of six unhappy hours spent on a crossing which in normal weather lasts 90 minutes or less. Nor will bad sailors be advised to go below deck when a strong wind is blowing and the sea is stormy. Comfortable electric trains will take them from England to France in 30 minutes. Motor-cars and lorries will be carried on special double-decker trains, each with room for 300 vehicles. The trains will run every five minutes. Tunnel fares for motor-cars will be 30% cheaper than the present rates for carriage by ship. The economic advantages are believed to be considerable. Freight costs are calculated to be half as high as they are today. The exchange of goods between Britain and the Continent is bound to become cheaper.

The "Chunnel" between Folkestone and Calais will be 32 miles long, 23 miles of it under water.

Considering all the advantages that are to be expected, it is surprising that Britain did not go ahead with the tunnel sooner, as it is a piece of engineering which can be carried out without great difficulty. And yet, the tunnel project is not supported in all British circles. In particular, the inhabitants of Dover are said to be disappointed.

Dover, a few miles away, is the busiest passenger port in the world. It handles more than 4 million passengers a year, and more than 664,000 cars. It recently spent several million pounds in tearing five acres of land away from the sea to increase its port capacity. Is all that money and effort to be wasted? What will become of the passenger ships and car ferries sailing to and fro? What of the sailors, porters and dockworkers? Last but not least, there is Britain's pride in being an island.

Can it still claim to be an island after it is connected with the Continent by "the most expensive hole in the world"?

In spite of all the protests, the "Chunnel" shares are rising.

How to Telephone

Look up the number in the directory.
For a local call from a call box, dial the number and wait.
In London leave out the 01- and just dial the rest of the number. Example: (01) 653 7560
When you get a reply, insert a 10 p piece.
If there is no reply, try again later.
For a trunk call from London or most towns, dial the whole number. Example: (051) 439 2411, or ask the operator.
(Operator) "Hold the line, please — I'll put you through."
"This is George Taylor speaking. May I speak to Mr Black?"

Die Leideform II (Passiv) (Formen s. L 24, I)

Im Englischen kann die Leideform gebildet werden:

1. Mrs Parks **will** always **be remembered** for her refusal to get up in a bus. An Mrs P. wird man sich erinnern ..., Mrs P. wird unvergessen bleiben wegen ihrer Weigerung	1. von allen Zeitwörtern mit **Wenfall-Ergänzung** (z. Teil abweichend v. Dt.; vgl. L 24, II)
Satzgegenst. | | Wemfall | Wenfall 2. Tatf.: They give | the animals | food. The animals **are given** | food. Den Tieren wird Futter gegeben. I **was offered** | a cigarette. Mir wurde eine Zigarette angeboten.	2. von Zeitwörtern mit **Wen- und Wemfall-Ergänzung** ohne *to*, wobei der Wemfall (Stellungs-Wemfall) zum Satzgegenstand wird (Wortliste s. L 27, II, 1)
3. It **can be carried out** without difficulty. Es kann leicht ausgeführt werden. The children **were taken good care of.** Für die Kinder wurde gut gesorgt.	3. von Zeitwörtern, die eng **mit einem Verhältniswort** verbunden sind; ebenso von einigen entsprechenden Ausdrücken (s. Liste unten)
4. Some engineers **are known** to prefer a bridge. Einige Ingenieure sind dafür bekannt, daß sie eine Brücke vorziehen. The advantages **are believed** to be considerable. Man glaubt, daß die Vorteile beträchtlich sind. Some people **are said** to be disappointed. Einige Leute sollen enttäuscht sein.	4. von einigen Zeitwörtern des **Dafürhaltens** u. ä. (z. B. *to believe, to know, to suppose*) mit nachfolgender Grundform Merke: *s.th.* or *s.o. is said to* etw. *od.* jd. soll (angeblich)
Beachte: The headline "Continent Isolated" **is** often **seen** in the daily papers. sieht man oft, ist oft zu sehen Stories of six-hour crossings **may be heard.** man kann ... hören	Beachte: Die engl. Leideform wird im Dt. oft besser durch die Tatform wiedergegeben, meistens mit „man".

Zeitwörter und entsprechende Ausdrücke mit Verhältniswort (zu 3.):

to deal with	sich befassen mit, behandeln	to depend on	sich verlassen auf
to hear of	hören von	to speak of s.o. as	von jdm. sagen, daß
to laugh at	lachen über	to think of	denken an [er ... sei
to look after	sich kümmern um, sorgen für	to think of s.o. as	jdn. halten für
to look upon s.o. as	jdn. betrachten als	to put an end to	(e-r Sache) ein Ende
to object to	etw. einwenden gegen	to take care of	sorgen für [machen
to pay for	bezahlen	to take possession of	in Besitz nehmen

I. Put into the right tense of the passive voice

Ex.: Building a tunnel under the English Channel (to dream) of for more than 170 years.
Building a tunnel under the English Channel has been dreamt of for more than 170 years.

1. The hole dug in 1880 marking the spot where the tunnel (to begin) on French soil can still (to see). 2. If everything goes well, travellers (to carry) by trains under the Channel by 2000. 3. Motor-cars (to carry) on special double-decker trains. 4. The economic advantages (to believe) to be considerable. 5. It is a piece of engineering which can (to deal with) without difficulty. 6. However, the inhabitants of Dover (to say) to be disappointed.

II. Put into the passive voice

1. We will always remember the first protests of the inhabitants of Dover. 2. Quite a number of people all over Britain joined them in their protests. 3. They did not trust the political development. 4. Others believed the Channel tunnel to be an economic adventure. 5. The European Community helped those in favour of the tunnel. 6. The engineers won't follow the plans of 1880.

III. Tourists are expected at the hotel

a) *The manager gives instructions to the staff*

Ex.: A key will be given *to each tourist.*
Each tourist will be given a key.

1. Double rooms will be given *to married couples.* 2. Flowers will be handed *to each female visitor.* 3. Drinks will be offered *to the gentlemen.* 4. The letters will be handed *to the guide.* 5. Water will be served *to those who don't touch alcohol.*

b) *When the tourists arrived:*

Ex.: A key was given *to each tourist.*
Each tourist was given a key.

1. Married couples were ... (go on)

40 North Sea Gas and Oil

At one time all that Britain got out of the North Sea was fish. Then, in 1964, natural gas was discovered off the east coast. Within less than ten years enough of it was found to make a complete change in Britain's gas industry.

News to be received even more eagerly was the discovery of oil off the Scottish coast in 1969. These oil fields are large enough to supply such quantities of the valuable liquid that the whole of Britain has become independent of the oil riches under the desert surface of the Middle East. The steady flow of oil being pumped through the North Sea pipelines to the shores of Scotland and Northern England has completely removed the fears of an oil shortage in Britain for the coming 30 years. Nowadays Britain is one of West Germany's largest oil suppliers.

The development of raw material in the North Sea demands extraordinary efforts of organization and capital. In order to protect the steel rigs against the attacks of storms and high waves, they have to be firmly fastened to the sea-bed, sometimes 300 feet deep. The costs of development are five times as high as on land.

In Scotland, where unemployment is rather high in comparison to the south of England, employment figures have risen on the East Coast. More than eighty companies have set up their headquarters in the city of Aberdeen where property prices in some areas have doubled in the last ten years. Before starting to look for the black liquid, the oil companies are forced to insure themselves against all sorts of risks like accidents, damage to property, and pollution. No wonder London insurance companies were the first to profit. Their shares have risen considerably. Thus the production of North Sea oil is giving fresh hope to large parts of Britain's industry.

However, there are always two sides to a coin. Fishing and other local industries in the North are already anxious about the new development. There are fears of pollution of both air and sea. It is to be feared that pipelines not tight enough to prevent the oil from escaping will destroy the fish reserves of the North Sea. Cracks in the pipelines will also let the oil pollute the coast lines. Does modern science know how to check collisions of ships and rigs?

It is to be doubted that North Sea oil reserves will last much longer than 30 years. To feed her industry with the necessary energy, Britain will either have to go back to her coal mines or she will have to develop her atomic plants further.

No Sense of Humour

A: You look very sour. What's the matter?

B: I'm disappointed and so is my wife. The Goings are giving a party and we haven't been invited.

A: What a shame! You and the Goings have always been such good friends and neighbours.

B: As you can imagine, we were very shocked about it.

A: It's very rude of them. What could be the reason? Surely their memory can't be so short as to forget that you invited them to your daughter's 21st birthday party?

B: A few days ago we had Mr Going in for the evening. About 11 o'clock I made a harmless joke and said, "I hope Going is really going". My wife and I exploded with laughter, but he seemed angry and went immediately. These people have no sense of humour.

A: There was no harm in what you said. Obviously, some people can't take a joke.

Der Gebrauch der Grundform (Infinitiv)

Die Grundform des Zeitworts hat gewöhnlich *to* vor sich: *to* sing singen; *to be* or not *to be* — that is the question. Sein oder Nichtsein.

A. Die Grundform in der Leideform

Special measures **are not to be expected.** sind nicht zu erwarten **It is to be doubted** that the oil reserves will last. ist zu bezweifeln Oil **is to be found** off the coast. ist zu finden	Drückt die Grundform aus, daß etwas getan werden kann oder soll, so steht sie — dem Sinn entsprechend — in der Leideform (vgl. dagegen das Dt.!).
Aber: The office is **difficult to find.** Your question is **easy to answer.**	Aber: Nach einem Eigenschaftswort steht die Grundform meistens in der Tatform (wie im Dt.).

B. Die Grundform steht satzverkürzend

1. Enough natural gas was found **to supply** a large part of Britain. um zu versorgen **In order to be protected,** the steel rigs must be fastened. Damit sie geschützt sind	1. mit ***to*** oder ***in order to*** } um zu zum Ausdruck des Zwecks
2. The Scots know **how to take advantage of** North Sea oil. wie man Nutzen zieht aus They showed him **where to go.** wohin er gehen sollte	2. mit **how to,** *what to, when to, where to, whether to,* bes. nach *to ask, to decide, to explain, to know, to remember, to show, to tell*; im Dt. Nebensatz
3. a) They chose Miss Miller **to organize** the trip. die organisieren sollte I hope there will be a guide **to show** us round. der uns herumführen kann b) Insurance companies were the first **to profit.** waren die ersten, die profitierten	3. a) in der Bedeutung eines **Beifügungssatzes,** der ein Können oder Sollen ausdrückt b) nach *the first, the last, the next, the only* in der Bedeutung eines gewöhnlichen Beifügungssatzes

I. Use the passive infinitive

a) *Ex.:* The money *is to be paid* in advance.

1. These pills (to take) three times a day. 2. Large quantities of oil (to find) in the North Sea. 3. These sentences (to translate) into French. 4. The medicine (to shake) before use. 5. Many strange animals (to see) in Australia. 6. The patient (to keep) in bed.

b) Use *must be* ... or *can be* ...
Ex.: The money *must be paid* in advance.

II. Use *how to, what to, where to, whether to, when to*

Ex.: We know how we can deal with the problem of oil pollution.
We know how to deal with the problem of oil pollution.

1. We know where we can place the rigs. 2. We have learnt how we can avoid accidents. 3. Our engineers understand what they must do for the safety of ships. 4. The fishing industry knows how it can catch fish. 5. Our industry has learnt how it can find oil. 6. We know when we have to act. 7. We don't know whether we should pay the shipping industry for possible losses. 8. We'll decide what we must insure ourselves against.

III. Translate

Use the infinitive in all the sentences

Ein Problem, das gelöst werden muß

1. Großbritannien ist nicht das einzige Industrieland, das Öl aus der Wüste bekommt. 2. Es ist aber das erste Land, das seine Industrie im 18. Jahrhundert entwickelte. 3. Die erste Eisenbahn, die gebaut wurde, verkehrte zwischen Manchester und Liverpool im (Jahre) 1824. 4. Kohle war das bedeutendste Energieprodukt, mit dem Großbritanniens Industrie bis 1964 beliefert wurde. 5. Dann sollte das Öl die Rolle *(part)* der Kohle übernehmen *(to take over)*. 6. Mehr und mehr Öl, das die Bedürfnisse einer modernen Industrie befriedigen soll, kommt von den Ölfeldern des Mittleren Ostens und Nordafrikas. 7. Dieses Öl wird immer teurer. Wissen die Wissenschaftler, wie man das Energieproblem lösen kann?

41 From Empire to Commonwealth I

The victory of the English fleet over the Spanish Armada in 1588 was an important one and made England a sea-power. Now she was able to stretch her wings over the seas. A colony in North America and a trading company in India under Elizabeth I were the first attempts to build an Empire.

In the 17th century political as well as religious reasons favoured emigration to the east coast of North America. The fleet, under the command of splendid captains, won a final victory over another nation of sailors, the Dutch. In 1664 New Amsterdam became New York.

The 18th century was altogether marked by the English policy of maintaining the balance of power in Europe to prevent any country from becoming strong enough to be a danger to England. This policy put Britain on the side of the victor in European wars and she automatically received a big slice of the cake when the peace was signed. Thus Gibraltar was taken from the Spaniards, Canada and parts of India from the French. The Empire reached the height of its power with the defeat of the Boers in South Africa (1902). The Irishman in Dublin, the Chinese in Hong Kong, the Indian in Calcutta, the descendant of Dutchmen in Johannesburg, the white and the coloured, they all lived under the British flag.

During this steady growth of their Empire, the British had suffered only one setback, but a very serious one: the loss of their North American colonies. After defeating the British army, they separated from the mother country in 1783 and became the United States. This had taught the English a lesson. When Canada showed signs of unrest in the 19th century, the government granted home rule to this large colony. From then on all interior affairs were dealt with by the Canadians themselves. The first British dominion was born. It was followed at the beginning of the 20th century by Australia, New Zealand and the Union of South Africa, all of which enjoyed home rule by 1910. After the First World War these four dominions were granted complete independence. Together with the mother country they formed the British Commonwealth of Nations. Their common political link was loyalty to the Crown.

I. Das Eigenschaftswort mit Stützwort

Im Dt. kann ein Eigenschaftswort mit dem Geschlechtswort allein stehen (Welches Haus gehört euch? — *Das kleine.*) oder durch Vorsetzen des Geschlechtswortes zum Hauptwort gemacht werden (Was hast du *dem Blinden* gegeben?). Im Engl. dagegen muß im allgemeinen immer ein Hauptwort folgen.

1. The British had suffered only one setback, but **a very serious one.** einen sehr ernsten These maps (Landkarten) of the Commonwealth are all out of date. Aren't there any **more modern ones?** modernere	1. Als Ersatz für ein kurz zuvor genanntes Hauptwort tritt zum Eigenschaftswort das Stützwort *one, ones.*
2. Many **coloured people** have emigrated to Britain from the West Indies. viele Farbige The job was given to **a coloured man.** einem Farbigen Aber: Much has been done for **the poor.** für die Armen **The white** and **the coloured** — they all lived under the British flag. Die Weißen und die Farbigen	2. Zur Bezeichnung einzelner Personen tritt zum Eigenschaftswort ein Hauptwort, z. B. *man, woman, people* oder *one, ones.* Aber: Zur Bezeichnung einer ganzen Gattung von Personen kann das Eigenschaftswort allein stehen (mit Geschlechtswort, aber ohne Mehrzahl-*s*)

II. Völkernamen

Endung auf	Eigenschaftswort (Sprache)	Gesamtheit des Volkes	Einzelne Volksangehörige, z. B.
-sh, -ch	English, Irish French, Dutch	the English, the Irish the French, the Dutch	an Englishman two French ladies
-ss, -ese	Swiss, Chinese Japanese [dʒæpə'ni:z]	the Swiss, the Chinese the Japanese	a Swiss, a Chinese three Japanese
-an	German, Italian Russian, Canadian	the Germans, the Italians the Russians, etc.	a German, an Italian two Russians, etc.

Merke: 1. Zur Angabe der Nationalität wird das Eigenschaftswort verwendet:
Are you *English*? — No, I am *German.* Sind Sie Engländer(in)? — Nein, ich bin Deutsche(r).
2. Zusammensetzungen mit *man* und *woman* werden in einem Wort geschrieben: two Irishmen, an Englishwoman; alle anderen in zwei Wörtern: a Dutch gentleman, some French ladies, three Irish boys, many English people viele Engländer

Anmerkung: Länder werden — sofern man nicht an den rein geographischen Begriff denkt — als weiblich betrachtet: Britain and *her* Empire.

I. Setze passende Eigenschaftswörter mit *one(s)* ein

1. Our *old* car must always be repaired. We must soon buy ... 2. This hotel is too *expensive.* Isn't there ... in this district? 3. I have never seen Mr Parker in a *coloured* shirt. He always wears ... 4. This hat is too *big* for me. Please show me ... 5. I answered the *easy* questions myself, but my brother helped me with ...

II. Some countries and their inhabitants

England is inhabited by *the English.* They speak *English.* An inhabitant of England is *an Englishman* (or *Englishwoman*). Do you know any *English people?*
Say the same about the inhabitants of Holland, Italy, Switzerland, Spain, Japan [dʒə'pæn], Canada.

III. What Captain Drake told his officers

Ex.: England should beat the Spanish. She is strong enough.
England is strong enough to beat the Spanish.

1. Let's finish our game first. We have time enough. 2. We should win. We have experience enough. 3. Our ships will follow the Spanish fleet. They are fast enough. 4. Our guns will sink the Spanish ships. They are powerful enough. 5. The Spanish army will not land in England. It's not strong enough. 6. England will become a sea-power. She is great enough.

IV. Word-formation

a) *-(a)tion:*
Ex.: to quote — quotation, to found — foundation
1. to expect 2. to invite 3. to explain 4. to promote 5. to separate 6. to hesitate 7. to organize 8. to introduce

b) *-ce:*
Ex.: independent — independence
1. important 2. present 3. silent 4. intelligent 5. patient

42 From Empire to Commonwealth II

After the Second World War, India was granted freedom within the British Commonwealth of Nations, the result being three independent states, the Union of India, Pakistan and Ceylon. For the first time a coloured population was given self-government. As the word 'British' only applied to white member states, this word was dropped and the name most frequently used today is 'The Commonwealth'.

First the Union of India, then Pakistan wished their countries to become republics within the Commonwealth. Though no longer queen of these states, Elizabeth II remained the recognized head of the Commonwealth.

More and more parts of the Empire have been permitted to govern themselves since the last world war. Britain does not force any country to remain a member after independence has been granted. She saw Burma loosen her ties after becoming independent. Eire did the same in 1948. The Federation of Malaya, on the other hand, gladly stayed in this great group of nations. In 1961 the other members caused the Union of South Africa to give up her membership because of her racial policy.

In 1957 the first African Negro colony became independent under the name of Ghana. First recognizing the Queen as her monarch, Ghana, after three years, proclaimed herself a republic within the Commonwealth. The next African state to become a free member was Nigeria in 1960, with a black population of 36 million. More African colonies and the West Indian Federation followed. The countries with a coloured population already form the majority in the Commonwealth. They all have economic and cultural links with Britain and they expect her to help but not guide them in the future. On Christmas Day 1953 Queen Elizabeth II broadcast to her peoples throughout the Commonwealth the following message: "... Little did those daring heroes of Tudor and Stuart times realize what would grow from the settlements which they and later pioneers founded. From the Empire of which they built the frame there has arisen a world-wide fellowship of nations, of a type never seen before. In that fellowship, the

United Kingdom is an equal partner with many other proud and independent nations, and she is leading yet other nations to the same goal."

Her Prime Minister, Winston Churchill, did not share the hopes of seeing a family of friendly nations rise from the ashes of the former Empire. It was obvious to him that the members of the Commonwealth would move further apart. Meanwhile, they have even gone to war with each other. Was the Commonwealth idea an error? Was that the reason for Britain joining Europe? So many questions, so many doubts. Though the idea may have failed to be the string holding the former Empire together in one block, the attempt in itself deserves to be admired.

Der Wenfall mit Grundform (AcI)

	Ergänzung
I expect	him to come.
Ich erwarte,	daß er kommt.

Der Wenfall *(him)* und die Grundform *(to come)* bilden zusammen die Ergänzung.

1. Grundform ohne *to*

		Wenfall +	Grundform	
a) I	*heard*	**the Queen**	**broadcast**	her message.
On TV we	*saw*	**her**	**drive**	through the City.
b) In the 18th century England would not	*let*	**any power**	**become**	too strong.
The pressure of the other members	*made*	**S. Africa**	**leave**	the Commonwealth. zwang S.A., zu verl.

Der Wenfall mit der Grundform **ohne *to*** steht nach den Zeitwörtern:

a) der sinnlichen Wahrnehmung:
to see to hear to feel fühlen, spüren to watch beobachten, sehen

b) to let zulassen to make (veran)lassen

2. Grundform mit *to*

		Wenfall +	Grundform	
a) In 1846 Britain	*permitted*	**the Canadians**	**to deal**	with their interior affairs themselves.
b) Britain does not	*oblige*	**any country**	**to remain**	a member. verlangt von keinem Land, daß es Mitglied bleibt
The new states	*expect*	**Britain**	**to help**	them. erwarten von B., daß es
c) India and Pakistan	*wished*	**their countries**	**to become**	republics. wollten, daß ...
Britain would not	*like*	**more members**	**to separate.**	möchte nicht, daß ...

Der Wenfall mit der Grundform **mit *to*** steht nach den Zeitwörtern

a) der Erlaubnis: to allow, to permit erlauben, zulassen

b) des Forderns und des Veranlassens:
to cause veranlassen to oblige verpflichten; verlangen to require verlangen
to expect erwarten to order auffordern, befehlen to tell sagen, daß ... soll

c) des Wünschens und Nichtwünschens:
to want, to wish wünschen, wollen I should prefer es wäre mir lieber, wenn
I should like ich möchte, daß I should hate es wäre mir höchst unangenehm, wenn

Im Dt. meistens Nebensatz mit „daß".

I. Change the sentences

a) *Ex.:* The Queen arrived at Westminster Abbey. (We saw ...) — We *saw the Queen arrive* ...

1. She stepped out of her car. (A large crowd watched ...) 2. The band played 'God Save the Queen'. (We heard ...) 3. Someone pulled my arm. (I felt ...) 4. The children stayed up until nine o'clock to see the TV broadcast. (We let ...)

b) *Ex.:* Because of the thick fog the plane had to land in a potato-field. (Thick fog caused ...) Thick fog *caused the plane to land* in ...

1. I should be glad if you stayed at home at the weekend. (I should prefer ...) 2. I hope the guests will not arrive before we are ready. (I should hate ...) 3. Shall I phone for a taxi? (Would you like ...?) 4. The boss said that the workers must finish the job by the end of the week. (The boss ordered, told ...)

II. Form new sentences

a) *to make*

Ex.: The end of the Second World War. India demanded her independence.
... made India demand her independence.

1. Religious and political reasons. Parts of India separated. 2. The wish of coloured politicians. Many Commonwealth States became republics. 3. Practical reasons. Most Commonwealth States continued to use English as their official language. 4. The other members of the Commonwealth. The Union of South Africa gave up her membership. 5. Experience. Churchill doubted that the Commonwealth would be a success.

b) *to cause*

Ex.: The end of the Second World War. India demanded her independence.
Did the end of the Second World War cause India to demand her independence?

Englisch-deutsches Wörterverzeichnis

1. Die Wörter, die zu den Lesestücken, den Ergänzungsstücken, der Grammatik und den Übungen gehören, sind verbindlich; sie werden nur in der Lektion gebracht, in der sie zum erstenmal auftreten. Später werden sie als bekannt vorausgesetzt.
2. Idiomatische Wendungen sind *schräg gedruckt.* Ihre Einprägung ist besonders wichtig.

1 A Visit

a visit [ə 'vizit]	ein Besuch
Mr *(Abk. v. Mister)* ['mistə]	Herr (vor d. Namen)
Dent [dent]	(Familienname)
is [iz]	ist
Mrs *(Abk. v. Mistress)* ['misiz]	Frau (vor d. Namen)
Sim [sim]	(Familienname)
in [in]	in; innen, drinnen
is Mrs Sim in?	*ist Frau Sim zu Hause?*
Ann [æn]	Anna
yes [jes]	ja
minute ['minit]	Minute; Augenblick
please [pli:z]	bitte
to [tu, tə]	zu
it [it]	es
to fetch [tə 'fetʃ]	holen
fetch in ['fetʃ‿'in]	*holen Sie herein!*
bed [bed]	Bett
Mr Sim is in bed	*Herr Sim ist (liegt) im Bett*
he [hi:]	er
ill [il]	krank
an actor [ən‿'æktə]	ein Schauspieler
and [ænd, ənd]	und
to have [hæv]	haben
tea [ti:]	Tee
Mr Dent and Mrs Sim have tea	*Herr Dent und Frau Sim trinken Tee*
to say [sei]	sagen
(he) says [sez]	(er) sagt
to hand [hænd]	reichen
hand me ['hænd mi:]	reich mir!
cheese [tʃi:z]	Käse
biscuit ['biskit], *Mehrz.* biscuits ['biskits]	Keks
Mrs Sim has [hæz]	Frau Sim hat
Mrs Sim has cheese	*Frau Sim ißt Käse*
an egg [ən‿'eg]	ein Ei
Ken [ken]	(männl. Vorname)
better ['betə]	besser
is he better?	*geht es ihm besser?*
to give [giv]	geben
his [hiz]	sein(e, r)
finished ['finiʃt]	beendet
tea is finished	*die Teestunde ist vorbei*
to get [get]	holen
(he) gets [gets]	(er) holt
hat [hæt]	Hut
his hat [hiz 'hæt]	sein(en) Hut
(he) gives [givz]	(er) gibt
kiss [kis]	Kuß
sister ['sistə]	Schwester
Mr Dent's sister [dents]	Herrn Dents Schwester

2 A Stationer's Shop

stationer ['steiʃnə]	Schreibwarenhändler
shop [ʃɔp]	Laden, Geschäft
stationer's shop ['steiʃnəz ʃɔp]	Schreibwarengeschäft
Tom [tɔm]	(Kurzform f. Thomas)
(shop) assistant [ə'sistənt]	Gehilfe, Verkäufer(in)
the [ðə, ði]	der, die, das
city ['siti]	(Groß-)Stadt
City	(Name der Londoner Innenstadt)
who? [hu:]	wer?
boss [bɔs]	Chef
Smith [smiθ]	Schmied (hier: Familienname)
what? [wɔt]	was?
to sell [sel]	verkaufen
(he, she, it) sells [selz]	(er, sie, es) verkauft
the shop sells	*das Geschäft führt*
paper ['peipə]	Papier
(news)paper ['nju:sˌpeipə]	Zeitung
pen [pen]	Federhalter (einschl. Füllfederhalter und Kugelschreiber)
pencil ['pensl]	Bleistift
picture ['piktʃə]	Bild
postcard ['pəustkɑ:d]	Postkarte

picture postcard ['piktʃə 'pəustka:d]	Bildpostkarte, Ansichtskarte
tobacco [tə'bækəu]	Tabak
sweet [swi:t]	süß
a sweet	ein Bonbon
sweets, *Mehrz.* [swi:ts]	Süßigkeiten
Betty ['beti]	(Kurzf. f. Elizabeth)
white [wait]	weiß (hier: Familienname)
to enter [tu‿'entə]	eintreten, betreten
(he, she, it) enters ['entəz]	(er, sie, es) tritt ein, betritt
she [ʃi:]	sie
typist ['taipist]	Maschinenschreiber(in)
office ['ɔfis]	Amt, Büro
opposite ['ɔpəzit]	gegenüber
Miss [mis]	Fräulein (vor d. Namen)
nice [nais]	nett, hübsch
little ['litl]	klein
thing [θiŋ]	Ding
a nice little thing	*ein nettes kleines Ding*
face [feis]	Gesicht
shoe [ʃu:]	Schuh
she has shoes on	*sie hat Schuhe an*
to want [wɔnt]	wünschen
she wants [wɔnts]	sie möchte (haben)
to show [ʃəu]	zeigen
he shows [ʃəuz]	er zeigt
two [tu:]	zwei
The Times [taimz]	(wörtl.: Die Zeiten—
The Guardian ['ga:djən]	Der Wächter; engl. Tageszeitungen)
to go [gəu]	gehen
away [ə'wei]	weg
go away ['gəu‿ə'wei]	*geh mir weg!, aber nicht doch!*

not [nɔt]	nicht
this [ðis]	dieser, diese, dieses
these [ði:z]	diese (Mehrz.)
to buy [bai]	kaufen
daily ['deili]	täglich
The Daily Mail [ðə 'deili 'meil]	(wörtl.: Die tägliche Post; reichbebildertes Massenblatt)
entertaining [ˌentə'teiniŋ]	unterhaltend
article ['a:tikl]	Artikel
to open ['əupən]	öffnen, aufschlagen
he opens ['əupənz]	er öffnet, schlägt auf
this is ['ðis‿iz]	dies ist
wedding ['wediŋ]	Hochzeit
these are ['ði:z‿a:]	dies sind
to take [teik]	nehmen
she takes [teiks]	sie nimmt
expensive [iks'pensiv]	teuer
many ['meni]	viele
thanks, *Mehrz.* [θæŋks]	Dank
many thanks ['meni 'θæŋks]	*vielen Dank*
good-bye ['gud'bai]	*auf Wiedersehen*
to leave [li:v]	verlassen
she leaves [li:vz]	sie verläßt
to know [nəu]	kennen
I know [ai 'nəu]	ich kenne
what nonsense! ['wɔt 'nɔnsəns]	*was für ein Unsinn!*

3 An Evening Out

evening ['i:vniŋ]	Abend
out [aut]	draußen, außer Haus
an evening out	*ein Ausgehabend*
Bill [bil]	(Kurzf. f. William)
free [fri:]	frei
ticket ['tikit]	(Eintritts-, Fahr-) Karte
free ticket ['fri: 'tikit]	Freikarte
for [fɔ:]	für
Empire ['empaiə]	(brit. Welt-)Reich; (hier: Name eines Kinos)
that is ['ðæt‿iz]	das ist
big [big]	groß
cinema ['sinəmə]	Lichtspieltheater, Kino
pictures, *Mehrz.* ['piktʃəz]	Kino
what about the pictures? ['wɔt‿əbaut]	*wie wär's mit dem Kino?*
Sally ['sæli]	(Kurzf. f. Sarah)
what's on? ['wɔts‿'ɔn] = *what is on?*	*was wird gespielt, gegeben?*
green [gri:n]	grün
monster ['mɔnstə]	Ungeheuer
darling ['da:liŋ]	Liebling
that's = that is [ðæts]	
fine [fain]	fein, schön
let's take ['lets 'teik]	*laßt uns nehmen!, nehmen wir!*
taxi ['tæksi]	Taxi
why? [wai]	warum?
bus [bʌs]	Omnibus
we [wi:]	wir
plenty of ['plenti‿əv]	eine Menge, viel(e)
time [taim]	Zeit
film [film]	Film
to begin [bi'gin]	beginnen
ten [ten]	zehn
street [stri:t]	Straße
full [ful]	voll

car [kɑ:]	(Personen-)Wagen, Auto
the streets are full of cars [ˈful‿əv ˈkɑ:z]	die Straßen sind voller Autos
hour [ˈauə]	Stunde
rush hour [ˈrʌʃ‿auə]	Hauptverkehrszeit
traffic [ˈtræfik]	Verkehr
light [lait]	Licht
traffic lights, *Mehrz.* [ˈtræfik laits]	Verkehrsampel(n)
every [ˈevri]	jeder, jede, jedes
crossing [ˈkrɔsiŋ]	Kreuzung
at every crossing	an jeder Kreuzung
Piccadilly [ˌpikəˈdili]	(große Geschäftsstraße in London, die in den Piccadilly Circus mündet; s. Stadtplan auf Umschlag-Innenseite vorn)
at last [ət ˈlɑ:st]	endlich
theatre [ˈθiətə]	Theater
London's [ˈlʌndənz]	Londons
west [west]	Westen
end [end]	Ende
West End [ˈwest ˈend]	(Stadtteil Londons)
here [hiə]	hier
here we are [ˈhiə wi:‿ˈɑ:]	*wir sind da*
man, *Mehrz.* men [mæn, men]	Mann
entrance [ˈentrəns]	Eingang
at the entrance	am Eingang
to look [luk]	schauen
to look at [ˈluk‿æt]	schauen auf, anschauen, ansehen
but [bʌt, bət]	aber
what's this? [ˈwɔts ˈðis]	*was ist das?, was soll das?*

(I am) sorry [(aim) ˈsɔri]	(wörtl.: ich bin traurig) *es tut mir leid*
they are [ˈðei‿ɑ:]	sie sind
they are no good [ˈðei‿ə ˈnəu ˈgud]	*sie haben keinen Wert*
box [bɔks]	Schachtel
box-office [ˈbɔksɔfis]	(Theater-, Kino-) Kasse
left [left]	(der, die, das) linke
on the left [ɔn ðə ˈleft]	links
pocket [ˈpɔkit]	(Hosen-, Rock-) Tasche
my [mai]	mein(e)
never mind [ˈnevə ˈmaind]	*mach dir nichts draus! macht nichts!*
luck [lʌk]	Glück
better luck [ˈbetə ˈlʌk]	mehr Glück
next [nekst]	(der, die, das) nächste
next time [ˈnekst‿ˈtaim]	das nächste Mal
you [ju:]	du, ihr, Sie
sad [sæd]	traurig
drink [driŋk]	Getränk
let's have a drink	*trinken wir etwas!*
instead [inˈsted]	statt dessen, dafür

4 The Red Paint

red [red]	rot
paint [peint]	Farbe (zum Anstreichen), Anstrich
brown [braun]	braun (hier: Familienname)
small [smɔ:l]	klein
house, *Mehrz.* houses [haus, ˈhauziz]	Haus
Wimbledon [ˈwimbldən]	(Vorort v. London)

home [həum]	Heim
Home, sweet home	wörtl.: *Heim, süßes Heim* (engl. Sprichwort)
trautes Heim, Glück allein	
motto [ˈmɔtəu]	Wahlspruch
Mr Brown's motto [ˈbraunz]	Herrn Brauns Wahlspruch
downstairs [ˈdaunˈstɛəz]	die Treppe hinunter, nach unten; unten
he is downstairs	*er ist unten*
to sit [sit]	sitzen
room [ru(:)m]	Raum, Zimmer
sitting-room [ˈsitiŋrum]	Wohnzimmer
where? [wɛə]	wo?
garden [ˈgɑ:dn]	Garten
in the garden	*im Garten*
there is [ˈðɛər‿ˈiz, ðəz]	es ist, es gibt
there are [ˈðɛər‿ˈɑ:, ˈðɛər‿ə]	es sind, es gibt
beautiful [ˈbju:təful]	schön
flower [ˈflauə]	Blume
he looks at the evening paper	*er schaut in die Abendzeitung*
nothing [ˈnʌθiŋ]	nichts
interesting [ˈintristiŋ]	interessant
nothing interesting	nichts Interessantes
book [buk]	Buch
boring [ˈbɔ:riŋ]	langweilig
too *(nachgestellt)* [tu:]	auch
TV = television [ˈti:ˈvi:, ˈteliˌviʒən]	Fernsehen
What about TV?	*Wie wär's mit Fernsehen?*
good [gud]	gut
programme [ˈprəugræm]	Programm, Sendung
there is a good programme on	*es kommt eine gute Sendung*
today [təˈdei]	heute

then [ðen]	dann, da
idea [ai'diə]	Idee, Gedanke
he gets an idea	*es kommt ihm ein Gedanke*
to think [θiŋk]	denken
brush [brʌʃ]	Bürste, Pinsel
bathroom ['bɑ:θrum]	Badezimmer
how [hau]	wie
how many? ['hau 'meni]	wie viele?
he goes [gəuz]	er geht
upstairs ['ʌp'stɛəz]	die Treppe hinauf, nach oben; oben
to paint [peint]	malen, anstreichen
one [wʌn]	eins; ein, eine
after one hour [ɑ:ftə 'wʌn‿'auə]	nach einer Stunde
bath [bɑ:θ]	Bad; Badewanne
chair [tʃɛə]	Stuhl
floor [flɔ:]	Fußboden
wall [wɔ:l]	Wand, Mauer
window ['windəu]	Fenster
frame [freim]	Rahmen
all [ɔ:l]	alle
door [dɔ:]	Tür
to knock at the door ['nɔk‿ət]	an die Tür klopfen
no [nəu]	kein(e)
answer ['ɑ:nsə]	Antwort
there is no answer	*es kommt keine Antwort*
to cry [krai]	rufen, schreien
she cries [kraiz]	sie ruft
What's this?	*Was ist denn das?*
awful ['ɔ:ful, 'ɔ:fl]	furchtbar, schrecklich
colour ['kʌlə]	Farbe
what an awful colour!	*was für eine schreckliche Farbe!*

Mary ['mɛəri]	Maria
to like [laik]	lieben, gern haben, mögen
I like the colour	*die Farbe gefällt mir*
Why not paint the door green?	*Warum nicht (gleich) die Tür grün streichen?*
blue [blu:]	blau
that wall ['ðæt 'wɔ:l]	jene Wand, die Wand dort
yellow ['jeləu]	gelb
those window frames [ðəuz]	jene Fensterrahmen, die Fensterrahmen dort
pink [piŋk]	rosa
hair [hɛə]	Haar
grey [grei]	grau
my hair goes grey	*mein Haar wird grau*
when [wen]	wenn
black [blæk]	schwarz
day [dei]	Tag

5 Spoilt Holidays

spoilt [spɔilt]	verdorben
holidays ['hɔlədiz]	Ferien, Urlaub
Turner ['tə:nə]	(Familienname)
before his holidays [bi'fɔ:]	vor seinen Ferien
to come [kʌm]	kommen
home [həum]	heim, nach Hause
from [frɔm, frəm]	von
very ['veri]	sehr
tired ['taiəd]	müde
head [hed]	Kopf
headache ['hedeik]	Kopfweh

to have a headache	*Kopfweh haben*
hot [hɔt]	heiß, sehr warm
health [helθ]	Gesundheit
to do [du:]	tun
it does you good [it 'dʌz ju: 'gud]	*es tut dir gut*
to the bathroom [tə ðə 'bɑ:θrum]	zum Badezimmer
water ['wɔ:tə]	Wasser
to turn on the water ['tə:n‿'ɔn]	das Wasser aufdrehen
to fill [fil]	füllen
jacket ['dʒækit]	Jacke
he takes off his jacket ['teiks‿'ɔf]	er zieht seine Jacke aus
pullover ['pul,əuvə]	Pullover
tie [tai]	Krawatte, Schlips
shirt [ʃə:t]	(Herren-)Hemd
trousers, *Mehrz.* ['trauzəz]	(lange) Hose
sock [sɔk]	Socke
pants, *Mehrz.* [pænts]	Unterhose
to get in ['get‿'in]	hineingehen, (hin)einsteigen
a few [ə 'fju:]	einige, ein paar
right [rait]	(der, die, das) rechte; recht, richtig
just right ['dʒʌst 'rait]	gerade richtig
to shut [ʃʌt]	zumachen, schließen
eye [ai]	Auge
to enjoy [in'dʒɔi]	genießen
warmth [wɔ:mθ]	Wärme
pleasure ['pleʒə]	Vergnügen, Freude
now [nau]	nun, jetzt
shock [ʃɔk]	Schreck
he gets a shock	*er bekommt einen Schreck*
body ['bɔdi]	Körper

covered ['kʌvəd]	bedeckt
with [wið]	mit
spot [spɔt]	Fleck
on [ɔn]	auf, an
hand [hænd]	Hand
on his hand	an seiner Hand
finger ['fiŋgə]	Finger
arm [ɑ:m]	Arm
leg [leg]	Bein
foot, *Mehrz.* feet [fut, fi:t]	Fuß
chest [tʃest]	Brust
to jump [dʒʌmp]	springen
out of the bath ['aut‿əv]	aus dem Bad heraus
towel ['tauəl]	Handtuch
to rub [rʌb]	reiben
to rub hard [hɑ:d]	*fest reiben*
still [stil]	noch, immer noch
there [ðɛə]	dort, da
they are still there	*sie sind immer noch da*
to call [kɔ:l]	rufen
wife [waif]	(Ehe-)Frau
to come in ['kʌm‿'in]	hereinkommen
to see [si:]	sehen
husband ['hʌzbənd]	(Ehe-)Mann
her husband [hə:]	ihr Mann
skin [skin]	Haut
oh [əu]	Oh!
John [dʒɔn]	Johann, Hans
baby ['beibi]	Baby
you big baby!	*du Kindskopf!*
German ['dʒə:mən]	deutsch
German measles, *Mehrz.* ['dʒə:mən 'mi:zlz]	Röteln
pity ['piti]	Mitleid
what a pity!	*wie schade!*

6 Red Riding Hood and the Wolf

hood [hud]	Haube, Kappe
Red Riding Hood ['red 'raidiŋ hud]	Rotkäppchen
wolf, *Mehrz.* wolves [wulf, wulvz]	Wolf
Betsy ['betsi]	(Kurzf. f. Elizabeth)
to stand [stænd]	stehen
mirror ['mirə]	Spiegel
in front of the mirror [in 'frʌnt‿əv]	vor dem Spiegel
what is she doing?	*was tut sie?*
to put [put]	setzen, stellen, legen
to put on ['put‿'ɔn]	anziehen, aufsetzen
dress [dres]	Kleid
cap [kæp]	Mütze
best [best]	(der, die, das) beste
stocking ['stɔkiŋ]	Strumpf
mother ['mʌðə]	Mutter
to go and see ['gəu‿ənd 'si:]	besuchen
grandma = grandmother ['grænmɑ:, 'græn,mʌðə]	Oma, Großmutter
to take a bus	*mit dem Omnibus fahren*
number ['nʌmbə]	Nummer
the number eleven bus	Bus der Linie 11
basket ['bɑ:skit]	Korb
cake [keik]	Kuchen
fruit [fru:t]	Frucht; Obst
a basket with fruit in it	*ein Korb mit Obst (darin)*
young [jʌŋ]	jung
lady, *Mehrz.* ladies ['leidi, 'leidiz]	Dame
eighteen ['ei'ti:n]	achtzehn
a lady of eighteen	*eine Dame von 18 Jahren*
girl [gə:l]	Mädchen
people, *Mehrz.* ['pi:pl]	Leute, Menschen
a lot of people [ə 'lɔt‿əv]	eine Menge, viele Menschen
to wait (for) [weit (fɔ:)]	warten (auf)
bus stop ['bʌs‿stɔp]	Omnibushaltestelle
to ask [ɑ:sk]	fragen
to smile [smail]	lächeln
thank you ['θæŋkju]	danke!
kind [kaind]	freundlich
corner ['kɔ:nə]	Ecke
round the corner [raund]	*um die Ecke*
to start [stɑ:t]	starten, anfahren
to live [liv]	leben; wohnen
near [niə]	nahe (bei), in der Nähe von
park [pɑ:k]	Park
Hyde Park ['haid 'pɑ:k]	(Park in London)
way [wei]	Weg
where? [wɛə]	wo?, wohin?
to go	gehen; fahren
to drive [draiv]	fahren
snack-bar ['snækbɑ:]	Imbißstube
to stop [stɔp]	aufhören; halten, anhalten
to laugh [lɑ:f]	lachen
bad [bæd]	schlecht; schlimm; böse
to drive on ['draiv‿'ɔn]	weiterfahren
to jump out ['dʒʌmp‿'aut]	hinaus-, heraus-springen
to run [rʌn]	rennen, laufen
to run back ['rʌn 'bæk]	zurücklaufen
the car is gone [gɔn]	*der Wagen ist weg*
poor [puə]	arm

→ mit 8 abhören

7 A Letter

letter ['letə]	Brief
leaf, *Mehrz.* leaves [li:f, li:vz]	Blatt
road [rəud]	Straße (bes. Landstraße und Straße in einem Wohnviertel)
E. = east [i:, i:st]	Osten
E. 17 (= seventeen) ['i: sevn'ti:n]	(Postbezirk) Ost 17
Sunday ['sʌndi]	Sonntag
June 5th (*lies:* June the fifth) [dʒu:n, fifθ]	5. Juni
dear [diə]	liebe(r, s)
Dudley ['dʌdli]	(männl. Vorname)
new [nju:]	neu
the same ... as ['seim‿əz]	der-, die-, dasselbe ... wie
parents, *Mehrz.* ['pɛərənts]	Eltern
dining-room ['dainiŋrum]	Eßzimmer
kitchen ['kitʃin]	Küche
bedroom ['bedrum]	Schlafzimmer
lavatory ['lævətəri]	Toilette
front garden ['frʌnt 'gɑ:dn]	Vorgarten
back [bæk]	Rücken, Rückseite
back garden ['bæk 'gɑ:dn]	Garten hinter dem Haus
down [daun]	hinunter
the garden runs down to	*der Garten erstreckt sich bis*
railway ['reilwei]	Eisenbahn
to hear [hiə]	hören
train [trein]	Zug

we take no notice ['nəutis]	*wir nehmen keine Notiz, wir beachten es nicht*
as [æz, əz]	da
rent [rent]	Miete
cheap [tʃi:p]	billig
landlord ['lænlɔ:d]	Hauswirt, -besitzer
brother ['brʌðə]	Bruder
in the evening	*am Abend, abends*
often ['ɔfn]	oft
at home [ət 'həum]	daheim, zu Hause
sometimes ['sʌmtaimz]	manchmal
Shirley ['ʃə:li]	(weibl. Vorname)
to call on s.o. ['kɔ:l‿ɔn] (= someone) ['sʌmwʌn]	jdn. besuchen
always ['ɔ:lweiz]	immer
to talk about ['tɔ:k‿əbaut]	reden über
clothes, *Mehrz.* [kləuðz]	Kleidung, Kleider
visitor ['vizitə]	Besucher
welcome ['welkəm]	willkommen
even ['i:vən]	sogar, selbst; hier: auch
without [wi'ðaut]	ohne
friend [frend]	Freund
never ['nevə]	nie
bored [bɔ:d]	gelangweilt
we are never bored	*wir langweilen uns nie*
to water ['wɔ:tə]	bewässern; gießen
curtain ['kə:tn]	Vorhang
to hang [hæŋ]	hängen
to hang up ['hæŋ‿'ʌp]	aufhängen
or [ɔ:]	oder
carpet ['kɑ:pit]	Teppich
to nail down ['neil 'daun]	annageln
to write [rait]	schreiben

to read [ri:d]	lesen
to play [plei]	spielen
to play the piano ['plei ðə 'piænəu]	Klavier spielen
fortunately ['fɔ:tʃnitli]	glücklicherweise
thick [θik]	dick
neighbour ['neibə]	Nachbar
only ['əunli]	nur
dog [dɔg]	Hund
to howl [haul]	heulen
so [səu]	so, deshalb
child, *Mehrz.* children [tʃaild, 'tʃildrən]	Kind
noise [nɔiz]	Lärm
to spend [spend]	verbringen
with us ['wið‿əs]	mit uns, bei uns
to phone [fəun]	telefonieren, anrufen
before [bi'fɔ:]	bevor, ehe
love [lʌv]	Liebe
aunt [ɑ:nt]	Tante
Sarah ['sɛərə]	Sara
give my love to Aunt Sarah	*grüße Tante Sara herzlich von mir*
uncle ['ʌŋkl]	Onkel
Henry ['henri]	Heinrich
all the best ['ɔ:l ðə 'best]	*alles Gute*
yours [jɔ:z]	der Deinige; hier: dein
Charlie ['tʃɑ:li]	(Kosename f. Charles) Karli, Karlchen
stamp [stæmp]	Briefmarke
Walker ['wɔ:kə]	(Familienname)
church [tʃə:tʃ]	Kirche
Christchurch Road ['kraistʃə:tʃ 'rəud]	(Straßenname)
Bromley ['brɔmli]	(Vorort von London)
Kent [kent]	(Grafschaft, s. Englandkarte)

8 Charlie's New Home

Saturday ['sætədi]	Samstag
afternoon ['ɑ:ftə'nu:n]	Nachmittag
open ['əupən]	offen
to know [nəu]	wissen
suddenly ['sʌdnli]	plötzlich
loud [laud]	laut
to listen ['lisn]	horchen, hören
to pass [pɑ:s] the cheese	den Käse reichen
cup [kʌp]	Tasse
have another cup [ə'nʌðə kʌp]	*nimm noch eine Tasse*
again [ə'gen]	wieder
furniture *(nur Einzahl)* ['fə:nitʃə]	die Möbel
to shake [ʃeik]	zittern, schütteln
the furniture is shaking	*die Möbel zittern*
to happen ['hæpən]	geschehen, passieren
what's happening?	*was passiert hier?*
to pass [pɑ:s]	vorbeifahren, vorbeigehen
at this time	*zu dieser Zeit*
usually ['ju:ʒuəli]	gewöhnlich
to meet [mi:t]	sich treffen, sich begegnen
they usually meet here	*sie treffen sich gewöhnlich hier*
head [hed]	Kopf
to get up	aufstehen
they get on your nerves ['nə:vz]	*sie fallen dir auf die Nerven*
lovely ['lʌvli]	lieblich, hübsch
night [nait]	Nacht
outside ['aut'said]	draußen
voice [vɔis]	Stimme
to love [lʌv]	lieben, sehr mögen
you two ['ju: 'tu:]	*ihr zwei*

to come over [kʌm 'əuvə]	herüberkommen
music ['mju:zik]	Musik
to join s.o. [dʒɔin]	sich jemandem anschließen
they go to join their neighbour	*sie gehen zum Nachbarn*

9 The Big Store

store [stɔ:]	Kaufhaus
to know [nəu]	kennen
Harrods ['hærədz]	(großes Londoner Kaufhaus)
haircut ['hɛəkʌt]	Haarschnitt
do you want a haircut?	*wollen Sie sich die Haare schneiden lassen?*
to provide [prə'vaid]	besorgen, versorgen
the big store can provide it [kæn]	das große Kaufhaus kann es besorgen
to buy [bai]	kaufen
do you want to buy?	möchten Sie kaufen?
monkey ['mʌŋki]	Affe
sportsman ['spɔ:tsmən] *Mehrz.* -men	Sportler
motorboat ['məutəbəut]	Motorboot
everything ['evriθiŋ]	alles
to wish [wiʃ]	wünschen
to bring [briŋ]	bringen
to bring a dog along [ə'lɔŋ]	*einen Hund mitbringen*
waiting-room ['weitiŋrum]	Warteraum
ground floor ['graund'flɔ:]	Erdgeschoß
until [ən'til]	bis (zeitlich)

to come back [bæk]	zurückkommen
to leave	(ver-, zurück-)lassen
don't you like to leave it?	lassen Sie ihn nicht gerne zurück?
other dogs ['ʌðə]	andere Hunde
well [wel]	nun, na schön
you must [mʌst]	du mußt, Sie müssen
to carry ['kæri]	tragen
important [im'pɔ:tənt]	wichtig, bedeutend
the most important [məust]	(der, die, das) wichtigste
customer ['kʌstəmə]	Kunde
queen [kwi:n]	Königin
to shop [ʃɔp]	einkaufen
of course [əv 'kɔ:s]	natürlich
what can you do to pass the time?	was können Sie tun, um sich die Zeit zu vertreiben?
restaurant ['restərɔ̃:ŋ]	Restaurant, Gaststätte
golf	Golf
lesson ['lesn]	Lektion, Unterrichtsstunde
figure ['figə]	Figur
to get married ['mærid]	sich verheiraten
wedding dress	Hochzeitskleid
hairdresser ['hɛə,dresə]	Friseur
wine [wain]	Wein
waiter ['weitə]	Kellner
driver ['draivə]	Fahrer
in fact [in 'fækt]	*in der Tat*
bride [braid]	Braut
look around! [ə'raund]	schauen Sie sich um!
to use [ju:z]	gebrauchen
perhaps [pə'hæps]	vielleicht
your future wife ['fju:tʃə]	ihre zukünftige Frau
among [ə'mʌŋ]	unter (einer Menge)
pretty ['priti]	hübsch

various ['vɛəriəs]	verschieden
department [di'pɑ:tmənt]	Abteilung
you can't [kɑ:nt]	du kannst nicht, Sie können nicht
because [bi'kɔ:z]	weil
too far [fɑ:]	zu weit
to order ['ɔ:də]	bestellen
by phone [bai 'fəun]	telefonisch
order department	Bestellabteilung
midnight ['midnait]	Mitternacht
bacon ['beikən]	Speck
in time	rechtzeitig
for breakfast ['brekfəst]	zum Frühstück
do you know that...	weißt du, wissen Sie, daß...
funeral ['fju:nərəl]	Beerdigung
own [əun]	eigen
coffin ['kɔfin]	Sarg
factory ['fæktəri]	Fabrik

An English Lesson

English ['iŋgliʃ]	englisch
gentleman ['dʒentlmən]	Herr
ladies and gentlemen ['leidiz‿ənd 'dʒentlmən]	*meine Damen und Herren*
teacher ['ti:tʃə]	Lehrer(in)
to start [stɑ:t]	beginnen, anfangen
page [peidʒ]	Seite
at the top (bottom) of page 3 [tɔp, 'bɔtəm]	*oben (unten) auf Seite 3*
line [lain]	Linie, Zeile
last [lɑ:st]	(der, die, das) letzte
sentence ['sentəns]	Satz
to speak [spi:k]	sprechen
louder ['laudə]	lauter
to repeat [ri'pi:t]	wiederholen
word [wə:d]	Wort
together [tə'geðə]	zusammen
difficult ['difikəlt]	schwierig, schwer
to pronounce [prə'nauns]	aussprechen
to go on ['gəu‿'ɔn]	weitermachen
to translate [træns'leit]	übersetzen
the first [fə:st]	(der, die, das) erste
paragraph ['pærəgrɑ:f]	Absatz, Abschnitt
blackboard ['blækbɔ:d]	Wandtafel
chalk [tʃɔ:k]	Kreide
correct [kə'rekt]	richtig
wrong [rɔŋ]	falsch
mistake [mis'teik]	Fehler
to spell [spel]	buchstabieren
who knows how to spell the word?	*wer kann das Wort richtig buchstabieren?*
to answer ['ɑ:nsə]	(be)antworten
question ['kwestʃən]	Frage
exercise ['eksəsaiz]	Übung
exercise-book	(Schreib-)Heft

Exercises

I. ex. = example [ig'zɑ:mpl]	Beispiel
III. when?	wann?

10 At the Marriage Agency

marriage ['mæridʒ]	Heirat, Ehe
marriage agency ['eidʒənsi]	Heiratsvermittlung
baker ['beikə]	Bäcker (hier: Familienname)
next, please	*der Nächste, bitte*
woman, *Mehrz.* women ['wumən, 'wimin]	Frau
name [neim]	Name
to tell [tel]	sagen, erzählen
don't tell me ['dəunt 'tel mi]	sagen Sie mir nicht
age [eidʒ]	Alter
don't be in a hurry ['hʌri]	seien Sie nicht so in Eile
to hesitate ['heziteit]	zögern
to test	testen, prüfen
to dislike [dis'laik]	nicht mögen
pop music ['pɔp'mju:zik]	Popmusik
to dance [dɑ:ns]	tanzen
I haven't much time	ich habe nicht viel Zeit
to watch [wɔtʃ]	beobachten
to watch television	fernsehen
seldom ['seldəm]	selten
to hate [heit]	hassen
classical music ['klæsikəl]	klassische Musik
to prefer [pri'fə:]	vorziehen
do you do a lot of sports? [spɔ:ts]	*treiben Sie viel Sport?*
I just play tennis	*ich spiele nur Tennis*
to swim [swim]	schwimmen
I swim a bit [bit]	*ich schwimme ein wenig*
to find [faind]	finden
easy ['i:zi]	leicht
stranger ['streindʒə]	Fremde, (r)
party ['pɑ:ti]	Party, Gesellschaft
rarely ['rɛəli]	selten
romantic love [rəu'mæntik]	romantische Liebe
necessary ['nesisəri]	notwendig, nötig
successful [sək'sesful]	erfolgreich
don't be silly ['sili]	seien Sie nicht töricht
to last [lɑ:st]	dauern
long [lɔŋ]	lange
to believe [bi'li:v]	glauben

bad-tempered ['bæd'tempəd]	schlecht gelaunt
to get	erhalten, bekommen
early ['ə:li]	früh
early morning tea	Tee vor dem Frühstück
to make [meik]	machen, zubereiten
father ['fɑ:ðə]	Vater
overdue ['əuvə'dju:]	überfällig
whether ['weðə]	ob
money ['mʌni]	Geld
soon [su:n]	bald

11 A Week at the Seaside

week [wi:k]	Woche
sea [si:]	(die) See, Meer
at the seaside ['si:'said]	an der See
Monday ['mʌndi]	Montag
August ['ɔ:gəst]	August
bank [bæŋk]	Bank(haus)
bank holiday	Bankfeiertag, gesetzlicher Feiertag
family ['fæmili]	Familie
the Smith family ['smiθ 'fæmili]	*die Familie Smith*
first [fə:st]	(der, die, das) erste
Brighton ['braitn]	(Seebad an der Südküste Englands)
at Brighton	in Brighton
to arrive at [ə'raiv‿ət]	ankommen in
guest [gest]	Gast
guest-house ['gesthaus]	Fremdenheim, Pension
station ['steiʃən]	Bahnhof
near the station [niə]	in der Nähe des Bahnhofs
landlady ['læn,leidi]	(Haus-)Wirtin

to welcome ['welkəm]	willkommen heißen, begrüßen
them [ðem]	sie (Wenfall von 'they')
a smile [smail]	ein Lächeln
dinner ['dinə]	(Hauptmahlzeit mittags oder abends) hier: Abendessen
for dinner [fə 'dinə]	*zum Abendessen*
soup [su:p]	Suppe
meat [mi:t]	Fleisch
potato, *Mehrz.* -oes [pə'teitəu(z)]	Kartoffel
vegetables, *Mehrz.* ['vedʒitəblz]	Gemüse
peach [pi:tʃ]	Pfirsich
Freddie ['fredi]	(männl. Vorname)
son [sʌn]	Sohn
fly [flai]	Fliege
to make a face [feis]	*das Gesicht verziehen, ein langes Gesicht machen*
remark [ri'mɑ:k]	Bemerkung
to pass a remark [pɑ:s]	eine Bemerkung machen
food, *immer Einz.* [fu:d]	Lebensmittel, Essen
to blush [blʌʃ]	erröten, rot werden
to try [trai]	versuchen
to change [tʃeindʒ]	ändern, wechseln
to change the subject ['sʌbdʒikt]	das Thema wechseln
Sheila ['ʃi:lə]	(weibl. Vorname)
year [jə:, jiə]	Jahr
old [əuld]	alt
daughter ['dɔ:tə]	Tochter
the eighteen-year-old daughter ['eiti:njə:rəuld 'dɔ:tə]	die achtzehnjährige Tochter

tomato, *Mehrz.* -es [tə'mɑ:təu(z)]	Tomate
slim [slim]	schlank
to be slimming	*eine Schlankheitskur machen*
Tuesday ['tju:zdi]	Dienstag
weather ['weðə]	Wetter
to hurry ['hʌri]	eilen
beach [bi:tʃ]	Strand
to take [teik]	nehmen, mitnehmen
camera ['kæmərə]	Fotoapparat
suit [sju:t]	Anzug
swimsuit ['swimsju:t]	Badeanzug
pebble ['pebl]	Kieselstein
sands, *Mehrz.* [sændz]	Sand(strand)
photograph ['fəutəgrɑ:f]	Aufnahme, Bild
background ['bækgraund]	Hintergrund
to have got = to have [hæv 'gɔt]	haben
for that	dafür
to reply [ri'plai]	antworten
happy ['hæpi]	glücklich
to bathe [beið]	(im Freien) baden
Wednesday ['wenzdi]	Mittwoch
rain [rein]	Regen
nothing but ['nʌθiŋ bət]	nichts als
to send [send]	schicken
a picture postcard of	eine Ansichtskarte von
sun [sʌn]	Sonne
sunny ['sʌni]	sonnig
Thursday ['θə:zdi]	Donnerstag
more [mɔ:]	mehr
three more ladies	*drei weitere Damen*
to clear up ['kliər‿'ʌp]	sich aufklären
Friday ['fraidi]	Freitag
beauty ['bju:ti]	Schönheit
competition [,kɔmpi'tiʃən]	Wettbewerb

pier [piə]	Pier; Promenadensteg
chance [tʃɑ:ns]	Aussicht, Chance
to look	schauen; aussehen
fair hair ['fɛə 'hɛə]	blondes Haar
judge [dʒʌdʒ]	Richter
parade [pə'reid]	Parade
Lily Pond ['lili 'pɔnd]	(Eigenname)
star [stɑ:]	Stern; Star
to give out ['giv‿'aut]	ausgeben, verteilen
prize [praiz]	(Sieges-)Preis
to win [win]	gewinnen
mayor [mɛə]	Bürgermeister
band [bænd]	Musikkapelle
at the station	auf dem Bahnhof
front page ['frʌnt 'peidʒ]	erste Seite, Titelseite
copy ['kɔpi]	Abschrift; Durchschlag; Exemplar

Postcard

wonderful ['wʌndəful]	wunderbar, herrlich
we are having a wonderful time	*es ist herrlich (hier bei uns)*

Meals

meal [mi:l]	Mahl, Mahlzeit
what meals?	was für Mahlzeiten?
the English	die Engländer
large [lɑ:dʒ]	groß, breit; hier: reichlich
to have breakfast	frühstücken
in the morning ['mɔ:niŋ]	am Morgen, morgens
cornflakes ['kɔ:nfleiks]	Maisflocken
porridge ['pɔridʒ]	Hafer(flocken)brei
milk [milk]	Milch
sugar ['ʃugə]	Zucker
toast [təust]	geröstetes Brot, Toast
bread [bred]	Brot
butter ['bʌtə]	Butter
marmalade ['mɑ:məleid]	Orangenmarmelade
to drink [driŋk]	trinken
coffee ['kɔfi]	Kaffee
cup of coffee [kʌp]	Tasse Kaffee
at 11 o'clock [ə'klɔk]	um 11 Uhr
to have lunch [lʌntʃ]	zu Mittag essen
about 1 o'clock [ə'baut]	etwa um 1 Uhr
sweet [swi:t]	Süßspeise, Nachtisch
several ['sevrəl]	mehrere
jam [dʒæm]	Marmelade
some [sʌm]	einige, manche
most people ['məust 'pi:pl]	die meisten Leute
light [lait]	leicht
to have supper ['sʌpə]	zu abend essen

12 Christmas in England

Christmas ['krisməs]	Weihnachten
England ['iŋglənd]	England
Christmas Eve ['krisməs 'i:v]	Heiliger Abend
member ['membə]	Mitglied, Angehörige(r)
Cologne [kə'ləun]	Köln
to pack [pæk]	packen
to unpack ['ʌn'pæk]	auspacken
present ['preznt]	Geschenk
under ['ʌndə]	unter
tree [tri:]	Baum
parcel ['pɑ:sl]	Paket, Päckchen
from England	aus England
George [dʒɔ:dʒ]	Georg
Taylor ['teilə]	(Familienname)
tape [teip]	Tonband
tape-recorder ['teip-riˌkɔ:də]	Tonbandgerät
hello ['he'ləu]	hallo!, guten Tag!
this is George speaking	(am Telefon) *hier ist Georg*
(a) merry Christmas ['meri]	*fröhliche Weihnachten*
Germany ['dʒə:məni]	Deutschland
to seem [si:m]	scheinen
you don't seem to know	du scheinst nicht zu wissen
let me tell	*laßt mich erzählen*
something ['sʌmθiŋ]	etwas
Christmas card ['krisməs kɑ:d]	Weihnachtskarte
postman ['pəustmən]	Briefträger
hundreds of them ['hʌndrədz]	Hunderte davon
to dream of ['dri:m‿əv]	träumen von
too mild ['tu: 'maild]	zu mild
snow [snəu]	Schnee
we do have Christmas trees	Weihnachtsbäume haben wir (tatsächlich)
to light [lait]	anzünden
not until Christmas	*erst an Weihnachten*
Christmas Day ['krisməs 'dei]	1. Weihnachtsfeiertag
ordinary ['ɔ:dnri] usual	gewöhnlich
normal ['nɔ:məl]	normal
closing time ['kləuziŋ taim]	Ladenschlußzeit
(Christmas) carol ['kærəl]	Weihnachtslied
singer ['siŋə]	Sänger
in the street	*auf der Straße*
to remind s.o. (of) [ri'maind]	jdn. erinnern (an)

morning ['mɔ:niŋ]	Morgen; Vormittag
on Christmas morning	*am Weihnachtsmorgen*
to receive [ri'si:v]	empfangen, erhalten
to go to church [tʃə:tʃ]	*zur, in die Kirche gehen*
traditional [trə'diʃənl]	traditionell
turkey ['tə:ki]	Truthahn
Christmas pudding ['pudiŋ]	(Pudding mit viel Rosinen)
to wear [wɛə]	(Kleidung) tragen
bright [brait]	hell, freundlich
balloon [bə'lu:n]	Luftballon
mistletoe ['misltəu]	Mistel, Mistelzweig(e)
Marilyn ['mærilin]	(weibl. Vorname)
to forget [fə'get]	vergessen
it hangs from the lamp	*es hängt an der Lampe*
if [if]	wenn, falls
to step [step]	treten
under it ['ʌndər‿it]	darunter
hopeful ['həupful]	hoffnungsvoll
mouse, *Mehrz.* mice [maus, mais]	Maus
into ['intu, 'intə]	in (... hinein)
trap [træp]	Falle
to refuse [ri'fju:z]	ablehnen, sich weigern
everybody ['evribɔdi]	jeder(mann), alle
season ['si:zn]	(Jahres-)Zeit
joy [dʒɔi]	Freude
kindness ['kaindnis]	Freundlichkeit
friendship ['frendʃip]	Freundschaft
quarrel ['kwɔrəl]	Streit
to kiss [kis]	(sich) küssen
we should kiss [wi: ʃud 'kis]	wir sollten uns küssen
to make it up	*den Streit beilegen, sich wieder vertragen*
wish [wiʃ]	Wunsch
good luck ['gud 'lʌk]	*viel Glück*
Charlotte ['ʃɑ:lət]	Charlotte

Conversation in the Plane

conversation [ˌkɔnvə'seiʃən]	Unterhaltung
plane [plein]	Flugzeug
to fasten ['fɑ:sn]	festmachen
seat [si:t]	Sitz, Sitzplatz
seat belt ['si:tbelt]	Sitzgurt
to feel nervous [fi:l 'nə:vəs]	*sich nervös fühlen*
take-off ['teik-ɔf]	Abflug
to fly [flai]	fliegen
safe [seif]	sicher
nowadays ['nauədeiz]	heutzutage
to smoke [sməuk]	rauchen
to smoke a pipe [paip]	Pfeife rauchen
cigarette [ˌsigə'ret]	Zigarette
specially ['speʃəli]	besonders
stewardess ['stju:ədis]	Stewardess
neat [ni:t]	ordentlich, sauber; hier: unverdünnt, rein
two neat whiskies	zwei Whisky pur
slow [sləu]	langsam
by rail [reil]	mit der Eisenbahn
it takes 10 hours ['auəz]	*man braucht 10 Stunden*

13 Landing at Dover

to land [lænd]	landen
landing ['lændiŋ]	Landung
Dover ['dəuvə]	(Hafen an der Südostküste Englands)
Belgian ['beldʒən]	belgisch; Belgier(in)
boat [bəut]	Boot; Schiff, Dampfer
to steam [sti:m]	dampfen
harbour ['hɑ:bə]	Hafen
Dover Harbour	Hafen von Dover
passenger ['pæsindʒə]	Passagier, Fahrgast
on deck [ɔn 'dek]	auf Deck
luggage ['lʌgidʒ]	Gepäck
later ['leitə]	später
porter ['pɔ:tə]	Gepäckträger
on board [ɔn 'bɔ:d]	an Bord
by the gangway [bai ðə 'gæŋwei]	über die Laufplanke
policeman [pə'li:smən]	Polizist, Schutzmann
British ['britiʃ]	britisch
subject ['sʌbdʒikt]	Untertan; Staatsangehöriger
to the right	rechts, nach rechts
foreigner ['fɔrənə]	Ausländer
to the left	links, nach links
passport ['pɑ:s-pɔ:t]	Reisepaß
straight [streit]	geradewegs, direkt
customs, *Mehrz.* ['kʌstəmz]	Zoll(abfertigung)
to queue [kju:]	Schlange stehen
control [kən'trəul]	Aufsicht, Kontrolle
immigration [ˌimi'greiʃən]	Einwanderung
officer ['ɔfisə]	Offizier; Beamter
high [hai]	hoch
desk [desk]	Schreibtisch, Pult
to ask questions ['ɑ:sk‿'kwestʃənz]	*Fragen stellen*
to ask s.o. questions	*an jdn. Fragen richten*
signora, *ital.* [si:n'jɔ:rə]	Frau
Capone [kə'pəuni]	(ital. Familienname)
it is my turn [tə:n]	*ich bin an der Reihe*
madam ['mædəm]	gnädige Frau, meine Dame
landing card ['lændiŋ kɑ:d]	Landekarte (Kontrollkarte für Ausländer)

I beg your pardon?	*wie bitte?*
what card? ['wɔt 'kɑ:d]	was für eine Karte?
each [i:tʃ]	jede (r, s)
foreign ['fɔrən]	ausländisch
ship [ʃip]	Schiff
what ... for? ['wɔt 'fɔ:]	wozu?
to need [ni:d]	brauchen
registration [ˌredʒis'treiʃən]	Registrierung, Eintragung
to fill up ['fil‿'ʌp]	ausfüllen
what is your name?	*wie ist Ihr Name?, wie heißen Sie?*
Sophia [sə'fia]	(ital. weibl. Vorname)
Italian [i'tæljən]	italienisch; Italiener(in)
birth [bə:θ]	Geburt
place [pleis]	Platz, Ort
place of birth	Geburtsort
Rome [rəum]	Rom
Italy ['itəli]	Italien
date [deit]	Datum
what is your date of birth?	*wann sind Sie geboren?*
to visit ['vizit]	besuchen
Torelli [tə'reli]	(ital. Familienname)
Soho ['səuhəu]	(Stadtteil von London, bekannt wegen seiner vielen ausländischen Gaststätten)
long [lɔŋ]	lang
do you wish to ...?	möchten, wollen Sie ...?
to stay [stei]	sich aufhalten, bleiben
climate ['klaimit]	Klima
I have to go	ich muß gehen
customs hall ['kʌstəmz hɔ:l]	Zollabfertigung

suitcase ['sju:tkeis]	Koffer
which suitcase is yours? [jɔ:z]	(welcher Koffer ist Ihrer?) *welcher Koffer gehört Ihnen?*
to point to [pɔint]	zeigen, deuten auf
large [lɑ:dʒ]	groß
case = suitcase [keis]	
to declare [di'klɛə]	erklären; verzollen
nothing at all ['nʌθiŋ‿ət‿'ɔ:l]	überhaupt nichts, gar nichts
as [æz, əz]	während, als
gold [gəuld]	Gold; golden
watch [wɔtʃ]	(Taschen-, Armband-) Uhr
in all [in‿'ɔ:l]	im ganzen
silver ['silvə]	Silber; silbern
cigarette-case [ˌsigə'retkeis]	Zigarettenetui
will you please come with me?	*wollen Sie bitte mitkommen?*
main office ['mein 'ɔfis]	Hauptbüro
boat train ['bəut‿trein]	(Schiffs-)Anschlußzug

Porter! Porter!

sir [sə:]	(mein) Herr
to take [teik]	(hin-)bringen
baggage ['bægidʒ] *Am.*	Gepäck
I'll (= I shall) see you at the customs [ail]	(wörtl.: ich werde Sie beim Zoll sehen) *ich treffe Sie beim Zoll*
get me a seat	*besorgen Sie mir einen Platz*
non-smoker ['nɔn'sməukə]	Nichtraucherabteil
I'll (= I shall) do my best	*ich werde mein möglichstes tun*
to travel ['trævl]	reisen

first [fə:st]	hier: erster Klasse
second ['sekənd]	(der, die, das) zweite; hier: zweiter Klasse
charge [tʃɑ:dʒ]	Gebühr
fixed [fikst]	festgesetzt, fest
I leave that to you	*das überlasse ich Ihnen*
penny, *Mehrz.* pence ['peni, pens]	Penny (ca. 6 Pfg.)
thanks very much ['θæŋks veri 'mʌtʃ]	besten Dank

14 The Ideal Husband

ideal [ai'diəl]	ideal
Dick [dik]	(Kurzf. f. Richard)
married ['mærid]	verheiratet
couple ['kʌpl]	(Braut-, Ehe-) Paar
married couple	Ehepaar
flat [flæt]	(Etagen-)Wohnung
furnished flat ['fə:niʃt]	möblierte Wohnung
the town of Rochester ['taun‿əv 'rɔtʃistə]	die Stadt Rochester
life [laif]	Leben
clock [klɔk]	(Wand-, Turm-)Uhr
seven o'clock ['sevn‿ə'klɔk]	sieben Uhr
alarm clock [ə'lɑ:m klɔk]	Wecker
to ring [riŋ]	läuten, klingeln, schellen
to get up ['get‿'ʌp]	aufstehen
to rush [rʌʃ]	eilen, stürzen
to wash [wɔʃ]	(sich) waschen
to shave [ʃeiv]	(sich) rasieren
to dress [dres]	(sich) anziehen
at ten (minutes) past seven [pɑ:st]	um 10 nach 7

8–5046

a bunch of roses [bʌntʃ‿əv'rəuziz]	Rosenstrauß
half [hɑ:f]	halb
ready ['redi]	bereit, fertig
tray [trei]	Tablett
a pot of tea [pɔt]	eine Kanne Tee
boiled egg ['bɔild 'eg]	gekochtes Ei
a piece of toast [pi:s‿əv təust]	Stück Toast
a bottle of milk [bɔtl‿əv milk]	Flasche Milch
a bowl of sugar [bəul]	eine Schale Zucker
beside [bi'said]	neben
quarter ['kwɔ:tə]	Viertel
to take	(weg-, hin-)bringen *dagegen:* to bring = (her)bringen
to wash up ['wɔʃ‿'ʌp]	abwaschen, spülen
to wash up the dishes ['diʃiz]	(das) Geschirr abwaschen
plate [pleit]	Teller
saucer ['sɔ:sə]	Untertasse
glass [glɑ:s]	Glas
knife, *Mehrz.* knives [naif, naivz]	Messer
fork [fɔ:k]	Gabel
spoon [spu:n]	Löffel
tea-pot ['ti:pɔt]	Teekanne
tidy ['taidi]	aufgeräumt, in Ordnung
radio ['reidiəu]	Radio
to clean [kli:n]	säubern
a pair of shoes ['pɛər‿əv 'shu:z]	ein Paar Schuhe
this morning	*heute morgen, heute vormittag*
cleaner ['kli:nə]	Aufwartefrau, Putzfrau
to strike [straik]	schlagen
my watch is right	*meine Uhr geht richtig*
to set a watch by the radio	*eine Uhr nach dem Radio stellen*
the clock is slow	*die Uhr geht nach*
to catch [kætʃ]	fangen
to catch a train [trein]	*einen Zug erreichen*
to town	in die Stadt (= die nächstgelegene Stadt oder London)
to meet [mi:t]	(sich) treffen
night [nait]	Nacht, Abend
tonight [tə'nait]	heute abend
café ['kæfei]	kleines Restaurant
royal ['rɔiəl]	königlich
Café Royal ['kæfei 'rɔiəl]	(Name eines Restaurants)
O.K. ['əu 'kei]	in Ordnung, recht
we are going to have	*wir werden haben*
late [leit]	spät
to be late	*(zu) spät kommen*
umbrella [ʌm'brelə]	Schirm
to rain	regnen
I'm off [aim‿'ɔf]	ich gehe weg
to think [θiŋk]	denken; glauben, meinen

What's the Time?

what's the time?	*wieviel Uhr ist es?*
the right time	*die genaue Zeit*
by your watch	*nach Ihrer (deiner) Uhr*
fast [fɑ:st]	schnell
my watch is fast	*meine Uhr geht vor*
I must put my watch right	*ich muß meine Uhr richten*
my watch has stopped [stɔpt]	*meine Uhr ist stehengeblieben*
to wind up a watch ['waind‿'ʌp]	eine Uhr aufziehen
there's something wrong with my watch	*mit meiner Uhr stimmt etwas nicht*

Women's Clothes

skirt [skə:t]	(Damen-)Rock
blouse [blauz]	Bluse
jumper ['dʒʌmpə]	(Damen-)Pullover
suit [sju:t]	Kostüm, Anzug
nylon ['nailən]	Nylon
tights [taits]	Strumpfhose
underneath [ˌʌndə'ni:θ]	darunter
summer ['sʌmə]	Sommer
cotton ['kɔtn]	Baumwolle, Baumwoll-
woollen ['wulən]	wollen, Woll-
cardigan ['kɑ:digən]	Wolljacke, -weste
rainy ['reini]	regnerisch
coat [kəut]	Mantel
raincoat ['reinkəut]	Regenmantel
winter ['wintə]	Winter
silk [silk]	Seide; seiden
scarf, *Mehrz.* scarves [skɑ:f, skɑ:vz]	Schal
glove [glʌv]	Handschuh

15 Under the Roofs of London

roof [ru:f]	Dach
boarding-house ['bɔ:diŋhaus]	Pension
he said [sed]	er sagte
Warwick Terrace ['wɔrik 'terəs]	(Name einer Straße)
sure [ʃuə]	sicher

central ['sentrəl]	zentral (gelegen)
Paddington Station ['pædiŋtən 'steiʃən]	(Name eines Londoner Bahnhofs, s. Stadtplan)
you can't miss it	Sie können es nicht verfehlen
widow ['widəu]	Witwe
you know *(nachgestellt)*	..., wissen Sie
the rest [rest]	der Rest, das übrige, die übrigen
and all the rest	*und alles, was sonst noch dazugehört*
I stayed there two years ago [ə'gəu]	ich wohnte dort vor zwei Jahren
at once [ət 'wʌns]	sofort
to have a vision of ['viʒən]	*sich ein Bild ausmalen von* sich vorstellen
warm [wɔ:m]	warm
heart [hɑ:t]	Herz
warm-hearted ['wɔ:mhɑ:tid]	warmherzig
comfortable ['kʌmfətəbl]	bequem, behaglich
party ['pɑ:ti]	Gesellschaft
game [geim]	Spiel
laughter ['lɑ:ftə]	Lachen, Gelächter
to decide [di'said]	sich entschließen
the Tube [tju:b]	(wörtl.: die Röhre; volkstüml. Bezeichnung f. d. Londoner Untergrundbahn)
when [wen]	wenn, als
to turn to the right [tə:n]	*nach rechts abbiegen*
Queen Victoria's days	*die Zeiten Königin Viktorias* (1819-1901)
alike [ə'laik]	gleich sein
to recall [ri'kɔ:l]	ins Gedächtnis zurückrufen, erinnern an
rich [ritʃ]	reich
middle class ['midl klɑ:s]	Mittelstand
broad [brɔ:d]	breit
notice ['nəutis]	Notiz; Schild
'*Bed and breakfast*'	*Zimmer mit Frühstück*
to let [let]	lassen; vermieten
'*Rooms to let*'	Mz *Zimmer zu vermieten*
district ['distrikt]	Bezirk
dormitory ['dɔ:mitri]	Schlafsaal; hier: Schlaf-, Nachtquartier
a thousand ['θauzənd]	tausend
thousands of	Tausende von
clerk [klɑ:k]	Büroangestellter
student ['stju:dənt]	Student
to look for	schauen nach, suchen
I did [ai 'did]	ich tat
such [sʌtʃ]	solche(r, s)
narrow ['nærəu]	eng, schmal
hall [hɔ:l]	Flur, Diele
hope [həup]	Hoffnung
spirits ['spirits]	Stimmung
to drop [drɔp]	fallen / sinken; fallen lassen
his spirits dropped	*seine Stimmung sank*
sight [sait]	Sicht; Anblick
at the sight of	beim Anblick von
thin [θin]	dünn, mager
orange ['ɔrindʒ]	Orange; orange
coloured ['kʌləd]	farbig
orange-coloured	orangefarben
floor [flɔ:]	Fußboden; Stockwerk
on the top floor ['tɔp 'flɔ:]	im obersten Stockwerk
terms, *Mehrz.* [tə:mz]	Bedingungen, Preise
£ 17 = seventeen pounds [paundz]	17 Pfund (1 Pfund = ca. DM 6,–)
£ 17 a week	17 Pfund pro Woche, in der Woche
would you like to ...?	*möchten Sie ...?*
to nod [nɔd]	nicken
stairs [stɛəz]	Treppenhaus, Treppe
up the stairs	*die Treppe hinauf*
dark [dɑ:k]	dunkel
make yourself at home	wörtl.: (machen Sie sich's wie zu Hause) *machen Sie sich's bequem*
third [θə:d]	(der, die, das) dritte
every time I step ...	jedesmal wenn ich ... trete
into the street	auf die Straße
to think of	denken an
to wonder ['wʌndə]	sich fragen / wundern
inside ['in'said]	innerhalb, im Innern

Booking a Room

to book [buk]	(vor)bestellen
booking a room	(wörtl.: das Vorbestellen eines Zimmers) Zimmerbestellung
Kensington Gardens ['kensiŋtən 'gɑ:dnz]	(westl. Fortsetzung des Hyde Park)
hotel [həu'tel]	Hotel
Sq. = square [skwɛə]	Platz
W. 2 = West 2 ['dʌblju: 'tu:]	
to reserve [ri'zə:v]	reservieren
single room ['siŋgl 'rum]	Einzelzimmer
cold [kəuld]	kalt
running water ['rʌniŋ 'wɔ:tə]	fließendes Wasser
May [mei]	Mai
May 17/18th (*read:* May the seventeenth to eighteenth)	17./18. Mai

kindly ['kaindli]	freundlich(erweise)
to confirm [kən'fə:m]	bestätigen
kindly confirm	*ich bitte höflich um Bestätigung*
bird [bə:d]	Vogel (hier: Familienname)
double room ['dʌbl 'rum]	Doppelzimmer
quiet ['kwaiət]	ruhig
a room at the back	*ein Zimmer nach hinten*
key [ki:]	Schlüssel
lift [lift]	Aufzug, Fahrstuhl
he will show you up	*er wird Sie hinaufführen*
to call [kɔ:l]	hier: wecken
service ['sə:vis]	Dienst, Bedienung
to include [in'klu:d]	einschließen
the service is not included	*Bedienung ist nicht inbegriffen*
bill [bil]	Rechnung
tip [tip]	Trinkgeld
also ['ɔ:lsəu]	auch

16 He Says It the English Way

to say, said, said [sei, sed]	sagen, sagte, gesagt
he says it the English way	*er sagt es auf englische Art*
Englishman, *Mehrz.* Englishmen ['iŋgliʃmən]	Engländer
to do, did, done [du:, did, dʌn]	tun
to show, showed, shown [ʃəu, ʃəud, ʃəun]	zeigen
feeling ['fi:liŋ]	Gefühl
school [sku:l]	Schule
schoolboy ['sku:lbɔi]	Schuljunge
to learn, learnt (learned), **learnt** (learned) [lə:n, lə:nt (lə:nd)]	lernen
at school	in der Schule
to practise ['præktis]	(aus)üben; praktisch anwenden
a letter to	ein Brief an
lonely ['ləunli]	einsam
top [tɔp]	Spitze, Gipfel; (Baum-)Krone
July 3rd (*read:* July the third) [dʒu'lai]	3. Juli
since [sins]	seit
to go, went, gone [gəu, went, gɔn]	gehen
it has gone well	es ist gutgegangen
all the time	die ganze Zeit
the dog has missed you all the time	der Hund hat dich die ganze Zeit über vermißt
button ['bʌtn]	Knopf
the buttons have gone	*die Knöpfe sind abgegangen*
to worry ['wʌri]	sich Sorgen machen
I need not (needn't) do it ['ni:dnt]	ich brauche es nicht zu tun
to sew, sewed, sewn [səu, səud, səun]	nähen
to sew on ['səu‿'ɔn]	annähen
dirty ['də:ti]	schmutzig
anyway ['eniwei]	sowieso, ohnehin
to starve [stɑ:v]	(ver)hungern
cook [kuk]	Koch, Köchin
to have, had, had [hæv, hæd]	haben
tin [tin]	Konservendose
tinned [tind]	in, aus Dosen, Büchsen-
corned beef ['kɔ:nd 'bi:f]	Büchsen(rind)fleisch
pea [pi:]	Erbse
last [lɑ:st]	(der, die, das) letzte
garage ['gærɑ:dʒ]	Garage
to notice ['nəutis]	bemerken, feststellen
to forget, forgot, forgotten [fə'get, fə'gɔt, fə'gɔtn]	vergessen
to turn off [tə:n 'ɔf]	ausschalten
headlight ['hedlait]	Scheinwerfer (am Auto)
to be, was, been [bi:, wɔz, bi:n]	sein
to be on	an sein, (vom Licht) brennen
weekend ['wi:k'end]	Wochenende
battery ['bætəri]	Batterie
the battery was flat	*die Batterie war leer*
yesterday ['jestədi]	gestern
to send, sent, sent [send, sent]	senden, schicken
evening dress ['i:vniŋ 'dres]	Abendkleid
to hope [həup]	hoffen
to fit	passen
by the way	übrigens, nebenbei bemerkt
to kick [kik]	stoßen, treten
football ['futbɔ:l]	Fußball
through [θru:]	durch (... hindurch)
butcher ['butʃə]	Metzger, Fleischer
to break, broke, broken [breik, brəuk, 'brəukən]	(zer)brechen
to give, gave, given [giv, geiv, 'givn]	geben
I gave him a good hiding ['haidiŋ]	*ich gab ihm eine ordentliche Tracht Prügel*

to keep, kept, kept [ki:p, kept]	halten
company ['kʌmpəni]	Gesellschaft
to keep s.o. company	*jdm. Gesellschaft leisten*
her idea of this	ihre Vorstellung davon
to sit, sat, sat [sit, sæt]	sitzen
fire ['faiə]	Feuer
by the fire [bai ðə 'faiə]	am Kaminfeuer
cat [kæt]	Katze
kitten ['kitn]	junges Kätzchen
the cat has had kittens	*die Katze hat Junge bekommen*
armchair ['ɑ:m'tʃɛə]	Sessel
proud [praud]	stolz
rum [rʌm]	Rum
some rum	etwas Rum
cold [kəuld]	kalt; Kälte; Erkältung
empty ['empti]	leer
to make, made, made [meik, meid]	machen
punch [pʌntʃ]	Punsch
to cheer s.o. up ['tʃiər‿'ʌp]	jdn. aufheitern
to drink, drank, drunk [driŋk, dræŋk, drʌŋk]	trinken
to phone for a taxi	*nach einem Taxi telefonieren*
I could [ai 'kud]	ich konnte
to walk [wɔ:k]	zu Fuß gehen
to get, got, got [get, gɔt, gɔt]	bekommen
to come, came, come [kʌm, keim, kʌm]	kommen
Jack [dʒæk]	Hans
burglar ['bə:glə]	Einbrecher
last night ['lɑ:st 'nait]	die vergangene Nacht, gestern abend
to steal, stole, stolen [sti:l, stəul, 'stəulən]	stehlen
coat [kəut]	Mantel
fur coat ['fə: 'kəut]	Pelzmantel

At the Restaurant

to see, saw, seen [si:, sɔ:, si:n]	sehen
menu ['menju:]	Speisekarte
I haven't seen it yet	*ich habe sie noch nicht gesehen*
to help	helfen
could you help me? [kud]	könnten Sie mir behilflich sein?
I've forgotten my glasses ['glɑ:siz]	ich habe meine Brille vergessen
certainly ['sə:tnli]	sicherlich, gewiß
excellent ['eksələnt]	ausgezeichnet
course [kɔ:s]	Lauf, Kursus
three-course dinner	*Abendessen mit drei Gängen*
hungry ['hʌŋgri]	hungrig
I'd like something light [lait]	*ich möchte etwas Leichtes*
breast [brest]	Brust
chicken ['tʃikin]	Hähnchen, Hühnchen
breast of chicken	Hühnerbrüstchen
for a long time	*seit langem*
sausage ['sɔsidʒ]	Wurst
taste [teist]	Geschmack
to think, thought, thought [θɔ:t]	denken
to choose, chose, chosen [tʃu:z, tʃəuz, 'tʃəuzn]	wählen, auswählen
have you chosen one yet?	*haben sie schon eins gewählt?*
afterwards ['ɑ:ftəwədz]	danach; später

17 Betting, a National Amusement

betting ['betiŋ]	Wetten
national ['næʃənl]	national
amusement [ə'mju:zmənt]	Vergnügen
over ['əuvə]	über
betting shop	Wettbüro
Great Britain ['greit 'britn]	Großbritannien
reason ['ri:zn]	Grund
to avoid [ə'vɔid]	vermeiden
tax [tæx]	Steuer
at the same time	gleichzeitig
to lose, lost, lost [lu:z, lɔst]	verlieren
fortune ['fɔ:tʃən]	Vermögen
people make and lose fortunes this way	*Leute machen und verlieren Vermögen auf diese Art*
to spend, spent, spent [spend, spent]	ausgeben
horse [hɔ:s]	Pferd
to spend about £1,100 million on horse-racing ['hɔ:sreisiŋ]	*ungefähr 1,1 Milliarden Pfund für Pferderennen ausgegeben*
alone [ə'ləun]	allein
Derby ['dɑ:bi]	(bedeutendstes engl. Pferderennen)
great [greit]	groß, bedeutend
event [i'vent]	Ereignis
race-course ['reis-kɔ:s]	Rennbahn
to take, took, taken place [teik, tuk, 'teikən 'pleis]	stattfinden
Epsom ['epsəm]	
inhabitant [in'hæbitənt]	Einwohner
south of London ['sauθ‿əv 'lʌndən]	südlich von London

lord [lɔ:d]	Lord (Adelstitel)
to found [faund]	gründen
classic [ˈklæsik]	klassisch
race [reis]	Rennen
to stretch [stretʃ]	sich erstrecken
mile [mail]	Meile
metre [ˈmi:tə]	Meter
employee [ˌemplɔiˈi:]	Angestellter
absent [ˈæbsənt]	abwesend
nobody [ˈnəubədi]	niemand
first … [fə:st] secondly [ˈsekəndli]	erstens … zweitens
to know, knew, known [nəu, nju:, nəun]	kennen, wissen
result [riˈzʌlt]	Ergebnis, Resultat
to win, won, won [win, wʌn]	gewinnen
pleased [pli:zd]	erfreut
to lend, lent, lent [lend, lent]	leihen
I'm afraid I can't [əˈfreid]	*ich kann leider nicht*
the second time	das zweite Mal
month [mʌnθ]	Monat
to bet [bet]	wetten
at least [li:st]	wenigstens
bet [bet]	Wette
once a month [wʌns]	einmal im Monat
twice a month [twais]	zweimal im Monat
dad [dæd]	Vater (Koseform)
to begin, began, begun [biˈgin, biˈgæn, biˈgʌn]	beginnen
I bet you ten pounds [paundz]	*ich wette mit dir um zehn Pfund*
beard [biəd]	Bart
proud of	stolz auf
to pay, paid, paid [pei, peid]	zahlen
within [wiˈðin]	innerhalb
to teach, taught, taught [ti:tʃ, tɔ:t]	lehren
to teach s.o. a lesson	*jdm. eine Lektion erteilen*
just wait and see [dʒʌst]	*warte nur ab*
to tell, told, told [təuld]	sagen, erzählen
to serve [sə:v]	bedienen, dienen; jdm. etwas zufügen
servieren	
it serves you right	*es geschieht dir recht*
mum [mʌm]	Mutter (Koseform)

At the Village Shop

village [ˈvilidʒ]	Dorf
can I help you?	*kann ich Ihnen behilflich sein?, was darf's sein?*
how much is (are) …?	*was kostet (kosten) …?*
to cost, cost, cost [kɔst]	kosten
six pence [ˈsiksˈpens]	(ca. DM 0,37)
black-and-white	schwarzweiß
four pence [ˈfɔ:ˈpens]	(ca. DM 0,25)
to sell, sold, sold [sel, səuld]	verkaufen
abroad [əˈbrɔ:d]	im (ins) Ausland
for home or abroad?	*fürs In- oder Ausland?*
postage [ˈpəustidʒ]	Postgebühr, Porto
anything? [ˈeniθiŋ]	(irgend) etwas?
anything else? [ˈeniθiŋ ˈels]	sonst noch etwas?
anything else I can do for you?	(wörtl.: sonst noch etwas, das ich für Sie tun kann?) *darf es sonst noch etwas sein?*
envelope [ˈenvələup]	Briefumschlag
writing-paper [ˈraitiŋˌpeipə]	Briefpapier
match [mætʃ]	Streichholz
a box of matches [ˈmætʃiz]	eine Schachtel Streichhölzer
packet [ˈpækit]	Packung, Schachtel
brand [brænd]	Marke
Players [ˈpleiəz]	(Zigarettenmarke)
a cake of soap [səup]	ein Stück Seife
electric razor [iˈlektrik ˈreizə]	elektrischer Rasierapparat
a tube of tooth-paste [tju:b, ˈtu:θpeist]	eine Tube Zahnpasta
a bar of chocolate [bɑ:, ˈtʃɔkəlit]	eine Tafel Schokolade
shall I? [ʃæl]	soll ich?
to wrap up [ˈræp ˈʌp]	einpacken, -wickeln
to put, put, put [put]	setzen, legen, stellen; hier: (hinein)tun
plastic bag [ˈplæstik ˈbæg]	Kunststofftüte
to leave, left, left [li:v, left]	verlassen

18 A Ticket to Washington

a ticket to Washington [ˈtikit, ˈwɔʃiŋtən]	eine Fahrkarte nach Washington
to fly, flew, flown [flai, flu:, fləun]	fliegen
tomorrow [təˈmɔrəu]	morgen
business [ˈbiznis]	Geschäft
a New York businessman [ˈnju:ˈjɔ:k ˈbiznismən]	ein New Yorker Geschäftsmann
secretary [ˈsekrətri]	Sekretär(in)
to call the airline [ˈɛə-lain]	die Fluggesellschaft anrufen
return [riˈtə:n]	Rückkehr, Rück-

return flight [ri:'tə:n flait]	Rückflug
11 a.m. [i'levn 'ei 'em]	11 Uhr vormittags
on April 3rd (*read:* on April the third) ['eipril ðə‿'θə:d]	am dritten April
about 3 p.m. [ə'baut 'θri: 'pi:'em]	gegen 3 Uhr nachmittags
to finish ['finiʃ]	beenden
to add [æd]	hinzufügen
are there any telegrams? ['teligræm]	sind irgendwelche Telegramme da?
not ... any	keine
to dictate [dik'teit]	diktieren
to dial 9734066 ['daiəl] (*read:* nine-seven-three-four-o- [əu] double six)	wählen (beim Telefon)
necessary arrangements ['nesisəri ə'reindʒments]	notwendige Vorkehrungen
March 31st (March the thirty-first) [mɑ:tʃ]	31. März
while he was on his way [wail]	während er unterwegs war
airport ['ɛə-pɔ:t]	Flughafen
to be missing ['misiŋ]	fehlen
to return [ri'tə:n]	zurückkehren
have you seen my tickets anywhere? ['eniwɛə]	haben Sie meine Flugscheine irgendwo gesehen?
have you any idea where you left them? [ai'diə]	haben Sie irgendeine Ahnung, wo Sie sie gelassen haben?
to find, found, found [faind, faund]	finden
out of the office [aut‿əv]	aus dem Büro
possible ['pɔsəbl]	möglich
therefore ['ðɛəfɔ:]	deswegen

to take, took, taken [tuk, 'teikən]	nehmen
trip [trip]	Reise
during his stay ['djuəriŋ, stei]	während seines Aufenthaltes
busy ['bizi]	beschäftigt
extra day ['ekstrə]	Extra-, weiterer Tag
for [fɔ:]	denn
like other tourists ['tuərist]	wie andere Touristen
president ['prezidənt]	Präsident
the White House ['wait 'haus]	(offiz. Sitz des am. Präsidenten)
to travel back by plane ['trævl]	mit dem Flugzeug zurückreisen
to reach [ri:tʃ]	erreichen
at 15.45 hours	um 15.45 Uhr
rather tired ['rɑ:ðə 'taiəd]	ziemlich müde
to drive, drove, driven [draiv, drəuv, 'drivn]	fahren
grass [grɑ:s]	Gras
immediately [i'mi:djətli]	sofort
to stare (at) [stɛə]	(an)starren
anything wrong? [rɔŋ]	stimmt etwas nicht?
to run, ran, run [ʌ, æ, ʌ]	laufen, rennen
the house next door	Nachbarhaus
to stand, stood, stood [u]	stehen
mouth [mauθ]	Mund
wide [waid]	weit
to crash [kræʃ]	abstürzen
police [pə'li:s]	Polizei
dead [ded]	tot
to inform [in'fɔ:m]	informieren, benachrichtigen
death [deθ]	Tod
to be surprised [sə'praizd]	überrascht sein

deep [di:p]	tief
breath [breθ]	Atem
he took a deep breath	er holte tief Atem
finally ['fainəli]	endlich, schließlich
somebody must have found my tickets ['sʌmbədi]	jemand muß meine Flugkarten gefunden haben
by train	mit dem Zug
to be lucky ['lʌki]	Glück haben
I was born lucky [bɔ:n]	ich wurde als Glückspilz geboren

In a Railway Carriage

railway carriage ['reilwei 'kæridʒ]	Eisenbahnwagen
excuse me [iks'kju:z]	*entschuldigen Sie (bitte)!*
I'm afraid so [ə'freid]	*Ich fürchte ja; leider ja*
to occupy ['ɔkjupai]	besetzen
occupied	besetzt
nearly ['niəli]	beinahe
Leamington Spa ['lemiŋtən 'spɑ:]	(Badeort in Mittelengland)
Birmingham ['bə:miŋəm]	(Industriestadt in Mittelengland)
I've got to change [tʃeindʒ]	ich muß umsteigen
upon [ə'pɔn]	auf
Stratford-upon-Avon ['strætfəd əpɔn 'eivən]	(Stadt in Mittelengland; Shakespeares Geburtsort)
ticket-collector ['tikitkə'lektə]	Schaffner
difference ['difrəns]	Unterschied
fare [fɛə]	Fahrpreis
return fare	Rückfahrpreis
departure [di'pɑ:tʃə]	Abfahrt

connection to [kə'nekʃən]	Verbindung nach
arrival [ə'raivəl]	Ankunft
all right ['ɔ:l'rait]	in Ordnung, recht
that's all right	*schon gut, bitte sehr*

Exercises

I. the day after tomorrow	übermorgen
the day before yesterday	vorgestern
New Year's Day ['nju: jə:z 'dei]	Neujahr
Easter ['i:stə]	Ostern
Whitsun ['witsn]	Pfingsten

19 A Sunday in Hyde Park

world [wə:ld]	Welt
all over the world	*in der ganzen Welt*
people who ...	Leute, die ...
walk [wɔ:k]	Spaziergang
to go for a walk	*einen Spaziergang machen, spazierengehen*
weekday ['wi:kdei]	Wochentag, Werktag
on weekdays	*werktags*
playground ['plei-graund]	Spielplatz
democracy [di'mɔkrəsi]	Demokratie
political [pə'litikəl]	politisch
non-political ['nɔn 'pəlitikəl]	unpolitisch
speaker ['spi:kə]	Sprecher, Redner
kind [kaind]	Art
of all kinds	aller Art
speech [spi:tʃ]	Rede
to make a speech	*eine Rede halten*
soap-box	Seifenkiste
to hear, heard, heard [hiə, hə:d]	hören
opposite ['ɔpəzit]	entgegengesetzt
opinion [ə'pinjən]	Meinung
yard [jɑ:d]	yard (ca. 90 cm)
6 yards apart [ə'pɑ:t]	6 Meter voneinander entfernt
nobody minds	*niemand nimmt Anstoß, hat etwas dagegen*
not even ['i:vən]	nicht einmal
practical ['præktikəl]	praktisch
tolerance ['tɔlərəns]	Toleranz, Duldsamkeit
tall [tɔ:l]	groß, (hoch) gewachsen
fellow ['feləu]	Bursche, Kerl
to let, let, let [let]	lassen
to listen (to s.o.) ['lisn]	horchen, (jdm.) zuhören
prison ['prizn]	Gefängnis
different ['difrənt]	verschieden
country ['kʌntri]	Land
sinner ['sinə]	Sünder
to start s.th.	etwas anfangen, beginnen
if I had not started ...	wenn ich nicht ... begonnen hätte
hopeless ['həuplis]	hoffnungslos
drinker ['driŋkə]	Trinker
one night	eines Nachts
dream [dri:m]	Traum
from now on	*von nun an, von jetzt ab*
to come to an end	zu Ende gehen, untergehen
terrible ['terəbl]	schrecklich
war [wɔ:]	Krieg
disease [di'zi:z]	Krankheit
to follow ['fɔləu]	folgen
man, *Mehrz.* men	Mann, Mensch
to die [dai]	sterben
flood [flʌd]	Flut
devil ['devl]	Teufel
government ['gʌvnmənt]	Regierung, Herrschaft
to rule [ru:l]	beherrschen, regieren
to awake, awoke, awoke [ə'weik, ə'wəuk]	erwachen
a light had come upon me [ə'pɔn]	ein Licht war über mich gekommen
drop	Tropfen
alcohol ['ælkəhɔl]	Alkohol
since [sins]	seither
Doomsday ['du:mzdei]	Jüngster Tag, Jüngstes Gericht
brotherhood ['brʌðəhud]	Bruderschaft
league [li:g]	Bund, Verband
Doomsday Brotherhood League	Bruderschaft des Jüngsten Gerichts
to join s.th. [dʒɔin]	sich einer Sache anschließen, beitreten
to become, became, become [bi'kʌm, bi'keim, bi'kʌm]	werden
for 50 pence a year	*für 50 Pence im Jahr*
to welcome s.o. to ['welkəm]	jdn. willkommen heißen in
red light	Zeichen der Gefahr, Warnsignal
I'm sure you'll find	*ich bin sicher, daß Sie finden, Sie finden sicher*
happiness ['hæpinis]	Glück
peace [pi:s]	Frieden
fight [fait]	Kampf
against [ə'genst]	gegen

sin [sin]	Sünde
path [pɑ:θ]	Pfad
pure [pjuə]	rein

Asking the Way

to ask the way [ɑ:sk]	*nach dem Weg fragen*
nearest ['niərist]	nächst(gelegen)
Underground station ['ʌndəgraund]	U-Bahnstation
I ... myself [mai'self]	ich selbst
could you ... ?	könnten Sie ... ?
Waterloo Station ['wɔ:təlu: 'steiʃən]	(Londoner Bahnhof, s. Stadtplan)
quick [kwik]	schnell
what is the quickest way to ... ? ['kwikist]	*wie komme ich am schnellsten zu ... ?*
take the second turning on the left ['tə:niŋ]	*biegen Sie in die zweite Querstraße links ein*
to turn right	rechts einbiegen
about [ə'baut]	etwa, ungefähr
you'd better take a bus	*Sie täten besser daran, einen Bus zu nehmen; fahren Sie lieber mit dem Bus*
to lose one's way	sich verirren
then change onto a No. 52 bus	dann steigen Sie in einen Bus der Linie 52 um
how long will it take me ?	*wie lange werde ich (dazu) brauchen ?*
to get to the station	am Bahnhof anlangen
thank you so much	*herzlichen Dank*
not at all	*keine Ursache, bitte*
to mention ['menʃən]	erwähnen
don't mention it	*nicht der Rede wert, bitte sehr*

20 Teaching English

as in other countries	wie in (den) anderen Ländern
most countries	*die meisten Länder*
Europe ['juərəp]	Europa
European ['juərə'pi(:)ən]	europäisch Europäer(in)
household help ['haushəuld hɛlp]	Haushalthilfe
scarce [skɛəs]	rar, knapp
continent ['kɔntinənt]	Kontinent, Erdteil
the Continent	der europäische Kontinent
to be prepared to [pri'pɛəd]	bereit sein zu
to look after	aufpassen auf
household ['haushəuld]	Haushalt
to work [wə:k]	arbeiten
hospital ['hɔspitl]	Krankenhaus
special ['speʃəl]	besondere(r, s)
class [kla:s]	klasse
evening classes	Abendkurse
language ['læŋgwidʒ]	Sprache
classroom ['kla:srum]	Klassenzimmer
verb [və:b]	Zeitwort
irregular verb [i'regjulə]	unregelmäßiges Zeitwort
tense [tens]	(grammatische) Zeit, Tempus
to eat, ate, eaten [i:t, et, 'i:tn]	essen
Dutch [dʌtʃ]	holländisch
she puts up her hand	*sie streckt ihre Hand hoch*
flesh [fleʃ]	Fleisch (des lebenden Körpers)
you ought to ['ɔ:t‿tə]	Sie sollten
to remember [ri'membə]	sich erinnern an, sich (etw.) merken
to rhyme [raim]	sich reimen
to sink, sank, sunk [siŋk, sæŋk, sʌŋk]	sinken
to be able to ['eibl]	können
to draw, drew, drawn [drɔ:, dru:, drɔ:n]	zeichnen; ziehen
animal ['æniməl]	Tier
ox, *Mehrz.* oxen [ɔks, 'ɔksən]	Ochse
calf, *Mehrz.* calves [kɑ:f, kɑ:vz]	Kalb
sheep, *Mehrz.* sheep [ʃi:p]	Schaf
pig [pig]	Schwein
what kind of animal ?	*was für ein Tier ?*
student ['stju:dənt]	Student; (erwachsener) Schüler
cow [kau]	Kuh
to point out ['pɔint‿'aut]	erklären, darauf hinweisen ausführen
drawing ['drɔ:iŋ]	Zeichnung
direct [di'rekt]	direkt, gerade
line [lain]	Linie
beef [bi:f]	Rindfleisch
(beef)steak [('bi:f)steik]	Beefsteak
to explain [iks'plein]	erklären
the calf which [witʃ]	das Kalb, welches (das)
to take for	halten für
goat [gəut]	Ziege
donkey ['dɔŋki]	Esel
cutlet ['kʌtlit]	(Kalbs-)Schnitzel
veal [vi:l]	Kalbfleisch
mutton ['mʌtn]	Hammelfleisch

pork [pɔ:k]	Schweinefleisch
to prepare [pri'pɛə]	vorbereiten, zubereiten
Austrian ['ɔstriən]	österreichisch; Österreicher(in)
you see	*sehen Sie, wissen Sie*
Germanic [dʒə:'mænik]	germanisch
Norman, *Mehrz.* Normans ['nɔ:mən(z)]	Normanne
to conquer ['kɔŋkə]	erobern
to speak French	Französisch sprechen
master ['mɑ:stə]	Meister, Herr
to sit down	sich setzen
Anglo-Saxon ['æŋgləu'sæksən]	angelsächsisch
in French	*auf französisch*
origin ['ɔridʒin]	Ursprung
to understand, understood, understood [ˌʌndə'stænd, ˌʌndə'stud]	verstehen
mixture ['mikstʃə]	Mischung

We Attend Evening Classes

to attend evening classes [ə'tend]	(einen) Abendkurs(e) besuchen
present ['preznt]	anwesend, da
Curry ['kʌri]	(Familienname)
what's the matter with him?	*was ist mit ihm los?*
to speak, spoke, spoken [spi:k, spəuk, 'spəukən]	sprechen
fast [fɑ:st]	schnell
pronunciation [prəˌnʌnsi'eiʃən]	Aussprache
meaning ['mi:niŋ]	Bedeutung
to look up a word	ein Wort nachschlagen
dictionary ['dikʃənri]	Wörterbuch
similar ['similə]	ähnlich
paragraph ['pærəgrɑ:f]	Abschnitt
text	Text
to interrupt [ˌintə'rʌpt]	unterbrechen
to collect [kə'lekt]	sammeln
textbook ['tekstbuk]	Lehrbuch

21 Alone Among Millions

wanted ['wɔntid]	(in Zeitungsanzeigen) gesucht
companion [kəm'pænjən]	Kamerad(in), Begleiter(in); Gesellschafterin
to apply to [ə'plai]	sich wenden an, sich bewerben bei
apply Box K 31	Zuschriften unter Chiffre K 31
advertisement [əd'və:tismənt]	(Zeitungs-)Anzeige
personal ['pə:snl]	persönlich
column ['kɔləm]	Spalte
personal column	Spalte „Persönliches", „Verschiedenes"
Sunday Times ['sʌndi 'taimz]	(große engl. Sonntagszeitung)
to start s.th. [stɑ:t]	hier: etw. in Gang bringen
she was a companion to	sie war Gesellschafterin bei
Bunby ['bʌnbi]	(Familienname)
to take s.o. out	jdn. ausführen
wheel [wi:l]	Rad
wheel chair ['wi:l tʃɛə]	Rollstuhl
the park near by	der Park in der Nähe, der nahegelegene Park
to read, read, read [ri:d, red, red]	lesen
to read to s.o.	jdm. vorlesen
unhappy [ʌn'hæpi]	unglücklich
although, though [ɔ:l'ðəu, ðəu]	obwohl
to treat [tri:t]	behandeln
to be homesick ['həum-sik]	Heimweh haben
obvious ['ɔbviəs]	offensichtlich
she obviously missed	offensichtlich vermißte sie
international [ˌintə(:)'næʃənl]	international
head office ['hed‿ɔfis]	Hauptgeschäftsstelle, Hauptsitz
branch [brɑ:ntʃ]	Zweig; Zweigstelle
aim [eim]	Ziel
to promote [prə'məut]	fördern
between [bi'twi:n]	zwischen
nation ['neiʃən]	Nation, Volk
to write, wrote, written [rait, rəut, 'ritn]	schreiben
invitation [ˌinvi'teiʃən]	Einladung
dance [dɑ:ns]	Tanz
youth [ju:θ]	Jugend
youth hostel ['ju:θ hɔstəl]	Jugendherberge, Jugendheim
to accept [ək'sept]	annehmen
glad [glæd]	froh, erfreut
gladly ['glædli]	gern
hall [hɔ:l]	Halle, Saal
dance hall ['dɑ:ns hɔ:l]	Tanzsaal
'Paul Jones' ['pɔ:l 'dʒəunz]	Marschwalzer (Tanzspiel)
already [ɔ:l'redi]	schon
in full swing	*in vollem Gang*
to form [fɔ:m]	bilden

inner ['inə]	(der, die, das) innere
circle ['sə:kl]	Kreis
ring	Ring
	um ... herum
	(sich) bewegen
	sie bewegten sich gerade → im Moment
	Richtung
	Melodie
	nach der Melodie von
	Marsch
	mitten drin
	Walzer
	sich jdm. zuwenden
	wie zuvor
	weitergehen
	einige Zeit (lang)
	(sich) treffen, begegnen, kennenlernen
	sind wir uns nicht schon 'mal begegnet?
	Franzose
	zum dritten Mal
	meine Lieblingsmelodie
	Lied
	(ich) selbst
	(wörtl.: es ist genannt) *es heißt*
	hüte dich vor
	nicht mehr
	fleißig arbeiten
	willig
	sich freuen auf
	geselliges Treffen

excursion [iks'kə:ʃən]	Ausflug
discussion [dis'kʌʃən]	Diskussion, Gespräch

A Date

date [deit]	Datum; Verabredung
have you anything on?	*haben Sie etwas vor?*
how about going for a walk?	*wie wär's mit einem Spaziergang?*
to pick s.o. up	*jdn. (mit dem Wagen) abholen*
outside Woolworths ['autsaid 'wulwə(:)θs]	vor Woolworth
all right ['ɔ:l 'rait]	*in Ordnung, recht*
are you on the phone?	*haben Sie Telefon?*
see you on Saturday	*auf Wiedersehen am (bis) Samstag*

22 Safety Last

safety ['seifti]	Sicherheit
safety last	etwa: *Sicherheit an letzter Stelle* (Abwandlung des bekannten Mottos: 'Safety first')
to buy, bought, bought [bai, bɔ:t]	kaufen
second-hand ['sekənd'hænd]	gebraucht
car-dealer ['kɑ:ˌdi:lə]	Autohändler
in cash [kæʃ]	bar
to belong to [bi'lɔŋ]	gehören
including [in'klu:diŋ]	einschließlich
tyre ['taiə]	(Auto-)Reifen
engine ['endʒin]	Maschine; Motor
Marjorie ['mɑ:dʒəri]	(weibl. Vorname)

to go for a drive [draiv]	*eine (Auto-)Fahrt machen, spazieren fahren*
to press [pres]	drücken
starter ['stɑ:tə]	Anlasser
to press the starter	auf den Anlasser drücken
gear [giə]	Gang (beim Auto)
bottom gear ['bɔtəm 'giə]	erster Gang
to put the car into bottom gear	*den ersten Gang einschalten*
off they went	*sie fuhren los*
to leave, left, left [li:v, left]	(ver-, zurück-) lassen
they left the town behind them	sie ließen die Stadt hinter sich zurück
to speed, sped, sped [spi:d, sped]	eilen, sausen, flitzen
to speed along a road [ə'lɔŋ]	eine Straße entlangsausen
speedometer [spi'dɔmitə]	Geschwindigkeitsanzeiger, Tachometer
needle ['ni:dl]	Nadel; Zeiger
70 miles an hour	70 Meilen in der Stunde, 70 Stundenmeilen
speed [spi:d]	Geschwindigkeit
at top speed ['tɔp 'spi:d]	mit Höchstgeschwindigkeit
mountain ['mauntin]	Berg
valley ['væli]	Tal
lake [leik]	See
Lake District ['leikˌdistrikt]	(Seengebiet in Nordengland)
effort ['efət]	Bemühung, Anstrengung

racing driver ['reisiŋ 'draivə]	Rennfahrer
careful ['kɛəful]	vorsichtig
to spoil, spoilt, spoilt [spɔil, spɔilt]	verderben
fun [fʌn]	Spaß
she spoils my fun	*sie verdirbt mir den Spaß*
distance ['distəns]	Entfernung, Strecke; hier: Raum
crash [kræʃ]	Krachen; (schwerer) Zusammenstoß
it's my fault [fɔ:lt]	*ich bin schuld*
puncture ['pʌŋktʃə]	Loch (im Reifen), (Reifen-)Panne
to run into a tree .	*gegen einen Baum fahren*
to slow down	die Geschwindigkeit herabsetzen, langsamer fahren
I shall [ʃæl]	ich werde
more than [ðæn, ðən]	mehr als
brake [breik]	Bremse
to get near a village	in die Nähe eines Dorfes, zu einem Dorf kommen
limit ['limit]	Grenze
speed limit ['spi:d ˌlimit]	Geschwindigkeitsgrenze, zugelassene Höchstgeschwindigkeit
to change into second gear	in den zweiten Gang schalten
beyond the village [bi'jɔnd]	jenseits des Dorfes, hinter dem Dorf
to prepare for [pri'pɛə]	(sich) vorbereiten auf; hier: ansetzen zu
speed record ['spi:d ˌrekɔ:d]	Geschwindigkeitsrekord
he tried the starter [traid]	er probierte am Anlasser herum
the engine would not start	der Motor wollte nicht anspringen
probably ['prɔbəbli]	wahrscheinlich
loose [lu:s]	lose
wire ['waiə]	Draht
to repair [ri'pɛə]	reparieren
to climb [klaim]	klettern
to climb out	herausklettern, (hin)aussteigen
to lift	(hoch)heben
bonnet ['bɔnit]	Haube; Motorhaube
air [ɛə]	Gesichtsausdruck, Miene
expert ['ekspə:t]	Fachmann
screw [skru:]	Schraube
to push [puʃ]	schieben
garage ['gærɑ:dʒ]	Garage; Autoreparaturwerkstätte
mechanic [mi'kænik]	Mechaniker
petrol ['petrəl]	Benzin
gallon ['gælən]	Gallone (ca. 4,5 l)
she needs ...	(Fahrzeuge bezeichnet man manchmal mit 'she')
juice [dʒu:s]	Saft; hier: Sprit
tank	Tank
filling-station ['filiŋˌsteiʃən]	Tankstelle

A Breakdown

breakdown ['breikdaun]	Panne
to break down (broke, broken) ['breik 'daun, (brəuk, 'brəukən)]	(vom Auto) eine Panne haben
accident ['æksidənt]	Unfall
to bump (crash) into [bʌmp (kræʃ)]	auffahren auf, zusammenstoßen mit
flat [flæt]	flach, platt
flat tyre	Reifenpanne
we're out of petrol	*das Benzin ist (uns) ausgegangen*
heaven [ˌhevn]	Himmel
thank Heaven ['θæŋk 'hevn]	dem Himmel sei Dank
serious ['siəriəs]	ernst, ernsthaft
to give s.o. a lift	*jdn. (im Auto) mitnehmen*
thank you	(als Antwort auf ein Angebot) ja bitte
to drop s.o.	*jdn. absetzen, aussteigen lassen*
on the way back	*auf dem Rückweg*

23 Friday the Thirteenth

Rhona ['rəunə]	(weibl. Vorname)
superstitious [ˌsu:pə'stiʃəs]	abergläubisch
to wear, wore, worn [wɛə, wɔ:, wɔ:n]	(Kleidung usw.) tragen
lucky ['lʌki]	glückbringend, Glücks-
charm [tʃɑ:m]	Zauber; Amulett
lucky charm	Glücksbringer, Talisman
neck	Nacken, Hals
round the neck	um den Hals (herum)
the great day when	der große Tag, an dem
to apply for [ə'plai]	sich bewerben um
job [dʒɔb]	Arbeit, (Arbeits-)Stelle
with Webber & Co. (= company)	bei Webber & Co.

to give a look at	*einen Blick werfen auf*
hairdo ['hɛə-du:]	Frisur
to drop	fallen; fallen lassen
to break to pieces	*zerbrechen, auseinanderbrechen*
to turn white	weiß werden, erbleichen
sheet [ʃi:t]	Leintuch, Bettuch
as white as a sheet	(wörtl.: so weiß wie ein Bettuch) *kreidebleich*
bad luck	Unglück, Pech
building ['bildiŋ]	Gebäude
heavy ['hevi]	schwer (von Gewicht)
to fall, fell, fallen [fɔ:l, fel, 'fɔ:lən]	fallen
to go by	vorbeigehen, -fahren
splash! [splæʃ]	platsch!
clean [kli:n]	sauber, rein
jaguar ['dʒægjuə]	Jaguar
staff [stɑ:f]	Stab, Personal
staff manager ['stɑ:f ˌmænidʒə]	Personalchef
elegant ['eligənt]	elegant
fresh	frisch
dew [dju:]	Tau
to have a wash	*sich waschen*
to disappear [ˌdisə'piə]	verschwinden
confused [kən'fju:zd]	verwirrt
managing director ['mænidʒiŋ di'rektə]	Generaldirektor
to look up	aufblicken
ever ['evə]	je
to apologize [ə'pɔlədʒaiz]	sich entschuldigen
to withdraw, withdrew, withdrawn [wið'drɔ:, wið'dru:, wið'drɔ:n]	sich zurückziehen
to order ['ɔ:də]	befehlen
rough [rʌf]	rauh, barsch
in a rough voice	*in barschem Ton, barsch*
applicant ['æplikənt]	Bewerber(in)
short [ʃɔ:t]	kurz
shorthand ['ʃɔ:thænd]	Kurzschrift, Stenografie
120 words a minute*	
to tremble ['trembl]	zittern
to roar [rɔ:]	brüllen
firm [fə:m]	Firma
certificate [sə'tifikit]	Bescheinigung, Zeugnis
school leaving certificate	Schulabgangszeugnis; hier: Abschlußprüfung
general ['dʒenərəl]	allgemein
education [ˌedju(:)'keiʃən]	Erziehung, Bildung
advanced [əd'vɑ:nst]	fortgeschritten
level ['levl]	Niveau, Stufe
General Certificate of Education at Advanced Level (G.C.E.) ['dʒi: 'si: 'i:]	(Prüfung am Ende der Oberstufe)
history ['histəri]	Geschichte
to manage ['mænidʒ]	fertigbringen, zustande bringen
himself [him'self]	(er) selbst
astonished [əs'tɔniʃt]	erstaunt
examination [igˌzæmi'neiʃən]	Prüfung
to pass an examination	*eine Prüfung bestehen*
subject ['sʌbdʒikt]	(Unterrichts-)Fach

* In England wird die Kurzschriftgeschwindigkeit nicht nach Silben, sondern nach Wörtern pro Minute gemessen.

to whisper ['wispə]	flüstern
to engage s.o. [in'geidʒ]	jdn. einstellen, anstellen
to interview ['intəvju:]	interviewen
private ['praivit]	privat, persönlich; Privat-
I am wrong [rɔŋ]	*ich habe unrecht*

Luck, lucky — Happy, happiness

interview ['intəvju:]	Interview
to bring, brought, brought [briŋ, brɔ:t]	bringen
to splash	bespritzen
that was unfortunate [ʌn'fɔ:tʃnit]	das war Pech
five minutes late	*fünf Minuten zu spät*
Many happy returns of the day	Viel Glück zum Geburtstag

24 A Murder has been Planned

murder ['mə:də]	Mord
to plan [plæn]	planen
a murder has been planned	ein Mord ist geplant worden
to be operated on ['ɔpəreitid]	operiert werden
nurse [nə:s]	Krankenschwester
to cut, cut, cut [kʌt]	schneiden, aufschneiden
to be cut up by the doctors ['dɔktəz]	von den Ärzten aufgeschnitten werden
to sleep, slept, slept [sli:p, slept]	schlafen
operation [ˌɔpə'reiʃən]	Operation
stomach ['stʌmək]	Magen

stomach trouble ['trʌbl]	Magenbeschwerden
to cure [kjuə]	heilen, kurieren
patient ['peiʃənt]	Patient
to throw, threw, thrown [θrəu, θru:, θrəun]	werfen
blanket ['blæŋkit]	Decke, Bettdecke
cupboard ['kʌbəd]	Schrank
hasty ['heisti]	hastig
however [hau'evə]	jedoch
to bother about ['bɔðə]	sich kümmern um, sich sorgen um
tooth, *Mehrz.* teeth [tu:θ, ti:θ]	Zahn
false teeth [fɔ:ls]	falsche Zähne, Gebiß
yard [jɑ:d]	Hof
help	Hilfe
ladder ['lædə]	Leiter
exact [ig'zækt]	genau
there was no moon [mu:n]	*der Mond schien nicht*
to cross the road [krɔs]	die Straße überqueren
front door	Haustür
to lie, lay, lain [lai, lei, lein]	liegen
to greet [gri:t]	grüßen
friendly ['frendli]	freundlich
movement ['mu:vmənt]	Bewegung
tail [teil]	Schwanz
sign [sain]	Zeichen
silent ['sailənt]	still, ruhig
to remain [ri'mein]	bleiben
air [ɛə]	Luft
for this reason	*aus diesem Grund*
to keep open [ki:p]	offen halten
regular ['regjulə]	regelmäßig
breathing ['bri:ðiŋ]	Atem
to be fast asleep [fɑ:st ə'sli:p]	fest eingeschlafen sein
artificial light [ˌɑ:ti'fiʃəl]	künstliches Licht

clear [kliə]	klar, deutlich
to creep, crept, crept [kri:p, krept]	kriechen, schleichen
wooden ['wudn]	hölzern
usual ['ju:ʒuəl]	gewöhnlich
to touch [tʌtʃ]	berühren
leather ['leðə]	Leder
leather glove [glʌv]	Lederhandschuh
to pour [pɔ:]	gießen
contents, *Mehrz.* ['kɔntents]	Inhalt
liquid ['likwid]	Flüssigkeit
at the bottom of the stairs ['bɔtəm]	am unteren Ende der Treppe
touch [tʌtʃ]	Berührung
to warn [wɔ:n]	warnen
to close [kləuz]	schließen
to feel, felt, felt [fi:l, felt]	fühlen, sich fühlen
he felt as light as a feather ['feðə]	er fühlte sich so leicht wie eine Feder
to note [nəut]	bemerken
satisfaction [ˌsætis'fækʃən]	Befriedigung
to shut, shut, shut [ʃʌt]	schließen
absence ['æbsəns]	Abwesenheit
to ring up, rang, rung [riŋ, ræŋ, rʌŋ]	läuten, anrufen
on purpose ['pə:pəs]	*mit Absicht*
alibi ['ælibai]	Alibi
to continue [kən'tinju(:)]	fortsetzen, fortfahren
to be continued	Fortsetzung folgt

For

to sail [seil]	segeln
to sail for Germany	nach Deutschland fahren
to shout [ʃaut]	schreien, rufen
to shout for help	nach Hilfe rufen, schreien
to ask for s.th.	um etw. bitten
to send for s.o.	nach jdm. schicken

25 The Proof

proof [pru:f]	Beweis
unconscious [ʌn'kɔnʃəs]	bewußtlos
lorry ['lɔri]	Lastwagen
to wake up, woke, woken [weik, wəuk, 'wəukən]	aufwecken, aufwachen
somehow ['sʌmhau]	irgendwie
expression [iks'preʃən]	Ausdruck
to guess [ges]	erraten
person ['pə:sn]	Person
police-inspector [pə'li:s in'spektə]	Polizeiinspektor
news, *immer Einzahl* [nju:z]	Nachricht
to attempt [ə'tempt]	versuchen
to murder ['mə:də]	ermorden
anxious ['æŋkʃəs]	besorgt
to rob [rɔb]	ausrauben
to be alive [ə'laiv]	leben
robbery ['rɔbəri]	Raub
out of the question	außer Frage
since [sins]	da
jewel ['dʒu:əl]	Juwel
drawer ['drɔ:]	Schublade
inquiry [in'kwaiəri]	Nachfrage, Erkundigung
to make inquiries [in'kwaiəriz]	*Nachforschungen anstellen, sich erkundigen*
detail ['di:teil]	Einzelheit

to be quite ready to answer any questions	*durchaus bereit sein, jede Frage zu beantworten*
the police were on his track [træk]	*die Polizei war ihm auf der Spur*
not in the least [li:st]	nicht im geringsten
what you said was plain enough ['plein i'nʌf]	*was Sie sagten war klar genug*
poison ['pɔizn]	Gift
at your wife's bedside ['bedsaid]	neben dem Bett Ihrer Frau
actually ['æktʃuəli]	tatsächlich
to contain [kən'tein]	enthalten
enough [i'nʌf]	genug
to kill	töten
to poison	vergiften
calm [kɑ:m]	ruhig
besides [bi'saidz]	außerdem
to hurt, hurt, hurt [hə:t]	verletzen, weh tun
strange [streindʒ]	merkwürdig
manner ['mænə]	Benehmen, Manieren
to lie, lied, lied [lai, laid]	lügen
without shame [ʃeim]	ohne Scham
to insist [in'sist]	bestehen, beharren
dangerous ['deindʒrəs]	gefährlich
medicine ['medsin]	Medizin
to suffer from ['sʌfə]	leiden an
sleep [sli:p]	Schlaf
it wouldn't be surprising [sə'praiziŋ]	*es wäre nicht überraschend*
to suggest [sə'dʒest]	vorschlagen, andeuten
stuff [stʌf]	Stoff
to discover [dis'kʌvə]	entdecken
onto ['ɔntu]	auf
to knock over ['nɔk 'əuvə]	umstoßen
stiff [stif]	steif
to examine [ig'zæmin]	untersuchen

there was no doubt [daut]	es gab keinen Zweifel
hardly ['hɑ:dli]	kaum
he had hardly finished talking	*er hatte kaum aufgehört zu sprechen*
to scratch [skrætʃ]	kratzen
front leg	Vorderbein
to pull [pul]	ziehen
to spring, sprang, sprung [spriŋ, spræŋ, sprʌŋ]	springen
to lay, laid, laid [lei, leid]	legen
cheerful ['tʃiəful]	fröhlich
praise [preiz]	Lob
do you mind?	*haben Sie etwas dagegen?*
thorough examination ['θʌrə igˌzæmi'neiʃən]	gründliche Prüfung
to pause [pɔ:z]	eine Pause machen
sharp [ʃɑ:p]	scharf
to discuss [dis'kʌs]	diskutieren
case [keis]	Fall
we needn't discuss the case any longer	*wir brauchen den Fall nicht länger zu diskutieren*
to stick, stuck, stuck [stik, stʌk]	stecken bleiben, kleben
throat [θrəut]	Hals, Kehle
the words stuck in his throat	*die Wörter blieben ihm im Halse stecken*
to arrest s.o. [ə'rest]	jdn. verhaften
attempted murder [ə'temptid]	versuchter Mord

How are you?

how are you?	*wie geht es Ihnen?*
I'm very well	*es geht mir sehr gut*
thanks [θæŋks]	danke
to feel fine	*sich wohl fühlen*
mark [mɑ:k]	Ziel, Grenzlinie; Standard
I'm not up to the mark	*ich bin nicht (ganz) auf der Höhe*
weak [wi:k]	schwach
I feel rather weak	*ich fühle mich ziemlich schwach*
to sweat [swet]	schwitzen
I sweated heavily	*ich schwitzte stark*
I must have a temperature ['tempritʃə]	*ich muß Fieber haben*
to go to sleep	*einschlafen*
what's wrong with you?	*was ist los mit Ihnen? was fehlt Ihnen?*
that fish didn't agree with me [fiʃ, ə'gri:]	der Fisch ist mir nicht bekommen
I'm going to be sick	ich muß mich gleich übergeben
ear [iə]	Ohr
to ache [eik]	schmerzen
pill	Pille
to catch, caught, caught [kætʃ, kɔ:t]	fangen
to catch a cold	*sich erkälten*
to see a doctor ['dɔktə]	*zum Arzt gehen*
to send for the doctor	*nach dem Arzt schicken*
I'm doing quite well	*es geht mir schon viel besser*

26 The Man who was Waiting for his Wife

the man who	der Mann, der (welcher)
surprise [sə'praiz]	Überraschung
to feel hungry	*Hunger haben*

honest ['ɔnist]	ehrlich
to address s.o. [ə'dres]	jdn. anreden, ansprechen
to introduce s.o. [ˌintrə'dju:s]	jdn. vorstellen
captain ['kæptin]	Kapitän
to imagine [i'mædʒin]	sich vorstellen, sich ausdenken
what has happened to her ?	*was ist ihr zugestoßen ?, was ist mit ihr los ?*
true [tru:]	wahr
I've been waiting for three hours	ich warte schon seit drei Stunden
fool [fu:l]	Narr, Dummkopf
to make a fool of oneself	*sich lächerlich machen*
to allow [ə'lau]	erlauben, gestatten, zulassen
wallet ['wɔlit]	Brieftasche
I hadn't a penny	ich hatte keinen Pfennig
impossible [im'pɔsəbl]	unmöglich
after all	schließlich, eben doch
waitress ['weitris]	Kellnerin
manager ['mænidʒə]	Geschäftsführer
story ['stɔ:ri]	Geschichte
card [kɑ:d]	(Visiten-)Karte
to get home	*nach Hause kommen*
expression [iks'preʃən]	(Gesichts-)Ausdruck
to change [tʃeindʒ]	(sich) (ver)ändern, sich wandeln
to amount to [ə'maunt]	sich belaufen auf
£1.55 (one pound fifty-five pence)	ca. DM 9,30
the next time you have lunch, ...	(das nächstemal, wenn Sie ...) wenn Sie das nächstemal zu Mittag essen, ...
really ['riəli]	wirklich
thank you so much	*herzlichen Dank*
to rise, rose, risen [raiz, rəuz, 'rizn]	sich erheben, aufstehen
to part [pɑ:t]	sich trennen
familiar [fə'miljə]	bekannt, vertraut
someone else	jemand anders
to trick s.o.	jdn. hereinlegen
in no time	im Nu
to be ashamed of o.s. [ə'ʃeimd]	sich schämen

Menu

menu ['menju:]	Speisekarte, Menu
£9.25 (nine pound twenty-five pence)	ca. DM 36,—
luncheon (= lunch) ['lʌntʃən]	Mittagessen
cream of tomato soup [kri:m, tə'mɑ:təu]	Tomatencremesuppe
choice [tʃɔis]	(Aus-)Wahl
grilled sausages ['grild 'sɔsidʒiz]	gegrillte Würstchen
spaghetti [spə'geti]	Spaghetti
roast lamb ['rəust 'læm]	Lamm-, Hammelbraten
mint sauce ['mint 'sɔ:s]	Minzsoße, -tunke
roast beef ['rəust 'bi:f]	Rinderbraten
Yorkshire pudding ['jɔ:kʃə 'pudiŋ]	(dünner Eierauflauf, der vor allem zum Rinderbraten gegessen wird)
roast potatoes	(im Backofen) gebackene Kartoffeln
boiled potatoes [bɔild]	Salzkartoffeln
chipped potatoes [tʃipt] or: chips [tʃips]	Pommes frites
cabbage ['kæbidʒ]	Kohl
green peas	junge Erbsen
ice [ais]	Eis
vanilla ice-cream [və'nilə 'ais'kri:m]	Vanilleeis

In — On — At

actress ['æktris]	Schauspielerin
stage [steidʒ]	Bühne

27 Journey's End

journey ['dʒə:ni]	Reise
African ['æfrikən]	afrikanisch; Afrikaner(in)
slave [sleiv]	Sklave
sugar-planter ['ʃugə plɑ:ntə]	Zuckerplantagenbesitzer
the West Indies, *Mehrz.*	Westindien
trade [treid]	Gewerbe, Handel
slave-trade ['sleivtreid]	Sklavenhandel
throughout the Empire [θru(:)'aut, 'empaiə]	*überall im Weltreich, im ganzen Weltreich*
Negro ['ni:grəu]	Neger
grandson ['grænsʌn]	Urenkel(sohn)
great-grandson ['greit'grænsʌn]	Urenkel
a former slave ['fɔ:mə]	ein früherer Sklave
to land	landen
Liverpool ['livəpu:l]	(s. Englandkarte)
clever ['klevə]	klug
boy [bɔi]	Junge
grammar ['græmə]	Grammatik
grammar school ['græmə sku:l]	Gymnasium
Kingston ['kiŋstən]	(Hauptstadt von Jamaika)

Jamaica [dʒə'meikə]	Jamaika (die bedeutendste der westindischen Inseln; s. Karte)
to study ['stʌdi]	studieren
physics ['fiziks]	Physik
university [ˌju:ni'və:siti]	Universität
he used to [ju:st]	er pflegte
lift	Aufzug, Fahrstuhl
liftboy ['liftbɔi]	Fahrstuhlführer
as a liftboy	als Fahrstuhlführer
to earn [ə:n]	verdienen
wage(s), *meistens Mehrzahl* ['weidʒ(iz)]	Lohn
colleague ['kɔli:g]	Kollege
you see them ...	man sieht sie ...
bus conductor ['bʌs-kənˌdʌktə]	Omnibusschaffner
they are hardly found	(sie werden nicht leicht gefunden) sie sind kaum zu finden
profession [prə'feʃən]	(geistiger) Beruf
rare [rɛə]	selten
note [nəut]	Banknote, (Geld-)Schein
collection [kə'lekʃən]	Sammlung, Kollekte
position [pə'ziʃən]	Stellung, Stelle
physicist ['fizisist]	Physiker
a dozen ['dʌzn]	ein Dutzend
post [pəust]	Posten, Stelle
to fill a position	eine Stelle besetzen
polite [pə'lait]	höflich
lack of [læk]	Mangel an
success [sək'ses]	Erfolg
barrier ['bæriə]	Schranke, Hindernis
career [kə'riə]	Karriere, Laufbahn
almost ['ɔ:lməust]	fast

in despair [dis'pɛə]	in Verzweiflung, verzweifelt
government post ['gʌvnmənt 'pəust]	Stelle beim Staat, im öffentlichen Dienst
to offer ['ɔfə]	(an)bieten
social ['səuʃəl]	sozial
welfare ['welfɛə]	Wohlfahrt
federal government ['fedərəl]	Bundesregierung
Nigeria [nai'dʒiəriə]	Nigeria (s. Karte)
instructor [in'strʌktə]	Lehrer; Dozent
science ['saiəns]	Wissenschaft; Naturwissenschaft
(university) graduate ['grædʒuət]	Akademiker
science graduate	akademisch gebildeter Naturwissenschaftler
independence [ˌindi'pendəns]	Unabhängigkeit; Selbständigkeit
to proclaim [prə'kleim]	(öffentlich) ausrufen, verkünden; (feierlich) erklären
Commonwealth ['kɔmənwelθ]	(die brit.) Völkergemeinschaft
just like Jamaica	genauso wie Jamaika
common to them all ['kɔmən]	ihnen allen gemeinsam
to appoint [ə'pɔint]	ernennen
professor [prə'fesə]	Professor
he was appointed professor	*er wurde zum Professor ernannt*
Lagos University ['leigɔs]	Universität von Lagos
Africa ['æfrikə]	Afrika
to educate ['edju(:)keit]	erziehen, (aus)bilden
educated ['edju(:)keitid]	gebildet
to end	enden, beenden

ancestor ['ænsistə]	Ahn, Vorfahr
century ['sentʃuri]	Jahrhundert
four centuries before	vier Jahrhunderte zuvor, vorher

Identification

identification [aiˌdentifi'keiʃən]	Identifizierung; (Angabe der) Personalien
surname ['sə:neim]	(Familien-)Name
in block letters	in Druckschrift
Christian ['kristjən]	christlich; Christ
Christian name ['kristjənneim]	Vorname
Vera ['viərə]	Vera
Rose [rəuz]	Rosa, Rose
maiden name ['meidnneim]	Mädchen-, Geburtsname
single ['siŋgl]	ledig
Vienna [vi'enə]	Wien
Austria ['ɔstriə]	Österreich
sex [seks]	Geschlecht
male [meil]	männlich
female ['fi:meil]	weiblich
occupation [ˌɔkju'peiʃən]	Beruf
interpreter [in'tə:pritə]	Dolmetscher(in)
nationality [ˌnæʃə'næliti]	Nationalität, Staatsangehörigkeit
permanent ['pə:mənənt]	ständig, dauernd, anhaltend
address [ə'dres]	Adresse
permanent address	ständiger Wohnsitz
Raymond Road ['reimənd 'rəud]	(Straßenname)
840666 (*read:* eight-four-o-six-six-six)	
issue ['iʃu:]	Ausstellung
signature ['signitʃə]	Unterschrift

What do you say?

to get past s. o.	an jdm. vorbeigehen, -kommen
to mean, meant, meant [mi:n, ment]	bedeuten, meinen
I didn't mean it	*ich wollte es (das) nicht*
I beg your pardon	*(ich bitte um) Verzeihung, Entschuldigung*
to catch, caught, caught [kætʃ, kɔ:t]	fangen; hier: verstehen
not at all	*überhaupt nicht*
please do	hier: (bitte) rauchen Sie nur
I'd rather you didn't	*es wäre mir lieber, wenn Sie es nicht täten*

28 The World Food Crisis

crisis ['kraisis]	Krise
the only way	der einzige Weg
rise [raiz]	Anstieg
price [prais]	Preis
rise in prices ['praisiz]	Preisanstieg
price freeze [fri:z]	Preisstop
she had just come back	sie war gerade zurückgekommen
angry ['æŋgri]	böse, wütend
engineer [ˌendʒi'niə]	Ingenieur
increase ['inkri:s]	Erhöhung; Steigerung
salary ['sæləri]	Gehalt
increase in salary	Gehaltserhöhung
to have no money left	kein Geld übrig haben
especially [is'peʃəli]	besonders, insbesondere
to solve [sɔlv]	lösen
problem ['prɔbləm]	Problem
dear [diə]	hier: meine Liebe
cause [kɔ:z]	Ursache
to increase [in'kri:s]	wachsen, steigen; steigern, erhöhen
population [ˌpɔpju'leiʃən]	Bevölkerung
production [prə'dʌkʃən]	Produktion
all I know	*alles, was ich weiß*
it doesn't make any difference at all	es macht überhaupt keinen Unterschied
to realize ['riəlaiz]	sich im klaren sein
to produce [prə'dju:s]	produzieren
to develop [di'veləp]	(sich) entwickeln
developing country	Entwicklungsland
Asia ['eiʃə]	Asien
South America ['sauθ‿ə'merikə]	Südamerika
means [mi:nz]	Mittel
to feed, fed, fed [fi:d, fed]	ernähren
to grow, grew, grown [grəu, gru:, grəun]	wachsen
growing population	wachsende Bevölkerung
particularly [pə'tikjuləli]	besonders
India ['indjə]	Indien
Indian	indisch; Inder(in)
farmer ['fɑ:mə]	Bauer
to keep pace [peis]	Schritt halten
explosion [iks'pləuʒən]	Explosion
living ['liviŋ]	Lebensunterhalt
they failed to come	sie kamen nicht
to sweep, swept, swept [swi:p, swept]	fegen
valuable ['væljuəbl]	wertvoll
land [lænd]	Land
either ... or ['aiðə]	entweder ... oder
birth control ['bə:θ kən'trəul]	Geburtenkontrolle
resources [ri'sɔ:siz]	Hilfsquellen
both [bəuθ]	beide, beides
modern ['mɔdən]	modern
industry ['indəstri]	Industrie
organization [ˌɔ:gənai'zeiʃən]	Organisation
The United Nations Organization (UNO) [ju:'naitid 'neiʃənz‿ˌɔ:gənai'zeiʃən]	Die Vereinten Nationen
wealthy ['welθi]	wohlhabend
state [steit]	Staat
European Community [ˌjuərə'pi(:)ən kə'mju:niti]	Europäische Gemeinschaft
the United States [ju'naitid steits]	die Vereinigten Staaten
Japan [dʒə'pæn]	Japan
to be affected [ə'fektid]	betroffen sein
shortage ['ʃɔ:tidʒ]	Knappheit, Mangel
supply and demand [sə'plai‿ənd di'mɑ:nd]	Angebot und Nachfrage
present ['preznt]	augenblicklich
to feel sorry for	*Mitleid haben mit*

29 The Problem of Automation

automation [ˌɔ:tə'meiʃən]	Automation
dockworker ['dɔkwə:kə]	Dockarbeiter
port [pɔ:t]	Hafen
pupil ['pju:pl]	Schüler
comprehensive school [ˌkɔmpri'hensiv]	Gesamtschule
docks [dɔks]	Dock, Hafenanlagen
TV set	Fernsehapparat
machine [mə'ʃi:n]	Maschine

washing-machine	Waschmaschine
purchase ['pə:tʃəs]	Kauf
on hire-purchase ['haiə 'pə:tʃəs]	*auf Abzahlung*
the whole family [həul]	die ganze Familie
Spain [spein]	Spanien
sunshine ['sʌnʃain]	Sonnenschein
to save [seiv]	sparen
security [si'kjuəriti]	Sicherheit
social security	soziale Sicherheit; Sozialversicherung
what's the trouble?	*was ist los?*
container [kən'teinə]	Container (Großbehälter für den Verkehr von Werk zu Werk)
to cause [kɔ:z]	verursachen, veranlassen
trouble ['trʌbl]	Ärger, Sorge
ever since	seitdem
to appear [ə'piə]	erscheinen, auftauchen
to threaten ['θretn]	bedrohen
our jobs have been threatened ever since	*unsere Arbeitsplätze sind seitdem bedroht*
blood [blʌd]	Blut
to boil [bɔil]	kochen
it makes my blood boil	*es bringt mein Blut zum wallen*
to do something about it	*etwas dagegen tun*
to strike, struck, struck [straik, strʌk]	streiken; schlagen
the sooner the better [su:nə]	*je eher, desto besser*
to roll [rəul]	rollen
to look on	zuschauen
progress, *immer Einzahl* ['prəugres]	Fortschritt, Fortschritte
cost [kɔst]	Kosten

labour costs ['leibə]	Arbeitskosten
unemployment ['ʌnim'plɔimənt]	Arbeitslosigkeit
unemployment pay	Arbeitslosenunterstützung
point [pɔint]	Punkt
that's not the point	*darauf kommt es nicht an*
side [said]	Seite
to trouble s.o.	jdm. Sorgen bereiten
sum [sʌm]	Summe
to load [ləud]	laden, beladen
to unload ['ʌn'ləud]	ausladen, entladen
to retrain ['ri:'trein]	umschulen
at my age	*in meinem Alter*
one's	man ist
to face [feis]	ins Auge sehen
quite a problem [kwait]	*ein richtiges Problem*
for years	seit Jahren
computer [kəm'pju:tə]	Computer
consequence ['kɔnsikwəns]	Konsequenz, Folge
development [di'veləpmənt]	Entwicklung
certain industries ['sə:tn‿'indəstriz]	gewisse Industrien
employer [im'plɔiə]	Arbeitgeber
union ['ju:niən]	Gewerkschaft
to consider [kən'sidə]	betrachten, sich befassen mit

Weights and Measures

weight [weit]	Gewicht
measure ['meʒə]	Maß
amount [ə'maunt]	Menge, Betrag
beer [biə]	Bier
pub [pʌb]	Wirtshaus
pint [paint]	0,568 Liter
pound [paund]	Pfund (= 454 g)
ounce [auns]	Unze (= 28,35 g)
a 20 pound 2 ounce boy	ein 20 Pfund 2 Unzen schwerer Junge
American [ə'merikən]	amerikanisch; Amerikaner(in)
adult ['ædʌlt]	Erwachsener
height [hait]	Höhe, Größe
inch [intʃ]	Zoll (= 2,54 cm)
8 feet 10 inches ['intʃiz]	8 Fuß 10 Zoll
medical ['medikəl]	medizinisch
literature ['litəritʃə]	Literatur
to weigh [wei]	wiegen
stone [stəun]	Stein (= 6,35 Kilogramm)
hundredweight (cwt.) ['hʌndrədweit]	Zentner (51 kg)
World Trade Center ['sentə]	(wörtl.: Welthandelszentrum)
tower ['tauə]	Turm
side by side	*Seite an Seite*
worker ['wə:kə]	Arbeiter
average ['ævəridʒ]	Durchschnitt, Durchschnitts-
suspension bridge [səs'penʃən]	Hängebrücke
Verrazano Bridge [ˌverə'zɑ:nəu]	
length [leŋθ]	Länge
golden ['gəuldən]	golden
gate [geit]	Tor
San Francisco [ˌsænfrən'siskəu]	
above [ə'bʌv]	über
sea level ['si:ˌlevl]	Meeresspiegel

30 The Open Window

Nuttle ['nʌtl]	(Familienname)
at the baker's	*beim Bäcker*
chemist ['kemist]	Drogist, Apotheker
at the chemist's	*in der Drogerie, Apotheke*
meanwhile ['mi:n'wail]	inzwischen
introduction [ˌintrə'dʌkʃən]	Einführung, Vorstellung
letter of introduction	Empfehlungsschreiben
round here	hier herum, hier in der Gegend
niece [ni:s]	Nichte
soul [səul]	Seele
to admit [əd'mit]	zugeben, zugestehen
library ['laibrəri]	Bibliothek
illness ['ilnis]	Krankheit
on this very day	*eben an diesem Tag*
three years ago on this very day	*genau heute vor drei Jahren*
French window	Fenstertür (in den Garten)
wet [wet]	naß, feucht
to go shooting	auf die Jagd gehen
body	Körper; Leiche
that is why	*deshalb, darum*
raincoat ['reinkəut]	Regenmantel
shoulder ['ʃəuldə]	Schulter
dull [dʌl]	trüb
on an evening like this	an einem Abend wie diesem, wie heute
creepy ['kri:pi]	gruselig, unheimlich
tear [tiə]	Träne
handkerchief ['hæŋkətʃif]	Taschentuch
to blow, blew, blown [bləu, blu:, bləun]	blasen
nose [nəuz]	Nase
she blew her nose	*sie putzte sich die Nase*
at that moment ['məumənt]	in diesem Augenblick
do you mind the open window?	macht es Ihnen etwas aus, daß die Fenstertür offensteht?
this way	*auf diesem Wege, hier (herein)*
to be out for	hier: auf der Jagd sein nach
wild [waild]	wild
duck [dʌk]	Ente
wild duck	Wildente(n)
discomfort [dis'kʌmfət]	Unbehagen
prospect ['prɔspekt]	Aussicht
shooting prospects	Jagdaussichten
to fix [fiks]	befestigen
her eyes were fixed on …	ihre Augen waren geheftet, (fest) gerichtet auf …
wood [wud]	Wald
the wood beyond [bi'jɔnd]	der Wald jenseits davon, dahinter
fright [frait]	Schreck, Furcht
to turn	sich umdrehen
darkness ['dɑ:knis]	Dunkelheit
across [ə'krɔs]	(quer)über
towards (the French window) [tə'wɔ:dz]	auf (die Fenstertür) zu
gun [gʌn]	Gewehr
warning ['wɔ:niŋ]	Warnung
on the way back	*auf dem Rückweg*
to call at (s.o.'s house, office) (*dagegen:* to call on a person)	vorsprechen, hineinschauen bei
vicar ['vikə]	(Gemeinde-)Pfarrer
to borrow ['bɔrəu]	borgen
funny ['fʌni]	sonderbar, komisch
one might think [mait]	man könnte glauben
ghost [gəust]	Geist, Gespenst
joke [dʒəuk]	Witz, Spaß, Scherz
hobby ['hɔbi]	Hobby

Paying a Visit

to pay a visit	einen Besuch machen
how do you do?	*guten Tag!*
to disturb [dis'tə:b]	stören
I hope I'm not disturbing you	*hoffentlich störe ich nicht*
do sit down	*nehmen Sie doch bitte Platz*
will you have …?	möchten Sie …?
how do you like London?	*wie gefällt Ihnen London?*
whenever [wen'evə]	wann immer
to appreciate [ə'pri:ʃieit]	schätzen, würdigen
I do appreciate that	*ich weiß das zu würdigen*
delightful [di'laitful]	angenehm, entzückend
regards [ri'gɑ:dz]	Grüße
give my regards to …	*grüßen Sie … von mir*

31 Don't

when in Rome	wenn Sie in Rom sind
Roman ['rəumən]	römisch; Römer(in)
indeed [in'di:d]	in der Tat
proverb ['prɔvə:b]	Sprichwort
to behave [bi'heiv]	sich benehmen
everyone ['evriwʌn]	jeder(mann), alle

to behave as everyone else does	sich (so) benehmen wie alle anderen
on the right-hand side	*auf der rechten Seite, rechts*
to shake, shook, shaken [ʃeik, ʃuk, 'ʃeikən]	schütteln
to shake hands	*die Hand geben*
except [ik'sept]	außer
inside ['in'said]	Innenseite
pavement ['peivmənt]	Bürgersteig, Gehweg
she would hardly think you polite	sie würde Sie kaum für höflich halten
shovel ['ʃʌvl]	Schaufel
to remain seated	sitzen bleiben
to expect [iks'pekt]	erwarten
per cent [pə'sent]	vom Hundert, Prozent
plenty ['plenti]	viel, (über)genug
licensing hours ['laisənsiŋ‿auəz]	(für den Alkoholausschank) behördlich genehmigte Öffnungszeiten
compromise ['kɔmprəmaiz]	Kompromiß
to object to [əb'dʒekt]	Einspruch erheben gegen, gegen (etw.) sein
custom ['kʌstəm]	Sitte, Brauch
round	Runde
a lot	eine Menge, viel
driving-licence ['draiviŋˌlaisəns]	Führerschein
to awaken [ə'weikən]	(auf)wecken
at bedtime ['bedtaim]	zur Schlafenszeit
to keep awake [ə'weik]	wachhalten
host [həust]	Wirt, Gastgeber
draught [drɑ:ft]	(Luft-)Zug
to cough [kɔf]	husten

32 Stratford-on-Avon

Shakespeare ['ʃeikspiə]	
famous ['feiməs]	berühmt
outside the house ['aut'said]	(draußen) vor dem Haus
earth [ə:θ]	Erde
dramatist ['dræmətist]	Dramatiker
matinée, *franz.* ['mætinei]	Nachmittagsvorstellung
performance [pə'fɔ:məns]	Vorstellung, Aufführung
play [plei]	Spiel; Schauspiel, (Theater-)Stück
house full	(vom Theater) *ausverkauft*
season ['si:zn]	Saison, Spielzeit
wise [waiz]	weise, klug
in advance [in‿əd'vɑ:ns]	im voraus
to disappoint [ˌdisə'pɔint]	enttäuschen
pleasant ['pleznt]	erfreulich, angenehm; liebenswürdig
market ['mɑ:kit]	Markt
market town	Landstädtchen (mit Marktrecht)
half-timbered house ['hɑ:fˌtimbəd]	Fachwerkhaus
to date from	stammen aus (einer Zeit)
Elizabeth I	Elisabeth I. (engl. Königin v. 1558—1603)
step	Schritt
poet ['pəuit]	Dichter
satchel ['sætʃəl]	Schulmappe, -tasche
to shine, shone, shone [ʃain, ʃɔn]	scheinen, strahlen
snail [sneil]	Schnecke
unwilling ['ʌn'wiliŋ]	widerwillig
'As You Like It'	„Wie es Euch gefällt" (Titel einer Shakespeare-Komödie)
Latin ['lætin]	lateinisch; Latein
Greek [gri:k]	griechisch
cottage ['kɔtidʒ]	(in ländl. Stil erbautes) Haus
Hathaway ['hæθəwei]	(Familienname)
to marry ['mæri]	heiraten
opportunity [ˌɔpə'tju:niti]	Gelegenheit; Möglichkeit
intelligent [in'telidʒənt]	intelligent
well-known ['wel'nəun]	(wohl)bekannt
native town ['neitiv]	Geburtsstadt, Heimatstadt
to bury ['beri]	beerdigen, begraben
holy ['həuli]	heilig
Trinity ['triniti]	Dreieinigkeit
to be situated ['sitjueitid]	(Haus, Stadt) gelegen sein
river ['rivə]	Fluß
on the River Avon ['eivən]	am Avon
tombstone ['tu:m-stəun]	Grabstein
epitaph ['epitɑ:f]	Grabinschrift
to engrave [in'greiv]	(ein)gravieren, (ein)meißeln
to curse [kə:s]	verfluchen
bone	Knochen
the man who should move his bones	derjenige, der je seine Gebeine entferne
to rest	ruhen
to transform [træns'fɔ:m]	um-, verwandeln
to such an extent [iks'tent]	*in solchem Maße*

pilgrimage ['pilgrimidʒ]	Wallfahrt
to obtain [əb'tein]	erlangen, erhalten, bekommen
unless [ən'les]	wenn nicht
beforehand [bi'fɔ:hænd]	zuvor, im voraus
well beforehand	*ziemlich lange vorher*
secret ['si:krit]	Geheimnis
to last [lɑ:st]	dauern, andauern
popularity [ˌpɔpju'læriti]	Beliebtheit
anyone ['eniwʌn]	(irgend)jemand
human ['hju:mən]	menschlich
nature ['neitʃə]	Natur
age	hier: Zeit(alter)

33 Starting a New Life in Australia

starting a new life	*Beginn eines neuen Lebens*
Australia [ɔs'treiljə]	Australien
bar [bɑ:]	Bar
ocean ['əuʃən]	Ozean
ocean liner ['lainə]	Ozeandampfer
ice-cream parlour ['pɑ:lə]	Eisdiele
Sydney ['sidni]	größte Stadt Australiens
emigrant ['emigrənt]	Auswanderer
advantage [əd'vɑ:ntidʒ]	Vorteil
offer ['ɔfə]	Angebot
to take advantage of an offer	*ein Angebot wahrnehmen*
map [mæp]	(Land-)Karte
to refer to [ri'fə:]	sich beziehen auf
plan [plæn]	Plan
passage ['pæsidʒ]	Überfahrt
apart from [ə'pɑ:t]	abgesehen von
comfort ['kʌmfət]	Bequemlichkeit
it may be [mei]	es kann sein
you get to know people	*man lernt Leute kennen*
all by myself	*ganz alleine*
relatives ['relətivz]	Verwandte
I could do with	*ich könnte gebrauchen*
to range [reindʒ]	sich bewegen zwischen
32° (*read:* thirty-two degrees) [di'gri:z]	
degree	Grad
centigrade ['sentigreid]	Celsius
at noon [nu:n]	mittags
to supply [sə'plai]	beliefern
soft drinks [sɔft]	nicht alkoholische Getränke
refrigerator [ri'fridʒəreitə]	Kühlschrank
to own [əun]	besitzen
a chain of ice-cream parlours [tʃein]	eine Kette von Eisdielen
coast [kəust]	Küste
blind [blaind]	blind
possibility [ˌpɔsə'biliti]	Möglichkeit
on the right side	hier: auf der richtigen Seite
neighbourhood ['neibəhud]	Nachbarschaft
reasonable ['ri:znəbl]	vernünftig; hier: angemessen
to pass by	vorbeigehen
at night	nachts
crowds (of people) [kraud]	Menschenmengen
heat [hi:t]	Hitze
thus [ðʌs]	so, auf diese Weise
smooth [smu:ð]	glatt
steady ['stedi]	stetig
to regret [ri'gret]	bedauern
crowded ['kraudid]	überfüllt
city	Stadt
to emigrate ['emigreit]	auswandern
space [speis]	Raum
Australian [ɔs'treiljən]	australisch; Australier(in)
citizen ['sitizn]	Bürger, Staatsangehöriger

Australia

to cover ['kʌvə]	bedecken
square mile ['skwɛə 'mail]	Quadratmeile
capital ['kæpitl]	Hauptstadt
to equal ['i:kwəl]	gleichkommen
work-force ['wə:kfɔ:s]	Arbeitskraft
basic wage ['beisik 'weidʒ]	Grundgehalt
to average ['ævəridʒ]	im Durchschnitt betragen
wool [wul]	Wolle
quantity ['kwɔntiti]	Menge
metal ['metl]	Metall
iron ['aiən]	Eisen
zinc [ziŋk]	Zink
nickel ['nikl]	Nickel
quality ['kwɔliti]	Qualität
politics ['pɔlitiks]	Politik

34 The Boat Race

race [reis]	Rennen
boat race ['bəut reis]	Bootsrennen, Ruderregatta
in late March	*Ende März*
sporting event ['spɔ:tiŋ i'vent]	Sportereignis, -veranstaltung
Briton ['britn]	Brite
to give up	aufgeben

occupation [ˌɔkjuˈpeiʃən]	Beschäftigung
to take the opportunity of … [ˌɔpəˈtju:niti]	die Gelegenheit ergreifen zu …
old boy	*alter Freund, mein Lieber*
to beat, beat, beaten [bi:t, bi:t, ˈbi:tn]	schlagen
Joe [dʒəu]	(Kurzf. f. Joseph und John)
Oxford [ˈɔksfəd]	(s. Englandkarte;
Cambridge [ˈkeimbridʒ]	die ältesten Universitäten in England)
meeting [ˈmi:tiŋ]	Versammlung
mass meeting [ˈmæs ˈmi:tiŋ]	Massenversammlung
larger than any mass meeting	größer als irgendeine, jede Massenversammlung
the States	die (Vereinigten) Staaten
it's no use [ju:s]	*es nützt nichts, es hat keinen Zweck*
Hammersmith [ˈhæməsmiθ]	(Vorort von London)
yet [jet]	doch, dennoch, trotzdem
coach [kəutʃ]	(einstöckiger) Omnibus
bicycle [ˈbaisikl]	Fahrrad
on foot [ɔn ˈfut]	zu Fuß
sardine [sɑ:ˈdi:n]	Sardine
like sardines in a tin	*„wie die Heringe"*
I succeed in [səkˈsi:d]	es gelingt mir
bank [bæŋk]	Ufer
danger [ˈdeindʒə]	Gefahr
launch [lɔ:ntʃ]	kleiner (Vergnügungs-) Dampfer
advice, *immer Einzahl* [ədˈvais]	Rat, Ratschlag
to get wet through	durchnäßt werden, bis auf die Haut naß werden
sense [sens]	Sinn
what was the sense in that?	*welchen Sinn hatte das alles?*
strong	stark, kräftig
at the back [bæk]	hinten
to row [rəu]	rudern
like mad	wie verrückt
over	vorüber, vorbei
the River Thames [temz]	die Themse
excitement [ikˈsaitmənt]	Aufregung
outboard motor [ˈautbɔ:d ˈməutə]	Außenbordmotor
energy [ˈenədʒi]	Energie, Kraft
I can't help …ing	*ich kann nicht umhin, zu …*
I could have (saved)	ich hätte (sparen) können
trouble [ˈtrʌbl]	Mühe
in spite of [spait]	trotz
in spite of disliking this, he …	*obwohl er dies nicht mochte, …*
this might apply to any kind of sport [mait]	*dies könnte für jede Art Sport gelten*
you might just as well say	*du könntest genau so gut sagen*
it isn't worth bothering about [wə:θ]	*es lohnt sich nicht, sich darum zu kümmern*
to be interested in [ˈintristid]	interessiert sein an
to mind [maind]	etwas dagegen haben
they don't mind waiting	*sie haben nichts dagegen zu warten*
match [mætʃ]	(Kampf-)Spiel
strength [streŋθ]	Stärke
skill [skil]	Geschicklichkeit
experience [iksˈpiəriəns]	Erlebnis

What's the Weather like?

what's … like?	*wie ist …?*
cloud [klaud]	Wolke
in the sky [skai]	*am Himmel*
forecast [ˈfɔ:-kɑ:st]	Vorhersage
mainly [ˈmeinli]	hauptsächlich
mainly fair	vorwiegend heiter, freundlich
settled [ˈsetld]	beständig
to stay fine	schön bleiben
it looks like rain	*es sieht nach Regen aus*
thunderstorm [ˈθʌndə-stɔ:m]	Gewitter
it's pouring with rain [ˈpɔ:riŋ]	*es schüttet, regnet in Strömen*
nasty [ˈnɑ:sti]	gräßlich
ugly [ˈʌgli]	ekelhaft, scheußlich
foggy	neblig
fog	Nebel
to snow [snəu]	schneien
to freeze, froze, frozen [fri:z, frəuz, ˈfrəuzn]	gefrieren
dry [drai]	trocken
fairly [ˈfεəli]	ziemlich
cool [ku:l]	kühl

35 Sales Psychology

sale [seil]	Verkauf
psychology [saiˈkɔlədʒi]	Psychologie
sales psychology [ˈseilz saiˈkɔlədʒi]	Verkaufspsychologie

supermarket ['sju:pə,mɑ:kit]	Supermarkt
to apply some methods ['meθədz]	einige Methoden anwenden
by 20 per cent [bai‿'twenti‿pə'sent]	*um 20%*
partly ['pɑ:tli]	teilweise
to realize an increase ['riəlaiz]	*eine Erhöhung erzielen*
to arrange differently [ə'reindʒ 'difrəntli]	anders ordnen
the articles on show [ʃəu]	*die ausgestellte Ware*
fast sellers ['seləz]	gut gehende Ware
salt [sɔ:lt]	Salz
within easy reach [ri:tʃ]	in Reichweite
public ['pʌblik]	Publikum
to block [blɔk]	blockieren
shelf, *Mehrz.* shelves [ʃelf, ʃelvz]	Regal
in any case [keis]	auf jeden Fall
slow sellers [sləu]	schlecht gehende Ware
toothbrush ['tu:θbrʌʃ]	Zahnbürste
comb [kəum]	Kamm
lipstick ['lip-stik]	Lippenstift
powder ['paudə]	Puder
to observe [əb'zə:v]	beobachten
habit ['hæbit]	(An-)Gewohnheit
to have the habit of doing something	*die Gewohnheit haben, etwas zu tun*
to place [pleis]	plazieren, stellen
to build, built, built [bild, bilt]	bauen
to build up ['bild‿'ʌp]	aufbauen
heap [hi:p]	Haufen
to advertise ['ædvətaiz]	ankündigen, annoncieren
handsome ['hænsəm]	hübsch

profit ['prɔfit]	Profit, Gewinn
importance [im'pɔ:təns]	Bedeutung
lighting ['laitiŋ]	Beleuchtung
general effect ['dʒenərəl i'fekt]	allgemeine Wirkung
to recommend [,rekə'mend]	empfehlen
record ['rekɔ:d]	Schallplatte
soft [sɔft]	weich
the sound of music [saund]	der Klang der Musik
to intend [in'tend]	beabsichtigen
to spread, spread, spread [spred]	verbreiten
spirit ['spirit]	Geist
over the whole year	*das ganze Jahr hindurch*
all sorts of things	*alles mögliche*
toy [tɔi]	Spielzeug
ices ['aisiz]	Eisspeisen
nut [nʌt]	Nuß
out of sight [sait]	außer Sicht
four-year-olds	Vierjährige
I had them placed [pleist]	*ich ließ sie stellen*
to satisfy ['sætisfai]	befriedigen
satisfying	befriedigend
fact [fækt]	Tatsache
complete [kəm'pli:t]	vollständig, ganz
I have never completely understood	*ich habe niemals ganz verstanden*
the figure 9 ['figə]	die Zahl 9
observation [,ɔbzə(:)'veiʃən]	Beobachtung
I put my observation to the test	*ich stellte meine Beobachtung auf die Probe*

to mark [mɑ:k]	bezeichnen, auszeichnen
favourite ['feivərit]	Favorit
they were greater favourites	*sie waren beliebter*
the meat priced at 99 p [praist]	*das Fleisch zu 99 Pence*
to be in demand [di'mɑ:nd]	*verlangt werden*
as far as prices are concerned [kən'sə:nd]	*was die Preise betrifft, angeht*
to charge [tʃɑ:dʒ]	berechnen
recently ['ri:sntli]	kürzlich
apple ['æpl]	Apfel
in good condition [kən'diʃən]	in gutem Zustand
extreme [iks'tri:m]	extrem, äußerst
ripe [raip]	reif
generous ['dʒenərəs]	großzügig
by the afternoon	bis zum Nachmittag
in writing this	*indem ich dies schreibe*
to draw attention to the fact [ə'tenʃən]	*die Aufmerksamkeit auf die Tatsache lenken*
responsibility [ris,pɔnsə'biliti]	Verantwortung
to prove [pru:v]	beweisen
salesman ['seilzmən]	Verkäufer
in addition [ə'diʃən]	*noch dazu*
ability [ə'biliti]	Fähigkeit
grateful ['greitful]	dankbar
close [kləus]	nahe, dicht
attention	Aufmerksamkeit
close attention	sorgfältige Aufmerksamkeit
Yours faithfully, ['feiθfuli]	Hochachtungsvoll

Exercises

I. guide [gaid]	Reiseleiter, Fremdenführer
illustrated guide [ˈiləstreitid ˈgaid]	illustrierter Reiseführer
in the country	*auf dem Lande*
information, *immer Einzahl* [ˌinfəˈmeiʃən]	Information
relation	Verhältnis, Beziehung
Public Relations Office [ˈpʌblik riˈleiʃənz ˈɔfis]	Fremdenverkehrsbüro

36 For Whites Only? I

hell [hel]	Hölle
coloured [ˈkʌləd]	farbig
lawyer [ˈlɔ:jə]	Rechtsanwalt
the deep South	der tiefe Süden der Vereinigten Staaten
to bear, bore, borne [bɛə, bɔ:, bɔ:n]	tragen
to bear the notice	*die Bekanntmachung führen*
anger [ˈæŋgə]	Ärger, Zorn
to explode [iksˈpləud]	explodieren
bomb [bɔm]	Bombe
patience [ˈpeiʃəns]	Geduld
for ever [fər‿ˈevə]	für immer
society [səˈsaiəti]	Gesellschaft
to stand (stood, stood) for something	etwas ertragen
to recognize [ˈrekəgnaiz]	erkennen
Montgomery [məntˈgʌməri]	(Stadt in USA)
Alabama [ˌæləˈbæmə]	(Südstaat der USA)
coloured woman	Farbige
interruption [ˌintəˈrʌpʃən]	Unterbrechung
department store	Kaufhaus
to employ [imˈplɔi]	beschäftigen, anstellen
half [hɑ:f]	Hälfte
front [frʌnt]	Vorderteil
middle [ˈmidl]	Mitte
from the middle to the back	von der Mitte nach hinten
part [pɑ:t]	Teil
to have a rest	sich ausruhen
knee [ni:]	Knie
to hurt, hurt, hurt [hə:t]	schmerzen
shortly after	kurz nachdem
to approach s.o. [əˈprəutʃ]	sich jdm. nähern
we can't have Niggers sitting	*wir können nicht dulden, daß Neger sitzen*
lazy [ˈleizi]	faul
I won't get up for anybody	*ich stehe für niemanden auf*
colored *Am.*	farbig
right	Recht
to settle something [ˈsetl]	etwas erledigen
to argue [ˈɑ:gju:]	streiten
scene [si:n]	Szene
do be reasonable [ˈri:znəbl]	*seien Sie doch vernünftig*
law	Gesetz
you've got to respect orders	*Sie müssen Befehle respektieren*
to force [fɔ:s]	zwingen
duty [ˈdju:ti]	Pflicht
come on!	*also, los!*
to be under arrest [əˈrest]	verhaftet sein
for disturbing the peace	*wegen öffentlicher Ruhestörung*
crime [kraim]	Verbrechen
to protest [prəˈtest]	protestieren
criminal [ˈkriminl]	Verbrecher
protest [ˈprəutest]	Protest
to lead, led, led [li:d, led]	führen
by force	*mit Gewalt*
slight [slait]	leicht, gering
she had not the slightest idea	*sie hatte nicht die geringste Ahnung*
refusal [riˈfju:zəl]	Ablehnung, Weigerung
to meet a demand [diˈmɑ:nd]	*einem Verlangen nachkommen*
beginning [biˈginiŋ]	Beginn, Anfang
nation-wide [ˈneiʃən ˈwaid]	nationsweit
movement [ˈmu:vmənt]	Bewegung
freedom [ˈfri:dəm]	Freiheit
power [ˈpauə]	Macht

At the Post-Office

post-office [ˈpəustˌɔfis]	Postamt
urgent [ˈə:dʒənt]	dringend; eilig
by air mail [ˈɛəmeil]	per Luftpost
a registered letter [ˈredʒistəd]	ein eingeschriebener Brief
to deliver [diˈlivə]	zustellen
to advise [ədˈvaiz]	raten
express [iksˈpres]	durch Eilboten
parcel post [ˈpɑ:sl ˈpəust]	Paketpost
printed matter [ˈprintid ˈmætə]	Drucksache
wire [waiə]*Am.*	Telegramm

form	Formular
to fill in a form	*ein Formular ausfüllen*
to hand in	abgeben
counter ['kauntə]	Schalter
letter-box ['letəbɔks]	Briefkasten

A Slight Misunderstanding

misunderstanding ['misʌndə'stændiŋ]	Mißverständnis, Mißverstehen
helpless ['helplis]	hilflos
postage stamp ['pəustidʒ stæmp]	Briefmarke
to stick on, stuck, stuck [stik, stʌk]	aufkleben
postal clerk ['pəustəl 'klɑ:k]	Postbeamter
it will do more good	*es ist besser, zweckmäßiger*
envelope ['envələup]	Briefumschlag

37 For Whites Only? II

leader ['li:də]	Führer
to hold, held, held [həuld, held]	halten
to hold a meeting	*eine Versammlung abhalten*
action ['ækʃən]	Handlung, Tat
a plan of action	Aktionsplan
equal ['i:kwəl]	gleich
bitter	bitter
because of	wegen
to act [ækt]	handeln
to organize ['ɔ:gənaiz]	organisieren
boycott ['bɔikət]	Boykott
work [wə:k]	Arbeit
Baptist minister ['bæptist 'ministə]	Baptistengeistlicher
to take (took, taken) on	annehmen, übernehmen
task [tɑ:sk]	Aufgabe
to spread (spread, spread) *the news*	*die Nachricht verbreiten*
packed [pækt]	überfüllt
to segregate ['segrigeit]	absondern, trennen
to humiliate [hju(:)'milieit]	demütigen
to kick about	herumtreten
brutal ['bru:tl]	brutal
oppression [ə'preʃən]	Unterdrückung
amazing [ə'meiziŋ]	erstaunlich
impression [im'preʃən]	Eindruck
we like the way we are treated	*wir mögen die Art, wie wir behandelt werden*
to save from	*retten vor*
patient ['peiʃənt]	geduldig
with anything less than	*mit irgendetwas Geringerem als*
justice ['dʒʌstis]	Gerechtigkeit
to march [mɑ:tʃ]	marschieren
to fight, fought, fought [fait, fɔ:t]	kämpfen
wherever [wɛər'evə]	wo auch immer
influence ['influəns]	Einfluß
to prevent s.o. from doing s.th. [pri'vent]	jdn. hindern etw. zu tun
to rush [rʌʃ]	rasen, stürzen
risky ['riski]	riskant
faith [feiθ]	Glaube
religion [ri'lidʒən]	Religion
to forbid, forbade, forbidden [fə'bid, fə'bæd, fə'bidn]	verbieten
to shoot, shot, shot [ʃu:t, ʃɔt]	schießen
enemy ['enimi]	Feind
to shoot his enemy	*auf seinen Feind schießen*
quarter ['kwɔ:tə]	Viertel
to react [ri(:)'ækt]	reagieren
to blame somebody for s.th. [bleim]	*jdm. die Schuld geben an etwas*
they would not give in	*sie wollten nicht nachgeben*
case [keis]	Fall
Supreme Court [su(:)'pri:m 'kɔ:t]	Oberster Gerichtshof
in favour of ['feivə]	*zugunsten von*
victory ['viktəri]	Sieg
segregation [ˌsegri'geiʃən]	Absonderung
school segregation	getrennte Schulen
driving force	treibende Kraft
battle ['bætl]	Schlacht
peaceful ['pi:sful]	friedlich
by peaceful means	*mit friedlichen Mitteln*
Nobel Peace Prize ['nəubel]	Nobel Friedenspreis
ideal [ai'diəl]	Ideal
to hire ['haiə]	anstellen, einstellen
to fire ['faiə]	feuern, entlassen
unskilled workers ['ʌn'skild]	ungelernte Arbeitskräfte
racial ['reiʃəl]	rassisch
struggle ['strʌgl]	Kampf

Useful Phrases for Business Letters

useful ['ju:sful]	nützlich
phrase [freiz]	Ausdruck, Redensart
to quote	angeben
low [ləu]	niedrig

in reply to	*in Beantwortung*
with reference to ['refrəns] *referring to* [ri'fə:riŋ]	*mit Bezug auf*
inquiry [in'kwaiəri]	Anfrage
we are glad to inform you [in'fɔ:m]	*wir teilen Ihnen (gerne) mit*
catalogue ['kætəlɔg]	Katalog
price-list ['praislist]	Preisliste
sample ['sɑ:mpl]	Probe, Muster
separate ['seprit]	getrennt, gesondert
cover ['kʌvə]	Hülle
under separate cover	*gesondert; mit getrennter Post*
to dispatch [dis'pætʃ]	ver-, absenden
to accept responsibility	Verantwortung übernehmen
delay [di'lei]	Verspätung, Verzögerung
terms of payment	Zahlungsbedingungen
cash [kæʃ]	bar, netto Kasse
discount ['diskaunt]	Abzug, Skonto
invoice ['invɔis]	Rechnung
within 30 days of date of invoice [wi'ðin]	*binnen 30 Tagen nach Rechnungsdatum*
payable ['peiəbl]	zahlbar
delivery [di'livəri]	Lieferung
c.o.d. = cash on delivery	*gegen Nachnahme*
claim [kleim]	Anspruch
your claims will be considered	*Ihre Ansprüche werden in Erwägung gezogen*
agreement [ə'gri:mənt]	Vereinbarung

Grammatik

to spend on advertising ['ædvətaiziŋ]	für Reklame ausgeben
bank account ['bæŋk‿ə'kaunt]	Bankkonto

38 London Through the Ages

London through the ages	London im Lauf der Jahrhunderte
to be to	sollen
residence ['rezidəns]	Wohnsitz; Residenz
cultural ['kʌltʃərəl]	kulturell, Kultur-
centre ['sentə]	Mittelpunkt, Zentrum
Winchester ['wintʃistə]	(s. Englandkarte)
south-eastern [sauθ'i:stən]	südöstlich
to protect [prə'tekt]	schützen
Westminster ['westminstə]	(Ortsname)
Parliament ['pɑ:ləmənt]	Parlament
to meet (met, met)	hier: zusammentreten
in comparison [kəm'pærisn]	im Vergleich
palace ['pælis]	Schloß, Palast
Whitehall ['wait'hɔ:l]	(heute Name einer Straße; s. Stadtplan)
abbey ['æbi]	Abtei
Westminster Abbey	(s. Stadtplan)
king [kiŋ]	König
to crown [kraun]	krönen
official [ə'fiʃəl]	Beamter
castle ['kɑ:sl]	Burg, Schloß
they would pass green fields	sie pflegten vorbeizukommen, sie kamen vorbei an ...
half-way ['hɑ:f'wei]	auf halbem Wege
cross	Kreuz
Charing Cross ['tʃæriŋ'krɔs]	(s. Stadtplan)
thirsty ['θə:sti]	durstig
busy ['bizi]	hier: belebt
Greater London	Groß-London
United Kingdom [ju:'naitid 'kiŋdəm]	Vereinigtes Königreich (England, Schottland, Wales, Nordirland)
solid ['sɔlid]	solide, fest, stabil
heart [hɑ:t]	Herz; Kern
commerce ['kɔmə(:)s]	Handel
export ['ekspɔ:t]	Ausfuhr, Export
exports ['ekspɔ:ts]	Exportgüter
national paper	überregionale Zeitung (die im ganzen Land gelesen wird)
total ['təutl]	Gesamt-
circulation [ˌsə:kju'leiʃən]	Auflage (von Zeitungen)
to print [print]	drucken
Fleet Street	(s. Stadtplan)
with the exception of [ik'sepʃən]	mit Ausnahme von
serious ['siəriəs]	ernst, seriös
shadow ['ʃædəu]	Schatten
St. Paul's Cathedral [snt 'pɔ:lz kə'θi:drəl]	St.-Pauls-Kathedrale (s. Stadtplan)
Londoner ['lʌndənə]	Londoner
local ['ləukəl]	Orts-
local train	Nahverkehrszug
the Underground ['ʌndəgraund]	die (Londoner) Untergrundbahn
suburb ['sʌbə:b]	Vorstadt, -ort
to lunch	zu Mittag essen
sandwich ['sænwidʒ]	Sandwich, belegtes Brot
to keep order	hier: nicht gegen die Ordnung verstoßen
discipline ['disiplin]	Zucht, Disziplin
traffic rush ['træfik rʌʃ]	Hauptverkehr
queue [kju:]	Reihe, (Menschen-) Schlange

to get out of a queue	*die Reihe durchbrechen*
nor ... [nɔ:]	noch ..., ... auch nicht
temper [ˈtempə]	Temperament; Stimmung, Laune; Gleichmut
to lose one's temper	*die Herrschaft über sich verlieren, wütend werden*
disciplined [ˈdisiplind]	zuchtvoll, diszipliniert
striking [ˈstraikiŋ]	auffallend
feature [ˈfi:tʃə]	(Charakter-)Zug, Merkmal

39 The Channel Tunnel

Channel [ˈtʃænl]	Ärmelkanal
tunnel [ˈtʌnl]	Tunnel
politician [ˌpɔliˈtiʃən]	Politiker
hole [həul]	Loch
ground [graund]	Grund, Boden
to dig, dug, dug [dig, dʌg]	graben
spot [spɔt]	Stelle
soil [sɔil]	(Erd-)Boden
soldier [ˈsəuldʒə]	Soldat
both ... and	sowohl ... als auch
camp [kæmp]	Lager
for military reasons [ˈmilitəri]	*aus militärischen Gründen*
to destroy [disˈtrɔi]	zerstören
to put an end to	beenden
fear [fiə]	Befürchtung, Furcht
hesitation [ˌheziˈteiʃən]	Zögern
reality [ri(:)ˈæliti]	Wirklichkeit
to be about to become reality	*im Begriff sein, Wirklichkeit zu werden*
according to plan [əˈkɔ:diŋ]	*nach Plan, planmäßig*
traveller [ˈtrævlə]	Reisender
southern [ˈsʌðən]	Süd-
headline [ˈhedlain]	Schlagzeile
to report [riˈpɔ:t]	berichten
isolated [ˈaisəleitid]	isoliert
crossing [ˈkrɔsiŋ]	Überfahrt
sailor [ˈseilə]	Seemann
to be a bad sailor	*nicht seefest sein*
below deck [biˈləu]	unter Deck
wind [wind]	Wind
stormy [ˈstɔ:mi]	stürmisch
France [frɑ:ns]	Frankreich
special double-decker trains [ˈdʌblˈdekə]	besondere Doppeldeckzüge
vehicle [ˈvi:ikl]	Fahrzeug
every five minutes	alle 5 Minuten
rate [reit]	Tarif
carriage by ship [ˈkæridʒ]	Transport mit dem Schiff
economic [ˌi:kəˈnɔmik]	wirtschaftlich
considerable [kənˈsidərəbl]	beträchtlich
freight costs [freit]	Frachtkosten
to calculate [ˈkælkjuleit]	berechnen
exchange [iksˈtʃeindʒ]	Austausch, Wechsel
to be bound to [baund]	zwangsläufig müssen
Chunnel = Channel Tunnel	
to go ahead with s.th. [əˈhed]	*voran machen mit etwas*
a piece of engineering [ˌendʒiˈniəriŋ]	ein Stück Ingenieursarbeit
to carry out	ausführen
difficulty [ˈdifikəlti]	Schwierigkeit
project [ˈprɔdʒekt]	Projekt
to support [səˈpɔ:t]	unterstützen
in particular [pəˈtikjulə]	insbesondere
disappointed [ˌdisəˈpɔintid]	enttäuscht
to handle [ˈhændl]	abfertigen
to tear, tore, torn [tɛə, tɔ:, tɔ:n]	reißen
to tear away	wegreißen, entreißen
acre of land [ˈeikə]	Morgen Landes
capacity [kəˈpæsiti]	Leistungsfähigkeit
to waste [weist]	verschwenden
is all that money to be wasted?	*soll all dies Geld verschwendet werden?*
car ferry [ˈferi]	Autofähre
to sail to and fro [seil, frəu]	hin und her fahren
last but not least	*nicht zuletzt, schließlich*
pride [praid]	Stolz
island [ˈailənd]	Insel
to claim [kleim]	beanspruchen
to connect [kəˈnekt]	verbinden
share	Anteil; hier: Aktie

How to Telephone

how to telephone [ˈtelifəun]	wie man telefoniert
(telephone) directory [diˈrektəri]	Telefonbuch
local call [ˈləukəl]	Ortsgespräch
call box [ˈkɔ:lbɔks]	(öffentl.) Telefonzelle
reply [riˈplai]	Antwort
to insert [inˈsə:t]	einführen; hier: hineinwerfen

['trʌŋk kɔ:l]	
operator ['ɔpəreitə]	Fernsprechbeamtin, Telefonistin
Hold the line, please.	*Bleiben Sie bitte am Apparat.*
I'll put you through	*ich verbinde*

40 North Sea Gas and Oil

north [nɔ:θ]	Norden
North Sea ['nɔ:θ 'si:]	Nordsee
gas [gæs]	Gas
oil [ɔil]	Öl
natural ['nætʃrəl]	natürlich
natural gas	Erdgas
off the coast [kəust]	*vor der Küste*
eager ['i:gə]	begierig
news to be received even more eagerly	*eine Nachricht, die noch begieriger aufgenommen werden sollte*
discovery [dis'kʌvəri]	Entdeckung
field [fi:ld]	Feld
to be likely to become ['laikli]	*wahrscheinlich werden*
riches, *immer Mehrz.* ['ritʃiz]	Reichtum, Reichtümer
desert ['dezət]	Wüste
surface ['sə:fis]	Oberfläche
the Middle East ['midl 'i:st]	der Nahe Osten
flow [fləu]	Fluß, Zufluß
to pump [pʌmp]	pumpen
pipeline ['paip-lain]	Leitungsrohr, Pipeline
shore [ʃɔ:]	Küste
northern ['nɔ:ðən]	nördlich
to remove [ri'mu:v]	abschaffen, entfernen
raw [rɔ:]	roh, Roh-
raw material [mə'tiəriəl]	Rohmaterial
to demand [di'ma:nd]	erfordern, verlangen
extraordinary [iks'trɔ:dnri]	außerordentlich
capital ['kæpitl]	Kapital
in order to ['ɔ:də]	um zu
steel [sti:l]	Stahl
rig [rig]	(schwimmende Bohrinsel)
attack [ə'tæk]	Angriff
storm [stɔ:m]	Sturm
wave [weiv]	Welle
firm [fə:m]	fest
sea-bed ['si:'bed]	Meeresboden
employment [im'plɔimənt]	Beschäftigung
lately ['leitli]	in letzter Zeit; kürzlich
headquarters ['hed'kwɔ:təz]	Zentrale, Hauptgeschäftsstelle
to set up headquarters	*Hauptgeschäftsstelle errichten*
Aberdeen [ˌæbə'di:n]	(Stadt im Norden Schottlands)
property prices ['prɔpəti]	Grundstückspreise
to double ['dʌbl]	(sich) verdoppeln
area ['ɛəriə]	Gebiet, Fläche
to insure [in'ʃuə]	versichern
risk	Risiko
property	Eigentum
damage to property ['dæmidʒ]	Schaden an Eigentum
pollution [pə'lu:ʃən]	Verschmutzung
trunk call	Ferngespräch
no wonder ['wʌndə]	kein Wunder
insurance company [in'ʃuərəns]	Versicherungsgesellschaft
to profit ['prɔfit]	profitieren
fishing industry	Fischereigewerbe
tight [tait]	dicht
to escape [is'keip]	entkommen
reserve [ri'zə:v]	Reserve
crack [kræk]	Riß
to pollute [pə'lu:t]	verschmutzen
coast line ['kəustlain]	Küstenlinie
to check [tʃek]	verhindern
collision [kə'liʒən]	Zusammenstoß
to doubt [daut]	bezweifeln, zweifeln
coal [kəul]	Kohle
mine [main]	Bergwerk
atomic [ə'tɔmik]	atomar
plant [plɑ:nt]	Fabrikanlage
atomic plant	Kernkraftwerk

No Sense of Humour

sense [sens]	Sinn
humour ['hju:mə]	Humor
sense of humour	Sinn für Humor
sour ['sauə]	sauer
to invite [in'vait]	einladen
what a shame [ʃeim]	wie schade!
shocked [ʃɔkt]	schockiert
rude [ru:d]	grob, unverschämt
surely ['ʃuəli]	sicherlich, gewiß
memory ['meməri]	Gedächtnis
to have somebody in	*jdn. bei sich zu Hause haben*
harmless ['hɑ:mlis]	harmlos
harm [hɑ:m]	Schaden, Leid
there was no harm in it	*es war doch harmlos*
to take a joke	*einen Scherz vertragen*

41 From Empire to Commonwealth I

fleet	Flotte
Spanish ['spæniʃ]	spanisch
Armada [ɑ:'mɑ:də]	Armada (Name der damaligen span. Flotte)
sea-power ['si:ˌpauə]	Seemacht
wing	Flügel
colony ['kɔləni]	Kolonie
trading company ['treidiŋ 'kʌmpəni]	Handelsgesellschaft
attempt [ə'tempt]	Versuch
as well as	ebenso wie, wie auch
religious [ri'lidʒəs]	religiös
to favour ['feivə]	begünstigen
emigration [ˌemi'greiʃən]	Auswanderung
command [kə'mɑ:nd]	Kommando, Befehl
splendid ['splendid]	prächtig
final ['fainl]	endgültig
the Dutch [dʌtʃ]	die Holländer
New Amsterdam ['æmstə'dæm]	Neu-Amsterdam
altogether [ˌɔ:ltə'geðə]	gänzlich, völlig
policy ['pɔlisi]	Politik (die jd. verfolgt)
to maintain [mein'tein]	beibehalten, aufrechterhalten
balance ['bæləns]	Gleichgewicht
victor ['viktə]	Sieger
automatically [ˌɔ:tə'mætikəli]	automatisch
slice [slais]	Scheibe, Schnitte; hier: Stück
Gibraltar [dʒi'brɔ:ltə]	Gibraltar
Spaniard ['spænjəd]	Spanier(in)
Canada ['kænədə]	Kanada
defeat [di'fi:t]	Besiegung; Niederlage
the Boers ['bəuəz]	die Buren
South Africa	Südafrika
Irishman ['aiəriʃmən]	Ire
Dublin ['dʌblin]	Hauptstadt von Irland (Eire)
Chinese ['tʃai'ni:z]	chinesisch; Chinese
Hong Kong [hɔŋ'kɔŋ]	Hongkong
Calcutta [kæl'kʌtə]	Kalkutta
descendant [di'sendənt]	Abkömmling
Johannesburg [dʒəu'hænisbə:g]	Johannesburg
flag	Fahne, Flagge
growth [grəuθ]	Wachstum, (An-)Wachsen
setback ['setbæk]	Rückschlag
to suffer a setback	einen Rückschlag erleiden
loss	Verlust
to defeat [di'fi:t]	besiegen
army ['ɑ:mi]	Armee, Heer
to separate from ['sepəreit]	sich trennen, lösen von
unrest ['ʌn'rest]	Unruhe
to grant [grɑ:nt]	bewilligen, gewähren
rule [ru:l]	Herrschaft
home rule	Selbstverwaltung
from then on	von da an
interior affairs [in'tiəriər‿ə'fɛəz]	innere Angelegenheiten, Innenpolitik
Canadian [kə'neidjən]	kanadisch; Kanadier(in)
dominion [də'minjən]	Dominion
at the beginning of	am Beginn, Anfang von
New Zealand [nju:'zi:lənd]	Neuseeland
Union of South Africa	Südafrikanische Union
all of which	die alle
to enjoy home rule	das Recht der Selbstverwaltung haben
by 1910	bis, um 1910
link	Band, Bindeglied
loyalty ['lɔiəlti]	Loyalität, Treue
crown [kraun]	Krone

Exercises

III. powerful ['pauəful]	mächtig, einflußreich

42 From Empire to Commonwealth II

independent [ˌindi'pendənt]	frei, unabhängig
Union of India ['indjə]	Indische Union
Pakistan [ˌpɑ:kis'tɑ:n]	Pakistan
Ceylon [si'lɔn]	Ceylon
self-government ['self'gʌvnmənt]	Selbstregierung, Autonomie
member states	Mitgliedstaaten
frequent ['fri:kwənt]	häufig
first	zuerst
republic [ri'pʌblik]	Republik
head	Oberhaupt
more and more	immer mehr
to permit [pə'mit]	erlauben, gestatten
to govern ['gʌvən]	regieren, verwalten
Burma ['bə:mə]	Birma
to loosen ['lu:sn]	lösen
tie [tai]	Bindung
Eire ['ɛərə]	Irland
federation [ˌfedə'reiʃən]	Bund, Föderation
Malaya [mə'leiə]	Malaya
the Federation of Malaya	die Malaiische Föderation
on the other hand	*andererseits; dagegen*

group [gru:p]	Gruppe
membership ['membəʃip]	Mitgliedschaft
Ghana ['gɑ:nə]	Ghana
monarch ['mɔnək]	Monarch
West Indian Federation	Westindische Föderation
majority [mə'dʒɔriti]	Mehrheit
to guide	führen, leiten
in the future	*in Zukunft*
to broadcast, broadcast, broadcast ['brɔ:dkɑ:st]	(im Rundfunk) senden
people, *Mehrz.* peoples	Volk
message ['mesidʒ]	Botschaft; Ansprache
to broadcast a message to	eine Rundfunkansprache richten an
little did they realize ['riəlaiz]	sie hatten überhaupt keine Vorstellung

to dare [dɛə]	wagen
daring ['dɛəriŋ]	wagemutig
Tudor ['tju:də]	(engl. Königshaus 1485—1603)
Stuart ['stjuət]	(engl. Königshaus 1603—1714)
to grow from, grew, grown [grəu, gru:, grəun]	(er)wachsen aus, entstehen
settlement ['setlmənt]	Siedlung
pioneer [ˌpaiə'niə]	Pionier, Vorkämpfer
to arise, arose, arisen [ə'raiz, ə'rəuz, ə'rizn]	sich erheben, entstehen
world-wide	weltweit
fellowship ['feləuʃip]	Brüderschaft, Gemeinschaft
type [taip]	Typ(e), (Eigen-)Art

equal ['i:kwəl]	gleich(gestellt, -berechtigt)
partner ['pɑ:tnə]	Partner
yet other nations	noch andere Nationen
goal [gəul]	Ziel
Prime Minister ['praim 'ministə]	Premier, Ministerpräsident
to share [ʃɛə]	teilen
ashes, *Mehrz.* ['æʃiz]	Asche
to go to war	*in den Krieg ziehen*
error ['erə]	Irrtum
to fail [feil]	versagen
string	Band, Schnur
block	Block
to admire [əd'maiə]	bewundern
to deserve to be admired [di'zə:v]	Bewunderung verdienen

Übersicht über das erstmalige Vorkommen der Vokabeln

Die Ziffern hinter den Vokabeln geben die Lektionen an. B = Ergänzungsstück, Ex = Exercises, Gr = grammatischer Teil. Nicht aufgenommen sind die Grundzahlen (1—12 bekannt ab L 4, 13—100 ab L 7), die Ordnungszahlen (bekannt ab L 17), die Monatsnamen (bekannt ab L 18) und Eigennamen.

a, an 1 Gr
abbey 38
ability 35
to be **able** to 20
about 11 B, 19 B
to be **about** to 39
what **about** 3
to talk **about** 7
above 29 B
abroad 17 B
absence 24
absent 17
to **accept** 21
to **accept** responsibility 37 B
accident 22 B
according to 39
bank **account** 37 Gr
accustomed to 34 Gr
to **ache** 25 B
acre 39
across 30
to **act** 37
action 37
actor 1
actress 26 B
actually 25
to **add** 18
in **addition** 35
address 27 B
to **address** s.o. 26
to **admire** 42
to **admit** 30
adult 29 B
in **advance** 32
advanced 23
advantage 33
to **advertise** 35
advertisement 21
advertising 37 Gr
advice 34
to **advise** 36 B
to be **affected** 28
to **afford** 26 Gr
I'm **afraid** 17, 18 B
Africa 27
African 27
after 4, 6 Gr
after all 26
afternoon 8
afterwards 16 B
again 8
against 19
age 10, 32
agency 10
ago 15
to **agree** with 25 B
agreement 37 B
to go **ahead** with s. th. 39
aim 21
air 22, 24
airline 18
airport 18
alarm clock 14
alcohol 19
alibi 24
alike 15
alive 25
all 4
in **all** 13
not at **all** 19 B, 28
all right 18 B
to **allow** 26
to be **allowed** to 20 Gr
almost 27
alone 17
along 22
to bring **along** 9
already 21
also 15 B
although, though 21
altogether 41
always 7
amazing 37
American 29 B
among 9
amount 29 B
to **amount** to 26
amusement 17
ancestor 27
and 1
anger 36
Anglo-Saxon 20
angry 28
animal 20
another 8
answer 4
to **answer** 9 B
anxious 25
any 18
not **any** 18
anybody 18 Gr
anyone 32
anything 18
anything else 17 B
anyway 16
anywhere 18
apart 19
apart from 33
to **apologize** 23
to **appear** 29
apple 35
applicant 23
to **apply** 35
to **apply** for 23
to **apply** to 21, 34
to **appoint** 27
to **appreciate** 30 B
to **approach** 24 Gr, 36
area 40
to **argue** 36
to **arise, arose, arisen** 42
arm 5
armchair 16
army 41
around 9, 21
to **arrange** 35
arrangement 18
arrest 36
to **arrest** 25
arrival 18 B
to **arrive** at 11
article 2, 35
artificial 24
as 7, 13, 21, 23 Gr
as a liftboy 27
as far as 35
as light **as** 24
as well **as** 41
ashamed of 26
ashes 42
Asia 28
to **ask** 6
to **ask** s.o. questions 13
to **ask** the way 19 B
to **ask** for s.th. 24 B
asleep 24
assistant 2
astonished 23
at 3
at last 3
at least 17
at six o'clock 14
at the baker's 30
at the beginning of 41
at that moment 30
atomic 40
attack 40
attempt 41
to **attempt** 25
to **attend** evening classes 20 B
attention 35
aunt 7
Australia 33
Australian 33
Austria 27 B
Austrian 20
automatically 41
automation 29
autumn 18 Gr
average 29 B
to **average** 33 B
to **avoid** 17, 34, 61
to **awake, awoke, awoke** 19
to **awaken** 31
away 2
awful 4

baby 5
back 7
back garden 7
to run **back** 6
to travel **back** 18
at the **back** 15 B, 34
background 11
bacon 9

10–5046

11–5046

Die Beugung des Zeitworts (Konjugation des Verbs, *Conjugation*)

	Tatform (Aktiv, *Active Voice*)		**Leideform** (Passiv, *Passive Voice*)
	Einfache Zeitform *(Ordinary Form)*	Verlaufsform *(Continuous Form)*	Einfache Zeitform *(Ordinary Form)*
Grundform Infinitiv *Infinitive* Gegenwart Vergangenh.	to paint *malen* to have painted *gemalt haben*	to be painting *(gerade) malen* to have been painting *(gerade) gemalt haben*	to be painted *gemalt werden* to have been painted *gemalt worden sein*
Gegenwart Präsens *Present Tense*	I, you paint he, she, it paints we, you, they paint *ich male*	I am you are he, she, it is we, you, they are painting *ich male (gerade)*	I am you are he, she, it is we, you, they are painted *ich werde gemalt*
Vergangenheit Präteritum *Past Tense*	I, you he, she, it we, you, they painted *ich malte*	I was you were he, she, it was we, you, they were painting *ich malte (gerade)*	I was you were he, she, it was we, you, they were painted *ich wurde gemalt*
Vollendete Gegenwart Perfekt *Present Perfect*	I, you have he, she, it has we, you, they have painted *ich habe gemalt*	I, you have he, she, it has we, you, they have been painting *ich habe (gerade) gemalt*	I, you have he, she, it has we, you, they have been painted *ich bin gemalt worden*
Vollendete Vergangenheit Plusquamperfekt *Past Perfect*	I, you he, she, it we, you, they had painted *ich hatte gemalt*	I, you he, she, it we, you, they had been painting *ich hatte (gerade) gemalt*	I, you he, she, it we, you, they had been painted *ich war gemalt worden*
Zukunft Futur I *Future Tense*	I, we shall you, he, they will paint *ich werde malen*	I, we shall you, he, they will be painting *ich werde (gerade) malen*	I, we shall you, he, they will be painted *ich werde gemalt werden*
Vollendete Zukunft Futur II *Future Perfect*	I, we shall you, he, they will have painted *ich werde gemalt haben*	I, we shall you, he, they will have been painting *ich werde (gerade) gemalt haben*	I, we shall you, he, they will have been painted *ich werde gemalt worden sein*
Bedingungsform Konditional I *Conditional*	I, we should you, he, they would paint *ich würde malen*	I, we should you, he, they would be painting *ich würde (gerade) malen*	I, we should you, he, they would be painted *ich würde gemalt werden*
Vollendete Bedingungsform Konditional II *Conditional Perfect*	I, we should you, he, they would have painted *ich würde gemalt haben*	I, we should you, he, they would have been painting *ich würde (gerade) gemalt haben*	I, we should you, he, they would have been painted *ich würde gemalt worden sein*

Verzeichnis der grammatischen Ausdrücke (mit Beispielen)

Laute

dt. Bezeichnung	lat. Bezeichnung	engl. Bezeichnung	Beispiele (deutsch)	Beispiele (englisch)
Selbstlaut	Vokal	vowel	a, e, i, o, u, ä, ö, ü	[æ], [e], [i], [ɔ] etc.
Mitlaut stimmhaft stimmlos	Konsonant	consonant voiced voiceless	b, c, d, f, g, h usw. b, d, g usw. p, t, k usw.	[b], [p], [v], [f], [ʃ] etc. [b], [d], [g], [v], [z] etc. [p], [t], [k], [θ] etc.

Wortarten

Hauptwort Einzahl Mehrzahl Beugung: Werfall (1. Fall) Wesfall (2. Fall, Besitzfall) Wemfall (3. Fall) Wenfall (4. Fall)	Substantiv Singular Plural Deklination: Nominativ Genitiv Dativ Akkusativ	noun singular plural declension: nominative genitive (possessive case) dative accusative	Hut, Schwester, Ei Hut, Schwester, Ei Hüte, Schwestern, Eier der Mann des Mannes dem Mann den Mann	hat, sister, egg hat, sister, egg hats, sisters, eggs the man the man's, of the man (to) the man the man
Geschlechtswort bestimmtes Geschlechtswort unbestimmtes Geschlechtswort	Artikel bestimmter Artikel unbestimmter Artikel	article definite article indefinite article	 *der* Hut, *die* Schwester, *das* Ei *ein* Hut, *eine* Schwester, *ein* Ei	 *the* hat, *the* sister, *the* egg *a* hat, *a* sister, *an* egg
Eigenschaftswort	Adjektiv	adjective	Das *schöne* Mädchen. Das Mädchen ist *schön*.	The *beautiful* girl. The girl is *beautiful*.
Umstandswort	Adverb	adverb	Das Mädchen singt *schön*. Wir singen sehr *oft*.	The girl sings *beautifully*. We sing very *often*.
Fürwort persönliches Fürwort besitzanzeigendes Fürwort	Pronomen Personalpronomen Possessivpronomen	pronoun personal pronoun possessive pronoun	 ich, du, er usw. *mein* Haus, *deine* Schuhe usw.	 I, you, he etc. *my* house, *your* shoes etc.

dt. Bezeichnung	lat. Bezeichnung	engl. Bezeichnung	Beispiele (deutsch)	Beispiele (englisch)
Fragefürwort	Interrogativpronomen	interrogative pronoun	wer? was? welcher Mann?	who? what? which man?
hinweisendes Fürwort	Demonstrativpron.	demonstrative pronoun	*dieses* Fenster, *jene* Stühle	*this* window, *those* chairs
bezügliches Fürwort	Relativpronomen	relative pronoun	Der Mann, *der (welcher)* auf seine Frau wartete.	The man *who* was waiting for his wife.
rückbezügliches Fürwort	Reflexivpronomen	reflexive pronoun (pronoun with *-self*)	Er stellte *sich* vor.	He introduced *himself*.
unbestimmte Fürwörter	indefinite Pronomen	indefinite pronouns	jeder, alle, kein(er), ein anderer, jemand, niemand	every, each, all, no, another, someone, nobody
Verhältniswort	Präposition	preposition	in, auf, an, vor, nach, mit	in, on, at, before, after, with
Bindewort	Konjunktion	conjunction	und, oder, aber, weil, obwohl	and, or, but, because, although
Zeitwort (Vollzeitwort)	Verb	verb	öffnen, warten, geben	to open, to wait, to give
Hilfszeitwort	Hilfsverb	auxiliary	haben, sein; können, müssen	to have, to be; I can, I must
Grundform	Infinitiv	infinitive	öffnen, warten, geben	to open, to wait, to give
Befehlsform	Imperativ	imperative	öffne(t)!, warte(t)!, gib! gebt!	open, wait, give
Mittelwort				
der Gegenwart	Partizip Präsens	present participle	öffnend, wartend, gebend	opening, waiting, giving
der Vergangenheit	Partizip Perfekt	past participle	geöffnet, gewartet, gegeben	opened, waited, given
Zeit[1]	Tempus	tense	(siehe Tabelle Seite 157)	
Tatform	Aktiv	active voice	Er öffnete die Tür.	He opened the door.
Leideform	Passiv	passive voice	Die Tür wurde geöffnet.	The door was opened.

Satzglieder

Satzgegenstand	Subjekt	subject	*Wir* hören den Lärm.	*We* hear the noise.
Satzaussage	Prädikat	predicate	Wir *hören* den Lärm.	We *hear* the noise.
Ergänzung	Objekt	object	Wir hören *den Lärm.*	We hear *the noise.*
Umstandsbestimmung,	adverbiale Best.	adverbial phrase		
z. B. der Zeit	der Zeit	of time	Wir hören den Lärm *jeden Tag.*	We hear the noise *every day.*
des Orts	des Orts	of place	Wir hören den Lärm *überall im Haus.*	We hear the noise *everywhere in the house.*

[1] Die Namen der einzelnen Zeiten (Tempora) finden sich in der Tabelle Seite 157.

Verzeichnis der wichtigsten unregelmäßigen Verben

(* bedeutet, daß auch die regelmäßige Form auf *-ed* vorkommt)

to arise [aiz]	arose [əu]	arisen [i]	sich erheben
to awake [ei]	awoke [əu]	awoke*	erwachen
to be	was	been	sein
to bear [ɛə]	bore [ɔ:]	borne [ɔ:]	(er)tragen; gebären
		born	geboren
to beat [i:]	beat [i:]	beaten [i:]	schlagen
to become [ʌ]	became [ei]	become [ʌ]	werden
to begin [i]	began [æ]	begun [ʌ]	beginnen, anfangen
to bend [e]	bent [e]	bent	beugen, biegen
to bet [e]	bet*	bet*	wetten
to bind [ai]	bound [au]	bound	binden
to bite [ai]	bit [i]	bit(ten) [i]	beißen
to bleed [i:]	bled [e]	bled	bluten
to blow [əu]	blew [u:]	blown [əu]	blasen
to break [ei]	broke [əu]	broken [əu]	(zer)brechen [ziehen
to breed [i:]	bred [e]	bred	brüten; züchten; er-
to bring [i]	brought [ɔ:]	brought	bringen
to broadcast [ˈɔ:,ɑ:]	broadcast*	broadcast	(im Rundfunk) senden
to build [i]	built [i]	built	bauen
to burn [ə:]	burnt* [ə:]	burnt*	(ver)brennen
to burst [ə:]	burst	burst	platzen
to buy [ai]	bought [ɔ:]	bought	kaufen
to cast [ɑ:]	cast	cast	werfen; (Metall) gießen
to catch [æ]	caught [ɔ:]	caught	fangen [suchen
to choose [u:z]	chose [əuz]	chosen [əu]	wählen, (sich) aus-
to come [ʌ]	came [ei]	come [ʌ]	kommen
to cost [ɔ]	cost	cost	kosten
to creep [i:]	crept [e]	crept	kriechen
to cut [ʌ]	cut	cut	schneiden
to deal [i:]	dealt [e]	dealt [e]	handeln, sich befassen
to dig [i]	dug [ʌ]	dug	graben [(mit)
to do [u:]	did [i]	done [ʌ]	tun
to draw [ɔ:]	drew [u:]	drawn [ɔ:]	ziehen, zeichnen
to dream [i:]	dreamt* [e]	dreamt*	träumen
to drink [i]	drank [æ]	drunk [ʌ]	trinken
to drive [ai]	drove [əu]	driven [i]	treiben, fahren
to eat [i:]	ate [et]	eaten [i:]	essen
to fall [ɔ:]	fell [e]	fallen [ɔ:]	fallen
to feed [i:]	fed [e]	fed	füttern
to feel [i:]	felt [e]	felt	(sich) fühlen
to fight [ai]	fought [ɔ:]	fought	kämpfen
to find [ai]	found [au]	found	finden
to flee [i:]	fled [e]	fled	fliehen
to fling [i]	flung [ʌ]	flung	schleudern, werfen
to fly [ai]	flew [u:]	flown [əu]	fliegen
to forbid [i]	forbad(e) [æ]	forbidden [i]	verbieten
to forget [fəˈget]	forgot [ˈɔ]	forgotten [ˈɔ]	vergessen
to forgive [i]	forgave [ei]	forgiven [i]	vergeben
to freeze [i:]	froze [əu]	frozen [əu]	(ge)frieren
to get [e]	got [ɔ]	got	bekommen; werden
to give [i]	gave [ei]	given [i]	geben
to go [əu]	went [e]	gone [ɔ]	gehen
to grind [ai]	ground [au]	ground	mahlen
to grow [əu]	grew [u:]	grown [əu]	wachsen; anbauen
to hang [æ]	hung [ʌ]	hung	(auf)hängen
to have	had	had	haben
to hear [iə]	heard [ə:]	heard	hören
to hide [ai]	hid [i]	hidden	(sich) verstecken
to hit [i]	hit	hit	schlagen; treffen
to hold [əu]	held [e]	held	halten
to hurt [ə:]	hurt	hurt	verletzen; weh tun
to keep [i:]	kept [e]	kept	(be)halten, aufbewah-
to kneel [i:]	knelt [e]	knelt	knien [ren
to know [nəu]	knew [nju:]	known [nəun]	kennen, wissen
to lay [ei]	laid [ei]	laid	legen
to lead [i:]	led [e]	led	leiten, führen
to lean [i:]	leant* [e]	leant*	lehnen
to leap [i:]	leapt* [e]	leapt*	springen
to learn [ə:]	learnt* [ə:]	learnt*	lernen; erfahren
to leave [i:]	left [e]	left	(ver)lassen

to lend [e]	lent	lent	leihen
to let [e]	let	let	lassen
to lie [ai]	lay [ei]	lain [ei]	liegen
to light [ai]	lit* [i]	lit*	anzünden, erleuchten
to lose [lu:z]	lost [ɔ]	lost	verlieren
to make [ei]	made [ei]	made	machen
to mean [i:]	meant [e]	meant	meinen; bedeuten
to meet [i:]	met [e]	met	begegnen, treffen
to mow [əu]	mowed [əu]	mown* [əu]	mähen
to pay [ei]	paid [ei]	paid	(be)zahlen
to put [u]	put	put	legen, setzen, stellen
to read [i:]	read [e]	read [e]	lesen
to ride [ai]	rode [əu]	ridden [i]	reiten, fahren
to ring [i]	rang [æ]	rung [ʌ]	läuten, anrufen (Tel.)
to rise [aiz]	rose [əu]	risen [i]	aufstehen; aufgehen (von Gestirnen)
to run [ʌ]	ran [æ]	run [ʌ]	rennen, laufen
to saw [ɔ:]	sawed [ɔ:]	sawn [ɔ:]	sägen
to say [ei]	said [e]	said	sagen
to see [i:]	saw [ɔ:]	seen [i:]	sehen
to seek [i:]	sought [ɔ:]	sought	suchen
to sell [e]	sold [əu]	sold	verkaufen
to send [e]	sent	sent	senden, schicken
to set [e]	set	set	setzen, stellen
to sew [əu]	sewed [əu]	sewn* [əu]	nähen
to shake [ei]	shook [u]	shaken [ei]	schütteln
to shine [ai]	shone [ɔ]	shone	scheinen, glänzen
to shoot [u:]	shot [ɔ]	shot	schießen
to show [əu]	showed [əu]	shown [əu]	zeigen [schrecken
to shrink [i]	shrank [æ]	shrunk [ʌ]	schrumpfen; zurück-
to shut [ʌ]	shut	shut	zumachen
to sing [i]	sang [æ]	sung [ʌ]	singen
to sink [i]	sank [æ]	sunk [ʌ]	sinken, versenken
to sit [i]	sat [æ]	sat	sitzen
to sleep [i:]	slept [e]	slept	schlafen
to slide [ai]	slid [i]	slid	gleiten
to smell [e]	smelt [e]	smelt	riechen
to sow [əu]	sowed [əu]	sown* [əu]	säen
to speak [i:]	spoke [əu]	spoken [əu]	sprechen
to speed [i:]	sped [e]	sped	sich sputen, beeilen
to spell [e]	spelt* [e]	spelt*	buchstabieren
to spend [e]	spent	spent	ausgeben; verbringen
to spill [i]	spilt*	spilt*	verschütten
to spin [i]	spun [ʌ]	spun	spinnen
to split [i]	split	split	spalten; platzen
to spoil [ɔi]	spoilt* [ɔi]	spoilt*	verderben
to spread [e]	spread [e]	spread	(sich) aus-, verbreiten
to spring [i]	sprang [æ]	sprung [ʌ]	springen
to stand [æ]	stood [u]	stood	stehen
to steal [i:]	stole [əu]	stolen [əu]	stehlen
to stick [i]	stuck [ʌ]	stuck	(an)stecken, (an)kleben
to sting [i]	stung [ʌ]	stung	stechen
to stink [i]	stank [æ]	stunk [ʌ]	stinken
to strike [ai]	struck [ʌ]	struck	stoßen, schlagen
to swear [ɛə]	swore [ɔ:]	sworn	schwören; fluchen
to sweep [i:]	swept [e]	swept	fegen, kehren
to swell [e]	swelled [e]	swollen [əu]	(an)schwellen
to swim [i]	swam [æ]	swum [ʌ]	schwimmen
to swing [i]	swung [ʌ]	swung	schwingen, schwenken
to take [ei]	took [u]	taken [ei]	nehmen; bringen
to teach [i:]	taught [ɔ:]	taught	lehren
to tear [ɛə]	tore [ɔ:]	torn [ɔ:]	zerreißen
to tell [e]	told [əu]	told	erzählen; (es) sagen
to think [i]	thought [ɔ:]	thought	denken, glauben
to throw [əu]	threw [u:]	thrown [əu]	werfen
to thrust [ʌ]	thrust	thrust	stoßen
to tread [e]	trod [ɔ]	trodden [ɔ]	treten
to understand	understood	understood	verstehen
to wake [ei] (up)	woke* [əu]	woke(n)* [əu]	(auf)wecken, -wachen
to wear [ɛə]	wore [ɔ:]	worn [ɔ:]	tragen (Kleider)
to weave [i:]	wove [əu]	woven [əu]	weben
to weep [i:]	wept [e]	wept	weinen
to win [i]	won [ʌ]	won	gewinnen
to wind [ai]	wound [au]	wound	winden
to wring [riŋ]	wrung [ʌ]	wrung	auswringen
to write [rait]	wrote [əu]	written [i]	schreiben

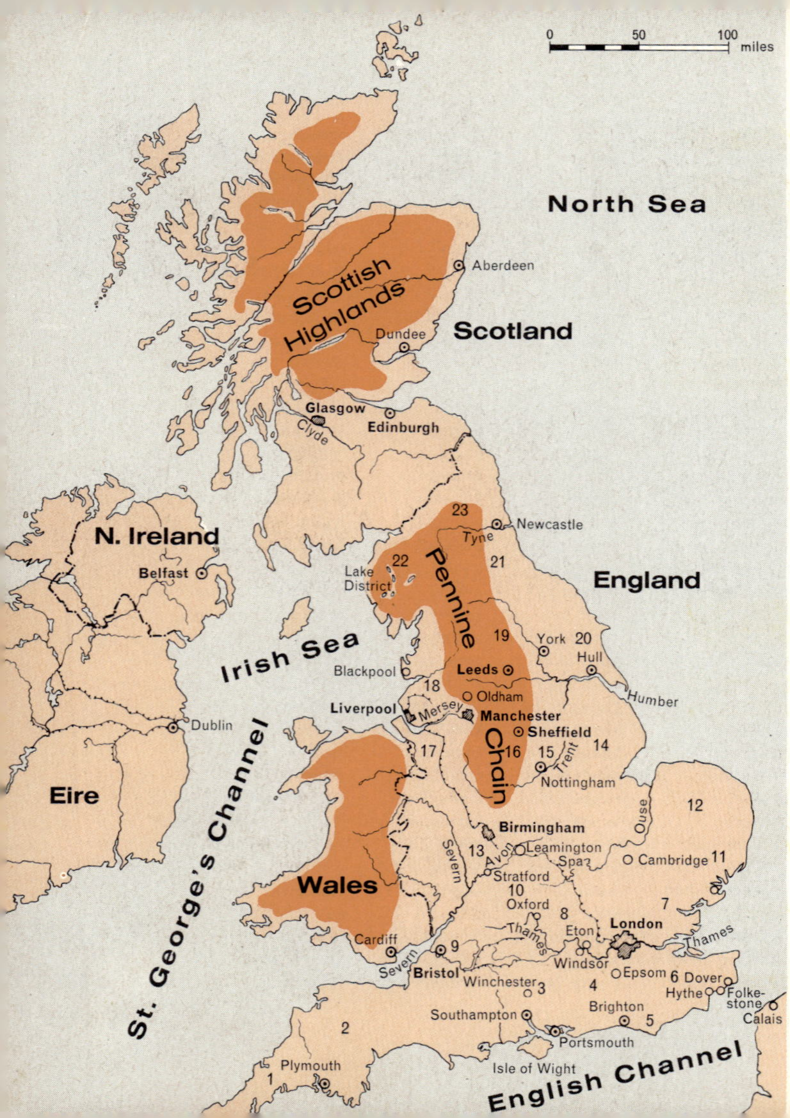

Great Britain

Great Britain consists of England, Scotland and Wales. Together with Northern Ireland it forms the United Kingdom (UK).
The population of the United Kingdom is 56 millions, its area 94,214 square miles. With 592 persons per square mile (or 229 per sq.km) the population density is one of the highest in the world. 75 per cent of the population live in towns; and every fourth inhabitant of the UK lives in the London Region (i. e. within a radius of 40—50 miles from Central London).

The Counties

The United Kingdom is divided into 92 counties, of which 23 are shown on the map numbered as follows:

1 Cornwall [ˈkɔ:nwal]
2 Devon [ˈdevn]
3 Hampshire [ˈhæmpʃə]
4 Surrey [ˈsʌri]
5 Sussex [ˈsʌsiks]
6 Kent
7 Essex [ˈesiks]
8 Buckinghamshire [ˈbʌkiŋəmʃə]
9 Avon [ˈeivən]
10 Oxfordshire [ˈɔksfədʃə]
11 Suffolk [ˈsʌfək]
12 Norfolk [ˈnɔ:fək]
13 Hereford and Worcester [ˈherifəd n ˈwustə]
14 Lincolnshire [ˈliŋkənʃə]
15 Nottinghamshire [ˈnɔtiŋəmʃə]
16 Derbyshire [ˈdɑ:biʃə]
17 Cheshire [ˈtʃeʃə]
18 Lancashire [ˈlæŋkəʃə]
19 North Yorkshire [ˈnɔ:θ ˈjɔ:kʃə]
20 Humberside [ˈhʌmbəsaid]
21 Durham [ˈdʌrəm]
22 Cumbria [ˈkʌmbriə]
23 Northumberland [nɔ:ˈθʌmbələnd]

Principal Cities (1972 mid-year population estimate)

Greater London	population	7,345,000	Sheffield	population	515,000
Birmingham	population	1,008,000	Leeds	population	500,000
Glasgow	population	862,000	Edinburgh	population	450,000
Liverpool	population	591,000	Bristol	population	422,000
Manchester	population	535,000	Teesside	population	394,000

Principal Ports

London	Import and export of goods of every kind.
Southampton	Ocean passenger traffic; import of citrus fruits; petroleum.
Liverpool	Export of British manufactured goods; import of grain, tobacco, wool.
Manchester	Import and export of petroleum.
Glasgow	Serves the industrial area of central Scotland; export of whisky.
Newcastle-upon-Tyne	Coal-shipping and ship repairing centre.
Belfast	Principal port of Northern Ireland; traffic across the Irish Sea.

Highest Mountains		
	Ben Nevis [benˈnevis] — Scotland	4,406 ft. (= 1 343 m)
	Snowdon [ˈsnəudn] — Wales	3,560 ft. (= 1 085 m)